Subjectivity and Literature from the Romantics to the Present Day

Edited by
Philip Shaw and Peter Stockwell

Pinter Publishers
London and New York

© The editors and contributors 1991

First published in Great Britain in 1991 by
Pinter Publishers Limited
25 Floral Street, London WC2E 9DS

All rights reserved. No part of this publication may be reproduced, stored in a retrieval system, or transmitted by any other means without the prior written permission of the copyright holder. Please direct all enquiries to the publishers.

British Library Cataloguing in Publication Data

A CIP catalogue record for this book is available from the British Library
ISBN 0 86187 1804

For enquiries in North America please contact PO Box 197, Irvington, NY 10533

Library of Congress Cataloging in Publication Data

A CIP catalog record for this book is available from the Library of Congress

Typeset by GCS, Leighton Buzzard, Beds.
Printed and bound in Great Britain by Biddles Ltd, Guildford and Kings Lynn

For our makers

Contents

List of Contributors

Acknowledgements

Foreword

Introduction   1

1 Exceeding Romanticism
   Philip Shaw   12

2 Is Emily Brontë a Woman?: Feminity, Feminism and the Paranoid Critical Subject
   Emma Francis   28

3 'What Language Can Utter the Feeling': Identity in the Poetry of Emily Brontë
   Kathryn Burlinson   41

4 Epiphany and Subjectivity in Charlotte Brontë's *Villette*
   Susan Watkins   49

5 'They Suck Us Dry': A Study of Late Nineteenth-century Projections of Vampiric Women
   Sian Macfie   58

6 Wallace Stevens: An Exemplary Subject
   Carolyn Masel   68

7 The Ideological Eye-witness: An Examination of the Eye-witness in Two Works by George Orwell
   Peter Marks   85

8 'Pretending to Be Me': Larkin *versus* 'Larkin'
   Peter MacDonald Smith   93

9 Language, Knowledge, and the Stylistics of Science Fiction
   Peter Stockwell   101

10 Narrative Voice and Focalization: The Presentation of the Different Selves in John Fowles' *The Collector*
   Dominique Costa   113

11 Feminism, Language or Existentialism: The Search for the
   Self in the Works of Clarice Lispector
   Barbara Mathie   121

12 Portrait of the Subject as a Young Man: The Construction of
   Masculinity Ironized in 'Male' Fiction
   Lynda Broughton   135

13 The Spaced-out Subject: Bachelard and Perec
   Jamie Brassett   146

14 The Death of Orality and the Rise of the Literate 'Subject'
   David Wilson   159

Index   173

List of Contributors

Philip Shaw is a Doctoral student in the Department of English at the University of Liverpool. He is due to submit a thesis on problems of reading in the history of romantic literature and philosophy.

Emma Francis took her B.A. and M.A. degrees at the University of Southampton and is now writing a Ph.D thesis on nineteenth-century women's poetry in the English Department at the University of Liverpool.

Catherine Burlinson is a lecturer in English at the University of Southampton. She is currently researching the work of Victorian women poets including Emily Brontë, Christina Rossetti and Elizabeth Barrett Browning.

Susan Watkins is a third-year research student in the English Department at the University of Sheffield. She is working on a Ph.D thesis on epiphany and female subjectivity in the prose fiction of Charlotte Brontë, D.H. Lawrence and Doris Lessing.

Sian Macfie is a research student in the English Department at Birkbeck College, University of London. She is interested in women's novels of the supernatural (1880–1900) and their relation to *fin-de-siècle* projections of the spiritual and demonic woman.

Carolyn Masel is a Doctoral student in the Department of Literature at the University of Essex, where she is working in the area of contemporary and modern poetry.

Peter Marks is a third-year Ph.D student in the Department of English Literature at the University of Edinburgh. His research topic is provisionally entitled 'The Polemical Essays of George Orwell: An Examination of Public Discourse in the Thirties'.

Peter Macdonald Smith is writing a Ph.D on 'Romanticism and Philip Larkin' in the English Department at the University of Bangor. His published work includes articles on modern poetry for *The New Welsh Review* and *English*.

Peter Stockwell is researching a Ph.D in discourse stylistics and the science-fiction genre in the English Department at Liverpool University. He has presented papers at several conferences and is a member of the Poetics and Linguistics Association.

Acknowledgements

The editors and contributors wish to acknowledge: Faber & Faber Ltd for permission to quote from *The Collected Poems of Wallace Stevens* by Wallace Stevens; Ian McEwan and Jonathan Cape for extracts from *First Love, Last Rites*; and the British Museum Prints and Drawings Department for Giovanni Battista Piranesi, *Carceri d'Inventione*, Plate 14, c. 1760.

Foreword

Books, like people, have birth dates and histories. This collection began life as a conference held at Liverpool University in October 1989. Our intention as conference organizers was to provide a forum for young academics to meet and exchange ideas on a topic of wide-ranging significance for a variety of research interests. From Kant to Foucault and from Wordsworth to Derrida, the quest for self-constitution within expressive language has been taken as a measure for the triumphs, the 'pathos', and the eventual 'defeat' of post-Enlightenment thought. To investigate the claims made for and against 'the subject' of that thought, and to coincide with the bicentenary of an inaugural event in its history, the conference assembled papers from a variety of disciplines under the original title of 'The Coming of the Subject: Making the Self from 1789–1989'. The event proved to be so successful that it was decided to present the papers in the form of a book.

This collection therefore represents the final stage in a conference 'process'. Papers presented orally and followed by general discussion were subsequently revised into a written register appropriate for publication for a wider academic audience. We believe, however, that the business of academics is not *simply* to produce books; face to face communication is a vital part of maintaining the links between those engaged in new and challenging areas of research. It is to be hoped that the process does not end here but that future conferences and publications will re-evaluate the issues dealt with by the contributors to this volume.

Obviously, with a collective enterprise of this kind, the editors owe much to the efforts of all those who attended and participated in the original conference. Firstly, we wish to thank all of those who have contributed to this volume for the speed and good humour with which they revised and prepared work to be re-presented in written form. Professor Vincent Newey was instrumental in providing support and advice at all stages. In this respect we would also like to thank the following: Paul Simpson, Geoff Ward, Brian Nellist, Linda Williams, Nick Davis, Brean Hammond, Simon Dentith, Suzanne Trill, Jane Morton, Andrew Foster, Joanna McIntyre, Susan Riley, Helen Chapman and Sara Wilbourne of Pinter Publishers for her persistence and encouragement in seeing the project through its final stages. Finally, our greatest debt must go to the English Department secretaries, Cathy Rees and Barbara Smith, for their infinite patience and skill when dealing with the consequences of our initial ineptitude.

Philip Shaw and Peter Stockwell
Liverpool, May 1990

Giovanni Battista Piranesi (1720-1778): Imaginary Prison, plate XIV of the *Carceri d'Invenzione*, c. 1761. Etching.

Introduction

> In the 'male' text, whatever the sex of the writer, the subject of discourse is male, and the narrative celebrates the characteristics of the hero: singular, sublime, mediating the world through the special consciousness of the transcendental subject, privileged, central, essential...

An assemblage of qualities, categories and classifications: in the 'male' text — defined here through the analysis of a short story, 'Homemade', by Ian McEwan, included in this volume (chapter 12) — the hero of romanticism melts imperceptibly into the subject of postmodernism where reading is at work everywhere. Speaking fluently at times, at other times in stutters, the 'I' is convulsed in a fitful scheme of self-assertion and self-negation. What a mistake it then becomes to have ever said the opening or the end of man. In marking these limits we stand rather, with Derrida, Deleuze and the later Foucault, on the *arrêt* or knife-edge of the question: a figure drawn in sand at the ocean's edge, soon to be erased by the incoming tide... later to be redrawn, reinvested, born again.[1]

To draw our subject into 'the change of terrain' that the distance between the romantic and the contemporary might cover, one thinks, for example of Piranesi's prison drawings, the famous *Carceri d'Inventione*.[2] Etched in the mid-eighteenth century, they present us now with the chillingly familiar logic of the body *in extremis*, a delirious effect produced by the machinery of a work whose obsession with the vertiginous possibilities of architecture leads its subject towards the outer darkness of representational collapse. Referring neither to inner nor outer space, they submit the viewer to the breakdown of perspective and the loss of centre; everywhere there is the same stairwell, the same passage, and the same ghostly figure, repeated endlessly until the flight from confinement breaks on the edge of a terrifying infinity. Here one searches in vain for ground on which to restore the disappearing boundaries between subject and object, spectator and prisoner. At a point just beyond our gaze the hallucinatory power of the *Carceri* works to destroy all such distinctions until, in the end, we experience the disturbing possibility that torturer and victim, subject and spectator are one and the same. As the stones fall apart there is no final resolution, only the process of redoubling that stands in the place where we had expected to find the origin or the 'truth' of Being: a dwelling for the birth/death of the subject.

In Piranesi's vision of the collapse of opening and closure, of freedom and constraint, there is a foreshadowing of the time — our own — when Immanuel Kant's philosophy of the Sublime will be forced into a meeting with the non-sense of delirium.[3] We will speak then of two foundations: the one in reason, the other in desire.

Writing in the preface to his own book on Kant, which was first published in 1963 and translated into English in 1984, the French philosopher Gilles Deleuze puts this relation into perspective. There is, he says, a 'deeply romantic Kant in the *Critique of Judgement*. In the two other Critiques, the various subjective faculties entered into relationships with each other, but these relationships were rigorously regulated in so far as there was always a dominant or determining faculty which imposed its rule on the others' (Deleuze 1984: xi). These faculties are: external sense, inner sense, imagination, understanding, and reason, each 'well-defined' and separated according to a certain hierarchical arrangement. Thus, in the *The Critique of Pure Reason*, the understanding was dominant 'because it determined inner sense through the intermediary of a synthesis of the imagination, and even reason submitted to the role which was assigned to it by the understanding' (p. xi). In the *Critique of Practical Reason*, on the other hand, reason was placed in the dominant role since 'it constituted the pure form of universality of the law, the other faculties following as they might (the understanding applied the law, the imagination received the sentence, the inner sense felt the consequences or the sanction)' (p. xi).

By the time of the *Critique of Judgement*, however, we find Kant wrestling with a problem that was already inherent in the troubled perspectives of the *Carceri*. Kant's undertaking, as Deleuze states, was extraordinary:

> if the faculties can, in this way, enter into relationships which are free and variable, but regulated by one or other of them, it must follow that all together are capable of relationships which are free and *unregulated*, where each goes to its own limit and nevertheless shows the possibility of some sort of harmony with the others... Thus we have the *Critique of Judgement* as the foundation of Romanticism. (Deleuze 1984: xi–xii)

What does this last statement mean? Deleuze describes the third *Critique* as 'a terrible struggle between imagination and reason, and also between understanding and inner sense, a struggle whose episodes are the two forms of the Sublime, and then Genius' (p. xii). Yet it is from this fundamental discord, experienced through the inadequacy of the imagination to comprehend, by reason, the magnitude of the Sublime, that the mind can feel itself 'set in motion' (*bewegt*). In bringing the various faculties into play, the Sublime is able to grant an infinite power of free reflection to the imagination and an unlimited conceptual power to the understanding; but what is here potentially disruptive, even damaging to the sense of composure which Kant (and also Coleridge) will later go on to describe as the essential characteristic of the original Genius, must first be regulated by an act of wilfull submission. Thus Kant's greatest coup after describing the terrifying effect of the Sublime is to immediately reinvest it as a brief but necessary element of discordancy within a universal system of harmonious accord. The Sublime is utilized as a function of that which makes us alive to the feeling of the law. If then, in the initial encounter with the Sublime, the imagination recoils upon itself and is reduced to impotence, it is not as an effect of the supersensible in nature but of reason which forces the mind to unite the magnitude of the sensible world into a comprehensive totality. As Deleuze (1984: 51) puts it, 'Imagination thus learns that it is reason which pushes it to the limit of its power, forcing it to admit that all its power is nothing in comparison to an Idea'. We are thus prepared for the advent of the moral law.

In this respect, however, we are reminded that Piranesi's is a Sublime of incarceration, and is therefore a parody of legislative reason. Perhaps the unidentified and seemingly multiple subject, the prisoner of the *Carceri*, has broken some fundamental law, a failure to enforce the submission of the imagination to the higher faculty of reason. The Sublime in this case has an indeterminate destination, and if reason brings us to a focus, it is only in order to deregulate, endlessly it seems, the conditions of our own self-legislation. Thus we join with Foucault and the Deleuze of *Anti-Oedipus* (Deleuze and Guattari 1984) to link the architecture of discipline and punishment to the architectonics of the subject whose natural tendency or line of flight has always been in a direction away from the confinements of reason, repetition and systematicity. But if we choose against the law, identifying with Deleuze and the later Foucault—a fundamental complicity between the 'truth' of enlightenment and the agencies of social repression (paranoia, neurosis: our ongoing failure to meet the standards of the universal)—are we then able to resist the return of the *Carceri* in some other more domesticated form?:

> the 'logic' of every relation to the outside is very complex and surprising. It is precisely the force and the efficiency of the system that regularly change transgressions into 'false exits'. Taking into account these effects of the system, one has nothing, from the inside where 'we are', but the choice between two strategies:
>
> a. To attempt an exit and a deconstruction without changing terrain, by repeating what is implicit in the founding concepts and the original problematic, by using against the edifice the instruments or stones available in the house, that is, equally, in language. Here, one risks ceaselessly confirming, consolidating, *relifting (relever)*, at an always more certain depth, that which one allegedly deconstructs. The continuing process of making explicit, moving toward an opening, risks sinking into the autism of the closure.
>
> b. To decide to change terrain, in a discontinuous and irruptive fashion, by brutally placing oneself outside, and by affirming an absolute break and difference. Without mentioning all the other forms of *trompe-l'œil* perspective in which such a displacement can be caught, thereby inhabiting more naively and more strictly than ever the inside one declares one has deserted, the simple practice of language ceaselessly reinstates the new terrain on the oldest ground.
> (Derrida 1982: 135)

If, in the *Carceri*, it is impossible to discover the cornerstone on which the edifice can be made to fall, it is because the image of the interior has been replaced with a more productive and fluid—one would say machine-like—vision of the dwelling. Likewise, it is still more difficult in a consciously postmodernist text, such as Ian McEwan's 'Homemade', to locate the point where irony works on the side of the reader to consolidate perspective and to reveal the moment where the glorification of violence is displaced by the critique of violence.

Through reading 'Homemade', one could say that the doctrine of the faculties has been thrown into delirious confusion. Utilizing the shock appeal of irony, inversion, and the formidable appeal of Gothic horror, the excesses of McEwan's literary style subvert any attempt on the part of the reader to reconstitute the habitual distinctions of gender, politics, legitimacy and truth. Writing of this kind, as Lynda Broughton's essay points out, is never 'clear'; its machinery is rather directed towards the re-evaluation of all forms of intellectual production, including the creation of distinctions, traditions and genres. But if the ironic subject of 'Homemade' rests uneasily in the company of those slightly more assured heroes of literary history — the writers of say, *The Prelude, Don Juan, Great Expectations, Middlemarch* — it is because it longs, with some futility, to escape the tantalizing claims of the romantic past. One discovers, for example, in the language Broughton uses to describe the characteristics of McEwan's anti-hero, a genealogy of terms that is indebted to the discourse of romanticism, and more specifically in reference to the Sublime and the transcendental, to the critical thought of Kant. As Derrida reminds us, there is a problem with changing terrain, a problem that has its own violence and the possibility of its own descent into the paranoiac structures of totality and oppression. It is not enough to say that one can merely exceed Kant by 'brutally placing oneself outside' since no proposition, however radical in its intent, can function without falling back on the anthropomorphic and metaphysical resources vested in language.[4]

Yet there is a way in which the violence of the critical act can be incorporated into the text. The question turns on the incline between truth and provocation, between say, Kant and Nietzsche, Hegel and Bataille, Dickens and Ian McEwan or, for Gilles Deleuze (1983: 108), on the violence of those 'forces which take hold of thought'. In tracing, therefore, the unutterable tenor of a thought that can be seen to persist through many of these essays, it may be that what a story such as 'Homemade' finds missing in the critique of the romantic self is in fact a genealogy of the passage which leads beyond Kant, the analysis of which seeks to uncover, or perhaps even to liberate, 'the will which hides itself and expresses itself in reason' (Deleuze 1983: 91). Seen in this way, literary violence is a reaction to the unthought background of the history of the self, a history that has, as its problematic origin, the difference or distance between the following set of pronouncements: 'Now, I say, man and, in general, every rational being exists as an end in himself'; 'man is an invention of recent date. And one perhaps nearing its end'.[5]

If Derrida reacts to this passage, it is because he mistrusts the potentially reductive metaphorics of terrains, buildings and houses; the placing of origins against ends in the 'economy of the eves' (Derrida 1982: 136). Instead of a change of place, what we need is a change of 'style'; 'and if there is style, Nietzsche reminded us, it must be *plural*' (p. 135). In other words there is no question of a simple choice between these two strategies, between Kant and Foucault, since they are really complementary to each other. Rather, we must choose both at once as if there were two ends of man: the end as *eschaton* and the end as *telos*. Here there is no question of doing away with the subject, instead one must analyse where it comes from and how it functions. When Derrida deconstructs man as a sovereign subject in command of the building blocks of reason and language, he is made to fragment within a system of textual relations, 'the psyche, society, the world' (Derrida 1978: 227). Within the writing system the concept of the subject performs only a legitimizing function and it is up to the reader to refrain from continuing to conceive of this function as a static, or non-evolutionary essence. In Derrida's example, and in Ian McEwan's text, the provocation of writing as an excessive and ironical form of play resists the classical notion of the subject which functions as the limit between the submission to 'truth' and the will to a more radical exploration of the questions of discourse, gender, power and privilege. In short, this is the task that many of the essays in this book address.

As the example from Lynda Broughton's essay shows, the discourse of Kantian reason persists, and often in the most unexpected places. Carolyn Masel, in her essay on the poetry of Wallace Stevens (chapter 6), points to the interest in the Sublime as the 'mode or genre in which deferral is necessary to transcendence'; alterity is dependent on the difference between self and other, 'he' and 'she', 'it' and 'they'. Yet, as Masel clearly shows, Stevens is able to move within this system in such a way as to present to romantic/Kantian thought the possibility of its own dissolution. Similarly, Peter Marks, in writing of George Orwell's creation of the 'eye-witness' (chapter 7), makes reference to the court-room drama as the *mise-en-scène* of self-determination, an implicit reminder of Kant's notion of the legislator-subject in which judgement is subjected to the high court of universal reason. But in setting up the *versus* of a conceptual opposition between self and other (the opposition also of 'Larkin *versus* "Larkin" ' in Peter MacDonald Smith's paper, chapter 8) we should not be surprised to discover that the outcome has always been rigged, that judge, defence and prosecution are locked in complicity.

If, as with Descartes, the speaking subject of Kant's imaginary courtroom is the *cogito*, it is only conceived following a line of absolute destruction represented by methodical doubt. Its specific existence, the *ergo sum* of the dominant reality, becomes a form of reconstitution, which has, in a very significant sense, always already been guaranteed by the *cogito* as an *a priori* whose effectiveness can never come under the same rigorous critique as all the other phenomena whose existence had been put into question. According to Deleuze and Guattari (1987: 130), in Descartes and in Kant the legislator-subject replaces 'the signifying despot' (God, the King), but with the following paradoxical effect: 'the more you obey the statements of the dominant reality, the more in command you are as subject of enunciation in mental reality, for in the end you are only obeying yourself! You are the one in command, in your capacity as a rational being. A new form of slavery is invented, namely, being slave to oneself, or to pure 'reason', the Cogito'. Furthermore, the *cogito* is 'a proceeding (*'procès'* or trial), that must always be recommenced, haunted by the possibility of betrayal, a deceitful God, and an evil Genius' (Deleuze and Guattari 1987: 128).

In Orwell's case the process of subjection is evident in the distance the narrator experiences between individual and collective desires, in the transfer of power from colonizer to colonized, in the swiftly closing gap between oppressor and oppressed. The conflict in a short story such as 'A Hanging', between the desire on the part of Orwell to provide an objective analysis of the effects of imperialism in Burma, whilst at the same time portraying the existential crisis of the narrator, is in reality an effect caused from the transferal of rule by a despotic regime (the British Raj) to the despotism of the self; the Western official whose victimization of the native Indians as an instrument of authoritarian rule becomes internalized through voluntary subjection to the slavery of the bad conscious, to the *cogito*, the court of reason. The fact that Marks draws out the equivocity produced by a text of this kind serves to remind us that the Kantian appeal to the supposedly universal conditions of taste and disinterestedness has always implicated in it the unexamined values of 'those who judge and evaluate' (Deleuze 1983: 1), and all ways of being, as Deleuze (1983: 102) reminds us (via Nietzsche), are either high or low, noble or base.

This is the point where idealist philosophy meets the challenge presented by materialist and feminist critiques of the subject. In this respect the readings of Emily and Charlotte Brontë (chapters 2, 3 and 4), have sought to engage a certain tradition within literary criticism in which the subject's encounter with the Sublime has been defined exclusively in terms of the masculine economy of loss and gain. Thus, in the formation of canons, we find the poetry of Emily Brontë denigrated to a secondary position in deference to the stabilizing authority of Wordsworth, Coleridge and Byron. Women's writing, as Christine Battersby has recently argued,[6] is subjected to a history of critical depreciation whose organon has been formed within the discourse of Kantian reason. In the nineteenth century especially, the differentiation between the characteristics considered Beautiful (and hence representative of female virtues) and those characteristics designated Sublime (belonging exclusively to the orders of a male intellectual élite), owes much to the tradition of theorizing sex differences which we find in Kant's early essay, *Observations on the Feeling of the Beautiful and Sublime* (1764): 'The fair sex has just as much understanding as the male, but it is a *beautiful understanding*, whereas ours should be a *deep understanding*, an expression which signifies identity with the sublime'.[7] If Emily Brontë's poetry was not granted serious attention in the Victorian period, as Emma Francis argues (chapter 2), the attempt to limit her work within the category of the Beautiful — a category that at the time would include the writings of Felicia Hemans, Christina Rossetti and Elizabeth Barrett Browning — would seem now as an act of desperate containment, an evasion of those elements in Brontë's poetry that would subvert, as it were, the Kantian hierarchy from within. In this sense Derrida has yet another forerunner for his distinction between the two strategies of philosophical deconstruction: Brontë's subversion rests on the question of her literary 'style', a violent oscillation between the restricted economies of gender and Genius. And this too is the position that Sian MacFie investigates in her paper on women and vampirism (chapter 5); 'sucking us dry' could well read as the repressed in late Victorian fiction, the moment where the female subject is positioned in the threateningly ambiguous role of the destroyer, the seducer, the outcast and the diseased. In true Gothic style, the venom from her bite seeps into the wounds of healthy philosophy, spreading contamination into the circulatory logic of the *cogito*.

The subversion of 'male' authenticity via the return of the (female) body is a notion also utilized by Barbara Mathie in her examination of the fictional works of Clarice Lispector (chapter 11). Here, Mathie argues, it is the theories of the Bulgarian philosopher Julia Kristeva, in her critique of the alienated subject of phallogocentric discourse, that are most relevant to the reading of this important and provocative author. Through the simultaneous use of feminist, existentialist and post-modernist approaches, Mathie brings a new understanding to Lispector, revealing how all three readings can be applied to the disordering of ego-logical, stratified conceptions of the self within a 'non-patriarchal' mode of fictional language.

Where Georges Bataille writes, in a similar fashion, of a suppressed interest in the material conditions of the body within the Western metaphysical tradition, the focus is once again on the tensional relation between two forces in the shared discourse of romanticism and postmodernism. Thus Philip Shaw, in 'Exceeding Romanticism' (chapter 1), argues that in attempting to construct philosophies of the intensive, or progressive impulse in romantic art, we inevitably create the grounds for a melancholic or nostalgic form of theoretical totality. This is brought through in Shaw's presentation of the themes of death and bodily decay as they occur in a cross-section of works ranging from *A Zed and Two Noughts*, by the postmodernist film-maker Peter Greenaway, through the writings of Wordsworth, Hegel and Ruskin to the post-Nietzschean tradition headed by Bataille and culminating in the works of Deleuze and Guattari.

The essays by Jamie Brassett and David Wilson also take as their cue a desire to exceed the reductive assumptions of the post-Kantian tradition. In 'The Spaced-out Subject: Bachelard and Perec' (chapter 13), Brassett outlines a critique of the subject in which space, as opposed to time, is regarded as the ordering principle of subjective experience. By telling 'stories in space' consciousness is experienced as 'heterogenous, fluid, and collective'. The notion of the 'self' that is thus developed through the 'topo-analysis' of these temporary or 'storeyed' formations is at once material, discontinuous and partial in form. If it escapes the process of idealization that we find in Kant it will be as a result of having escaped the spatio-temporal circle in which self is defined through its impossible relation to the other via the effects of difference.

Similarly, David Wilson, in a concluding essay on 'The Death of Orality and the Rise of the Literate "Subject" ' (chapter 14), attempts a critique of the subject-self that has continued to form the basis of Enlightenment speculations on the nature of conscious experience.[8] Utilizing the notion of 'orality' as it is developed in the work of Elizabeth Eisenstein and W.J. Ong, Wilson argues that it is only with the advent of print that our experience of individual subjectivity comes into being. In contrast to the view outlined in Brassett's essay, it is sound that functions as the 'unifying, involving phenomenon' and texts 'that allow for the possibility of abstraction (and hence alienation) by separating the knower from the known'. In other words, if the literate subject can reflect on the conditions of its own constitution through having taken recourse to the differential structure of writing, this will be, as Wilson suggests, at the expense of the values of collectivity and shared experience.

Several papers in this collection explore the themes of knowledge and self-creation. The work of Peter Stockwell and Dominique Costa (chapters 9 and 10), for example, are both concerned with how the subject is constructed through the process of reading. Through focusing on the varieties of subjective 'points of view' as these are produced in the text, both Stockwell and Costa treat the Kantian tradition as an idealized model that is actualized in the process of reading, in the study of the use and meaning of utterances in context (pragmatics). The conclusion is that consciousness is dependent in an ideal sense (the *ratio cognoscendi*) on narrative structures through which it can represent or reflect on its previous intentional states. At all times, however, the subjects presented in these respective analyses of 'The Night' (Ray Bradbury) and *The Collector* (John Fowles) are regarded as fragmented consciousnesses, whose reflections on meaning, truth and experience must remain provisional.

The incapacity of the subject to make its founded meanings of selfhood coincide with itself through the structure of language therefore raises some important questions to do with the supposed ideality of the Kantian ego. Implicit within Stockwell's discussion, in particular, is a critique of the reading subject's claim to be able to transcend experience and operate as the 'disinterested', unified referent of intentionality that speculative reason must require if it is to affirm the universality of the moral law. This is a view often challenged by the experimental perspectives of the science-fiction genre. 'We' (whoever 'we' are; in SF this is explored through the use of alien, animal and other non-human perspectives) bring 'our' empirical assumptions and expectations to the text which are manipulated in turn by the use of 'focalization' and 'viewpoints', differential structures which provide only a discontinuous and partial knowledge of the 'truth', truths that interact with and are affected by the material circumstances of the interpreter. Who then is the ideal or protean reader and does the problematization of knowledge that we encounter in experimental writing really serve to deregulate the 'fundamental' conditions of this form of subjective experience?

Here, one is reminded especially of Pierre Bourdieu whose work in the field of the social sciences has provided literary theorists and historians with an insight into the philosophical assumptions that lie behind the claims of academic professionalism. In *Distinction: A Social Critique of the Judgement of Taste* (1984), Bourdieu must be credited for having exposed the ideological mechanism by which theories of knowledge and 'pure' reason locate themselves in the opposition between transcendent and empirical. As Bourdieu states (1984: 490): 'The antithesis between culture and bodily pleasure (or nature) is rooted in the opposition between the cultivated bourgeoisie and the people'. The truly cultivated man is therefore measured by his capacity for sublimation; low desires must be eschewed if judgement is to transcend social relations. Yet every work of art is a conditioned object, including the philosophical or critical text. It also follows that every act of reading is conditioned and that even the most radical questionings announced by philosophy 'are in fact circumscribed by the interests linked to membership in the philosophical field' (p. 496):

> 'Empirical' interest enters into the composition of the most disinterested pleasures of pure taste, because the principle of the pleasure derived from these refined games for refined players [here Bourdieu singles out Derrida's attempts to transgress the third *Critique* through the excess of his 'seductive' style] lies, in the last analysis, in the denied experience of a social relationship of membership and exclusion. (Bourdieu 1984: 499)

In this respect we remember that the claim to have 'exceeded' Kant or Hegel or Derrida must first begin with the acceptance of a professional contract. As 'radical' readers we may agree to transgress the stock of consecrated texts from which the philosophers have learnt their trade but our readings, nevertheless, act as symbolic strategies which derive their sense of legitimacy from having operated within the terms dictated by the professional field. This rooted opposition between the reasonable terms of academia and that 'certain step of the dance' (Derrida 1982: 27) with which poststructuralism would put the subject into play, leads critical thought towards an inevitable encounter with the role of the political.

Despite the stated opposition on the part of many thinkers of the French intellectual left (here we must include, Foucault, Derrida, Lyotard and Deleuze), to 'the complete aestheticization of the political',[9] the resistance that many of these figures envisage is stated almost wholly in aesthetic terms. In other words, whilst at the beginning of this introduction we talked about the possibilities of a 'violent' critique of the subject, the provocation of this language seems to evaporate in the face of other and more pressing realities. If the 'self' is indeed a reification brought about through the technologies of power unleashed in the wake of the post-Enlightenment tradition, it still seems to be the case that French poststructuralism (from its turbulent inception in the events of May 1968 to the importance of its current standing within the professional field), consistently fails to locate the point(s) at which the subject can exercise its war of resistance. We must now ask how a philosophy of 'desire' (Nietzsche, Foucault and Deleuze) or of the 'event' (Lyotard) or of 'deconstruction' (Derrida) can ever hope to engage in the active resistance of the self to its political manipulation. Since it is academic language, as Bourdieu reminds us, that ceaselessly restates the grounds on which this critique takes place how is it to escape the charges of essentialism and irrelevance? The fact is, however, that contemporary theorists such as Felix Guattari still regard their work as capable of exercizing a transformation in the political scene, as the following example shows:

> I do not think it absurd to base a revolutionary politics on semiotic and analytical exercises that have broken with the dominant semiology; in other words, on ways of using the spoken and written word, pictures, gestures, groups and so on, that would direct along very different lines the relationship between the flux of signs and all the deterritorialized fluxes. In point of fact, it is getting caught up in the net of interpretative semiologies that the masses fail to realize the true springs of their power—that is their real control over industrial, technological, scientific, economic and social semiotics—and become bogged down in the phantasies of the dominant reality, and in the modes of subjectification and repression of desire imposed upon them by the bourgeoisie. (Guattari 1984: 106)

Here, the abandonment of the State apparatus is conceived, once more, through the radicalization of writing, in this case a 'nomadic' or 'schizophrenic' mode of writing that will permanently deregulate the carceral architecture of the subject under capitalism. But if this joins with Piranesi to form the abstract embodiment of a ceaselessly decoding arrangement of desires at work on the more concrete body of the State, it remains hard to see how such a loose arrangement of micro-politics can be put into effect without having to resort to the potentially oppressive structures of a 'dominant reality' or code. The textual politics of Deleuze and Guattari, along with those of Kristeva, Cixous and Lyotard, work, if at all, only as a form of critique and analysis. As such they lend themselves well to the Kantian tradition which constantly reforms even as the foundations are removed and forced into spasms of deregulation. This was the problem faced by Nietzsche and Bataille; it now remains to be seen how far this meeting between reason and pleasure can go before the 'kings of the castle' disappear once more with the incoming tide.

Notes

1. This sentence alludes to the close of Michel Foucault's *The Order of Things: an Archaeology of the Human Sciences* (1970).
2. For a general discussion of Piranesi's influence on the first generation of Romantic artists see Le Bris (1981: 32).
3. On the influence of the idealist tradition, in particular the philosophy of Kant, through nineteenth-century romantic theory and the New Critics to post-structuralism, see Sychrava (1989). See also Gasché (1986).
4. In this country Christopher Norris has been the most prominent of those theorists who would align Derrida in a more positive manner to the Kantian tradition. See especially Norris (1987: chapter 6).
5. Derrida quotes from Kant and Foucault as the epigram to his essay 'The Ends of Man'. See Derrida (1982: 111). This alignment was also used by the conference organizers in the original call for papers.
6. I am indebted to Christine Battersby of the Department of Philosophy at Warwick University for the use of her paper entitled 'Stages on Kant's Way: Morality and the Gendered Sublime' (unpublished draft). See also chapters 5 and 8 of *Gender and Genius: Towards a Feminist Aesthetics* (Battersby 1989) for further discussion of Kant, the romantic tradition and its harmful effects on the development of female genius. This work also includes some useful comments on writings by John Fowles and Wallace Stevens, authors discussed in this volume.
7. The reference to Kant, central to Battersby's discussion, is taken from Kant, I. (1960) *Observations of the Feeling of the Beautiful and the Sublime*, (tr. John T. Goldthwait), University of California Press, p. 78.
8. The editors have preserved the tone of the oral register within which David Wilson originally gave his paper to the conference. This seemed essential as his paper gives a rigorous critique of many of the assumptions that lie behind the conference title.
9. Lyotard from an interview given in 1988 and quoted in Callinicos (1989: 86). Callinicos' work challenges the 'idealist irrationalism' of postmodernist philosophy.

Bibliography

Battersby, C. (1989), *Gender and Genius: Towards a Feminist Aesthetics*, London, The Women's Press.
Battersby, C. (1990), 'Stages on Kant's Way: Morality and the Gendered Sublime' (unpublished draft).
Bourdieu, P. (1984), *Distinction: a Social Critique of the Judgement of Taste*, (tr. Richard Nice), London, Routledge and Kegan Paul.
Le Bris, M. (1981), *Romantics and Romanticism*, London, Macmillan.
Callinicos, A. (1989), *Against Postmodernism*, Cambridge, Polity Press.
Deleuze, G. (1983), *Nietzsche and Philosophy*, (tr. Hugh Tomlinson), Minneapolis, The University of Minnesota Press.
Deleuze, G. (1984), *Kant's Critical Philosophy: The Doctrine of the Faculties*, (tr. Hugh Tomlinson and Barbara Habberjam), London, The Athlone Press.
Deleuze, G. and Guattari, F. (1984), *Anti-Oedipus: Capitalism and Schizophrenia*, (tr. Robert Hurley, Mark Seem, and Helen R. Lane), London, The Athlone Press.
Deleuze, G. and Guattari, F. (1987), *A Thousand Plateaus: Capitalism and Schizophrenia*, (tr. Brian Massumi), London, The Athlone Press.
Derrida, J. (1978), *Writing and Difference*, (tr. Alan Bass), London, Routledge and Kegan Paul.
Derrida, J. (1982), *The Margins of Philosophy*, (tr. Alan Bass), Chicago, University of Chicago Press.

Foucault, M. (1970), *The Order of Things: an Archaeology of the Human Sciences*, (tr. Alan Sheridan), New York, Random House.
Gasché, R. (1986), *The Tain of the Mirror: Derrida and the Philosophy of Reflection*, Cambridge, Massachusetts, Harvard University Press.
Guattari, F. (1984), *Molecular Revolution: Psychiatry and Politics*, (tr. Rosemary Sheed), New York, Penguin.
Norris, C. (1987), *Derrida*, London, Fontana.
Sychrava, J. (1989), *Schiller to Derrida: Idealism in Aesthetics*, Cambridge, Cambridge University Press.

1 Exceeding Romanticism
Philip Shaw

I

> Me only cruel immortality
> Consumes: I wither slowly in thine arms,
> Here at the quiet limit of the world,
> A white-hair'd shadow roaming like a dream.
> Tennyson, (1987: 607), 'Tithonus', ll. 5–8[1]

Where do romantics and postmoderns meet?

The grotesque comedy of Tennyson's impossible insight into the bodily limits of immortality has been examined in recent years in *A Zed and Two Noughts* (1985), a film by the British director, Peter Greenaway. At first sight this is a work that would appear to have little relation to the concerns of 'Tithonus'. The title alone is diverting, alerting us more to the deployment of the film's self-generating 'system' — the letters of the alphabet — than to the pathos or tragedy we would normally expect to find in a work of romantic aesthetics. But there is a way of using *A Zed and Two Noughts* to scrutinize a little further the claims made both for and against romantic and postmodernist forms of expression. Greenaway, of course, is often criticized for the 'effortlessness' of his approach. Most comonly it is alleged that his work leaves us with nothing more than an undemanding, stylized product, a 'capitalist' object whose surface beauty fits in all too easily with the kitsch aesthetic of a designer *fin de siècle*. Well, this too: a perfect expression 'of the times'. But, in itself, such an appraisal seems lazy for Greenaway has a great deal more to say about a deconstructive approach to postmodernist art, and much of this will turn upon an older 'romantic' theme: the manipulation of time in a work's attempt to at once preserve and overcome the hallucinatory metonymy of the self's and the body's relation to the *otherness* of death. In this respect, what is perhaps most interesting about the film's productive system is not its efficiency, but its eventual breakdown: the stylistic implosion of a highly self-conscious organon.

Throughout *A Zed and Two Noughts* a recurring theme centres round the possibility of constructing the perfect recording machine, a totalizing device to appropriate and account for every last form of 'desiring production';[2] in this case the forces of decay that would normally exceed, or 'live on', the death of the habitual self. To this end, Greenaway's central 'figure', one of a pair of recently widowed brothers, records time-lapse films of dead animals undergoing decomposition. It is a motif that will eventually dominate the film's production, the brother's sub-contributions working almost as a quasi-cause for the forces of degeneration that were previously and properly unrepresentable. Each tiny narrative—an angel fish turning from transluscent silver to formless grey, the feathered carcass of a Leda's swan 'alive' with maggots—condenses the 'natural' time of the body's passing away into an exuberant *danse macabre*. Everything here is accelerated to the point where the phantasmic work of *de*composition comes to possess a much greater vivacity than the still lives of that other director's—Greenaway's—stylistic homage to Vermeer. It presents us with a significant contrast: the obsession with symmetry—the poised perfection of light captured in rooms, on faces— against the farcical dance of decay; the necrogenic presences of Dali and Buñuel.

A Zed and Two Noughts closes with one final absurdity: the symbolic unification of the two grieving brothers into a single, undifferentiated body. Injecting themselves with a lethal drug they attempt, with the aid of an autonomous self-generating machine, to photograph their own decomposition. A final act of representational control that would insert a further technological twist into the bitter lament of Tithonus's everlasting 'immortality'. But the point is that no one can own, in the Protestant sense of ownership ('when my time comes'), the continuing labour of dissolution. Biology refuses to accommodate itself to the codicils of incorporeal desire, to allow the temple of the body to live on, unviolated, beyond the punctual event of death. It is an event that shakes the belief in immortality and mocks the agonistic labours of romantic dualism. Thus, in the film, the final irony is left to the parasites, a 'natural' excess of slugs and snails that literally short-circuits the dream of a death without hidden remainders. The totalizing machine breaks down leaving darkness, once again liberated through the fecund energy of unlimited forces. Perhaps all along there was nothing more than a 'body without organs'—a machine designed to fail. Where does this strange allegory lead?

In this occult return, the laughable conclusion to Greenaway's film suggests comparison with Georges Bataille, labouring to overcome, through the uncovering of stinking decomposition, the reductive projects of Hegelianism. Post-Nietzschean French philosophy often makes this attempt to introduce romantic consciousness to a more dangerous *practice* of dissolution. It is a project that involves the insertion of a reminder, within the structures of the dialectic, of that which constantly evades the idea of its own seriousness. Thus throughout Bataille's work—philosophical, political and fictional—we encounter the purely 'material' bodies of excrement, flies and corpses: disgust and laughter joining in a single outburst. Perhaps Greenaway's work also acts like this, exceeding 'Tithonus', not tragically, but with a sense of grotesque exuberance—and always at the expense of its own highly stylized, self-representation:

> Everything that exists destroying itself, consuming itself and dying, each instant producing itself only in the annihilation of the preceding one, and itself existing as mortally wounded.[3]

II

The *force* of decay merges with Deleuze and Guattari's response to the paranoia of post-Enlightenment thought; their celebration, in *Anti-Oedipus*, of a state of pure intensity, 'like a cry suspended between life and death' (Deleuze and

Guattari 1984: 18). But we should remember that it is a position that would commit us to the dizzying extremes of pure presentation. Going beyond the law is a dangerous practice and it is more recently that the French philosopher Jean-François Lyotard has been drawn to the *question* of just what would be at stake in a discourse *at the maximum level of intensity*.[4]

In a sense, it is a question that cannot, or even, by an ironical turn, *should not* be asked — if, for no other reason, because it would be a means of re-employing non-logical difference' within the oppressive paradigms of philosophical intelligibility. Between, therefore, the stasis of verification and the fluidity of 'permanent revolution' (Lyotard 1974: 29) — Lyotard's own wrestling with the passage between Freud and Kant, Dionysos and the critical function — it seems there is something much 'older' than postmodernism, a phantasm relating the fundamental agonistics of the will to power with the reductive allure of theoretical totalization. For our purposes it is possible to transfer this relation and to point to the existence of two forces within the trajectory of European romanticism: the nostalgic and the progressive. If the latter promises a more affirmative, Dionysian, relationship with the drives and impulses of history, it remains to be seen for how far and for how long the principles of a 'permanent revolution' can be sustained in a language unpurged of non-evolutionary systems and projects; equilibriums shaped by the foreclosed structures of Newtonian physics and Biblical revelation. Accordingly, a large part of this study will be devoted to the movement by which the continuing presence of romantic language forces critique into the reconstruction of referential totalities at the very moment when romanticism, as pure intensity, would offer the possibility of an unlimited supersession of partial objects and evolutive processes. First, however, we had better be sure that our theoretical 'trace' has a common destination. What, in other words, does *romantic* desire perform in its attempt to exceed the habitual bounds of reason?

III

Gilles Deleuze has characterized the force of libidinal intensity as a product of the exhaustion of representation. What escapes the surface, or rather induces an a-signifying rupture upon the body of the concept, is the release of schizophrenic energy, an unrecuperable phantasm or *line of flight* away from the totalizing efficiency of Western architectonics: Oedipus, Capitalism — meta-narratives haunted, in Lyotard's analysis, by a more general oppression: 'the weakness and the nostalgic depression of having/not having the presence' (Lyotard 1978: 45). This last phrase seems an apt description for the characteristic tone of much romantic criticism. Yale's famous 'manifesto' on deconstruction, for example, a work self-avowedly tied in many ways to the 'psychological provenance' of romantic language, is steeped in the 'pathos' of the lost horizon; the disappearance of Being (Bloom et al., 1979: ix). Yet something in experimental art struggles, according to Lyotard, against this nostalgia. Through the violence of a force exerted by the purely figural, a more 'primal' phantasm breaks the law. But the transition from the melancholic ghosts of the romantic text to the more vengeful phantasms of post-Nietzschean free-play is a passage that seems to mark its own rhythmically weary correspondence. Through the necessity of communicative accountability the element of excess — most often the event of death itself as Bataille realized — is kept at a distance and is in fact put to work: the Kantian Sublime over the Freudian drive. It may then be true that even so-called experimental or 'postmodernist' art, via the Greenaway example, still manages to maintain a romantic interest with the existential import of the absolutely *other*. Through death as the unknowable beyond, thought is supplied with the (im)possibility of auto-affection and self-coincidence. Deferment, as Derrida has always insisted, provides the subject with the necessary illusion of its triumph over time, the *différance* that creates history as a product of loss and return; the inclusion/exclusion of energy and order.

The *versus* of this conceptual opposition being no more than a veil, however, we should not be surprised when the ghost of an unregulated desire haunts the more inclusive spirit of the all-encompassing grand narrative. Always, through the overdetermination of our 'desire' for rupture we wish to go a little further, to *a point beyond* the inextricably metaphysical. The problematics involved in this last sentence are obvious and in the case of Lyotard have resulted in the disownment of *Economie Libidinale* and the belief in *Just Gaming* (Lyotard 1985: 90) that 'Any philosophy of the will . . . is a monistic philosophy'.[5] The law exists as an insurmountable hierarchy and intensive discourse cannot make a clean break with reflective judgement. At best, and here Lyotard moves closer to Derrida, it is a matter of introducing within the romantic text a paraphrase or *différend*, deregulating the idea of knowledge as a foreclosed institution. But where Lyotard is more confident than Derrida is in the adaption of a post-Kantian notion of the Sublime, one that will involve a passage beyond the romantic insistence on 'the powerlessness of the faculty of presentation, on the nostalgia for presence felt by the human subject, on the obscure and futile will which inhabits him in spite of everything' (Lyotard 1984: 79). Lyotard, in other words, requires a Sublime that is somehow more heterogeneous in its effects than Kant himself would have allowed. If postmodernism can exceed romanticism it will be for a similar reason: something in A *Zed and Two Noughts* (via Bataille) disrupting all attempts to reconvert the subject's encounter with dispersion into a melancholy or nostalgic effect.

But romanticism has an almost irresistable pull. In working through our devotion to the unrepresentable levels of 'spiritual' being — the prospects of infinity that we encounter in the works of, say, Friedrich, Shelley and Wordsworth — it remains the case that interpretation, as the Yale example shows, is tied to the covers that bind what is still, essentially, *our* epoch. To adapt the words of Schlegel, we are still writing a critique

> that would be less a commentary on a literature that is already present, completed and withered, than the *organon* of a literature still to be completed, formed, or even begun.[6]

In 'the place of the absence of the work' (Lacoue-Labarthe & Nancy 1988: 102) a deceptive world quickly comes into being, with romantic absence playing the role of a recording surface that constantly falls back on the work of interpretation. Romanticism then becomes a very mystic effect since all of criticism's productive forces seem to issue from its disappearance. Blanchot's reading is especially pertinent; we know how to read romanticism because we accept 'discontinuity as *form*'[7] (Lacoue-Labarthe & Nancy 1988: 123) — an oxymoron effaced by its own rhythmic interplay, its claim on the work of our

(Kantian) understanding. But again is it possible, or indeed even desirable, to break the fetishism of form — to exceed the dictates of the nostalgic Sublime, Hegelian dialectic, the rule of metaphysics? If the detour into Greenaway's postmodernist work suggests anything at all, it lies in the realization that systematicity collapses via the work of something grotesque and unrecuperable. This is why the act of truly 'exceeding romanticism' may well require an affirmation of pure materiality and then...nothing more. In the light of this, Lyotard's complex mediation between intensity and reason begins to look very uncertain indeed.

A poem such as Wordsworth's 'Desultory Stanzas' (1946: 198–201), written in 1822 and added as a 'conclusion' to the *Memorials of a Tour of the Continent, 1820*, provides us with an exemplary account of the peculiar tensions romanticism and its critique faces. In the opening stanza the poet pictures himself surveying the proofs of the recently completed sequence:

> Is then the final page before me spread,
> Nor further outlet left to mind or heart?
> Presumptuous Book! too forwards to be read,
> How can I give thee license to depart? (lines 1–4)

In sealing off experience the book is 'presumptuous': 'too *forwards* to be read' (my emphasis); and in that ironic phrase we encounter the impossibility that inscribes the tain of memory and desire as relational poles. The closure of writing as a seal for the past is always at the cost of an end to the evolutionary flow of imagination and the re-creation of future horizons. In order to release the text from its own self-containment, Wordsworth requires the reinsertion of an element of discordancy. The book must once again become an unstable container for its themes. Hence the opening of the question in line 4 and the re-emergence of deterritorializing redundancies:

> One tribute more: unbidden feelings start
> Forth from their coverts; slighted objects rise;
> My spirit is the scene of such wild art
> As on Parnassus rules when lightening flies,
> Visibly leading on the thunder's harmonies. (lines 5–9)

This is Wordsworth returning to the scene of his 'high argument', the poet who would 'breathe in worlds/To which the heaven of heavens is but a veil'.[8] The accelerated syntax effects this renewal by moving from the end-stopped pentameters of the opening lines to the more fluid enjambements and phonetic intensives of 'rise', 'flies' and 'harmonies'; this last overburdened rhyme producing a final Alexandrine to break through whatever remains of the formalized beginning. From this over-production, repetition floods back into the work, only this time informed by breathless intensities that open up to the possibility of new and future existential configurations:

> All that I saw returns upon my view,
> All that I heard comes back upon my ear,
> All that I felt at this moment doth renew...(lines 10–13)

And the poet is projected once more into a region where 'wings alone could travel' to 'meet contending themes' (14-15). This is a space beyond nature and also beyond time:

> Where Mortal never breathed I dare to sit
> Among the interior Alps, gigantic crew,
> Who Triumphed o'er diluvian power!—and yet
> What are they but a wreck and residue,
> Whose only business is to perish!—true
> To which sad course, these wrinkled Sons of Time
> Labour their proper greatness to subdue;
> Speaking of death alone, beneath a clime
> Where life and rapture flow in plenitude sublime. (lines 19-27)

These, lines to rival the most extreme productions of the lucific imagination, reach the heights of romantic desire. But the will to death in lines 23-25—the ageing poet who must 'labour' his own provocations against mortality 'to subdue'—already contains the tone of a disciplinary submission to the corporal. For the space, however, of twelve syllables—the controlled excess of Wordsworth's metrical pattern in line 27—we touch, barely, the Sublime. But these traces of a possible subjective disintegration are domesticated or reterritorialized in the operative term of the following lines: '*Fancy* hath flung for me an airy bridge' (28). The recurrent excursions of this secondary category in the later poetry is a repressive strategy intended at once to deprivilege and preserve the poem's dependency upon an originary moment, to defer an unrepresentable source and an unthinkable point of termination. Fancy is self-consciously figurative, a 'playful' and 'unstable' metaphorical chain intended 'to quicken and beguile the temporal part of our nature'.[9] But its mechanism acts as romanticism's limit, returning the text to the earthbound time of its own creation. Deleuzean schizophrenia, if it exists at all in this text, is rechannelled through the incline running between sublimity and fancy. A final (literal) reterritorialization occurs with the introduction of proper nouns: Wordsworth stands on a real bridge overlooking the Rhone valley at Lucerne.

In the terms of deconstruction we may read the shifts from transcendence, to figure, to reality as a mask for the more subtle and pervasive fiction of the author, suspended over the apocalypse of the book. With this, the violent and artificial descent from the heights of the Sublime to the literal plain of reality is itself revealed as a metaphorical sequence through which life and death may be linked within 'amicable interchange' (43). However, this structural continuity is always threatened by an internal closure more silent and 'awful' than any that have gone before—a closure that not even the poet, held over the 'liquid flood' which like life 'slips from underneath us' (83-84), can resist: 'But list! the avalanche—the hush profound/That follows—yet more awful than that awful sound!' (44-5). Wordsworth's language of restoration works also 'unremittingly and *noiselessly*'[10] to dissolve even this last (metaphorical) suspension held over the event that is represented—through romanticism—as death, the *terminus a quo* of desire.

In drawing Wordsworth's poem to an impasse it is not yet the case that our reading overcomes the nostalgia for presence. Left suspended, so to speak, is the requirement that critique goes beyond a melancholic obsession with the representations of infinity. Deconstruction strangely begins to resemble romanticism, bound in a Promethean embrace to the fragmentation/

reconstruction of its own manifestation. The rock on which this particular reading exists continually reforms; any attempt to introduce a desultory excess as a form of permanent violation is effectively contained through the millenarianism of the 'whole design of Scripture history' (67).

With these concluding remarks on Biblical providence, the work is bound by a governing *telos* where faith in the power of the *word* to maintain fluidity and intentional horizons within unself-rivalling[11] boundaries, moves the text away from its linguistic origins towards an altogether more pervasive stability: the psychological hold of language as insurmountable law. Even during the time in which purely formal effects threaten to undo this provenance we have, nevertheless, to agree with de Man that romanticism 'gains [its] maximum of convincing power at the very moment when it abdicates any claim to the truth' (de Man 1979: 50). Language remains the ultimate territoriality.

At Yale, this type of reading has produced a literary deconstruction whose very 'sadness' in relation to romantic concerns with infinity and closure has tended to lock its participants within an agonistic, oppositional, and reactive relationship to the text. Again it is the case, even for someone as rigorously conscious of this tendency as de Man, that 'in formulating a theory' (of romanticism) our critiques achieve only 'a reconciliation on a depressive basis' (Lyotard 1978: 45). Put another way: language speaks and turns out to be a lie 'at the very moment when it asserts itself in the plenitude of its promise' (de Man 1979: 55). It is the inescapable pathos of this *aporia*, however, that turns out for Bataille to be 'the final question of man': how to make the negativity of death *unemployable* within the bounds of any sort of infrastructural dialectic.[12] In following this thought to its limit Bataille will come to wage a general war on representation, learning to laugh when his eyes 'persist in demanding objects that do not destroy them'.[13] The problem of grasping this laughter for its ability to effect a more permanent deregulation of econo-mimesis, as Bataille's successors continually recognize, may well be the next step in the movement away from—and then in the return to—a romantic, or nostalgic form of 'literary' deconstruction.

IV

In the absence of laughter, philosophy and poetry dwell on the 'use' of death within the formulation, deconstruction and eventual infinitization of linguistic and metaphysical sets. Within this context the comparison between Hegel and Wordsworth is obvious. In contemporary criticism they have been regarded by Derrida and Harold Bloom as the 'last' in their traditions. The possibilities of exceeding their work beyond the accusations of nihilistic emptiness is denied. Yet, writers dare to go beyond romanticism and metaphysics to the extent that in certain cases a new work threatens not so much to rival the precursor as to turn away from, ignore, or laugh in the face of its own presumptions. Bataille, as we have seen, is like this; he attempts to define himself, according to Queneau, not through 'opposition' (here with Hegel, but also for the purposes of this discussion with any form of dialectical representation), but, in a sense, through 'fraternization'.[14] The implications of this thought for Bloomian anxiety are compelling and will be allowed to overshadow my discussion.

To begin however, it will be necessary to re-stage a meeting between poetry and metaphysics. A useful and obvious entry point for the relation between Hegel and Wordsworth comes from the *The Phenomenology of Spirit* (1807) (Hegel 1977) and the *Essays: Upon Epitaphs* (1810) (Wordsworth 1974). These are texts in which death has a prominent role. Later we will trace the persistance and the subversion of this thought in the relation between Ruskin and Rilke. But first Hegel:

> Death, if that is what we want to call this non-actuality, is of all things the most dreadful, and to hold fast what is dead requires the greatest strength... But the life of Spirit is not the life that shrinks from death and keeps itself untouched by devastation, but rather the life that endures it and maintains itself in it. It wins its truth, only when, in utter dismemberment, it finds itself. (Hegel 1977: 32)

Bataille reads the metaphors of sacrifice and dismemberment within this text and becomes awakened to the repressed — later we will say 'sublated' — violence of Hegelian dialectic. The story has been well worked in recent years, principally by Derrida, but it serves here as an entry point for discussion of death's role in the formation of self-consciousness. The *Aufhebung* works through the paradox of desecration and preservation as if these could take place at the same time. And in a sense they do. The desire is for 'truth', self-identity, to live on through and within death, untouched by the material realities of dispersion and decomposition. But here, the problem for Bataille lies in Hegel's unwillingness to carry through the instance of personal violence to its full conclusion. Hegelianism, all too satisfied with the security and composure of a 'seamless' philosophy, actually betrays — through pseudo-affirmation — the experience of annulment through death. Bataille's demand is thus for an extension of the *Aufhebung*, so that it becomes an 'unchained violence' (Bataille 1970: 333) — against closure and systematicity, for 'in reality death reveals nothing... Once the animal being which supports it is dead, the human being itself has ceased to be' (p. 336).[15]

Through Hegel we are only fooled into the Absolute, and this becomes the source of Bataille's initial perplexity:

> For man finally to be revealed to himself he would have to die, but he would have to do so while living — while watching himself cease to be [a notion later figured in the impossible machinery of *A Zed and Two Noughts*]. In other words, death itself must become conscious (of itself) at the very moment at which it annihilates conscious being. (Bataille 1970: 336)

But beyond puzzlement, the absurdity of this insight leads Bataille towards the deeper truth of Hegelian negativity. What has the most importance is not the fact of death but its staging as a collaborator within the continuous linking-up of reflection, negation and self that characterizes the work of the *Phenomenology*. Hegel can no longer resist the invasion of literary and aesthetic categories into the dialectic for it is only through spectacle and sacrifice that we accomplish anything like 'self-consciousness'. Through the order of the ritual, death must be employed as 'the reassuring *other* side of the positive' (Derrida 1978: 259). But for Hegel this remains an unacknowledged spectacle. Incorporeal truth and material reality are constantly played off against each other in what will become the more specific dismemberment of philosophy —

the loss of a primordial intimacy between man and the world through the restricted economies of stratagems, profit and utility — functioning under the control of the dialectic. In writing of sacrifice, Bataille asks only that we witness this work as deceit and participate as willing victims in the celebration of an economy without reserve.

In recent years commentators have turned to Wordsworth's *Essays: Upon Epitaphs* as an entry point to romantic concerns with language and subjectivity. Like Hegel's philosophy, Wordsworth's graveyard community is constructed in order to affect a more functional relationship between the living and the dead. But again, like Hegel, we could say that no-one truly dies. Loss in Wordsworth is always provisional, with always the promise of 'abundant recompense' beyond deprivation. One thinks of the drowned man in Book V of *The Prelude* who

> ... 'mid that beauteous scene
> Of trees and hills and water, bolt upright
> Rose, with his ghastly face, a spectre shape —
> Of terror even. (V, lines 470–3)

Wordsworth, looking back on his boyhood, reports that at the time he found comfort in the thought that he had encountered 'such sights before' in books:

> Thence came a spirit hallowing what I saw
> With decoration and ideal grace,
> A dignity, a smoothness, like the words
> Of Grecian art and purest poesy. (V, lines 478–82)

Here 'knowledge' is 'not purchased with the loss of power' (V, 449), it proceeds instead *through* death as the 'hidden reserve' of its positive strength. Throughout the work, negativity forms the necessary interruption to Wordsworth's self-circling patterns of stability:

> The props of my affections were removed,
> And yet the building stood, as if sustained
> By its own spirit. (II, lines 294–6)

Thus we may say that the poetry has a 'restricted economy' in the sense intended by Bataille during his critique of the *Phenomenology*. Through the desire, in Wordsworth's first essay, to make 'Origin and tendency ... notions inseparably co-relative' (Wordsworth 1974: 51) death must be made to draw a profit:

> I confess, with me the conviction is absolute, that, if the impression and sense of death were not thus counterbalanced, *such a hollowness would pervade the whole system of things, such a want of correspondence and consistency, a disproportion so astounding betwixt means and ends*, that there could be no repose, no joy. (Wordsworth 1974: 52; My emphasis)

In the *Essays Upon Epitaphs*, in order to ensure the smooth running of the text as an interpretative and political machine, critical appendix to the *Excursion*, Wordsworth produces a rule for reading, the claim of which on the 'affections' will serve as a defence against internal ruptures. The work must become a pure showing, erasing its biological and material existence so that it may be implicated in a larger, more comprehensive system of interpretative autonomy. Hegel also works towards this transformation with the preface to the *Phenomenology*, and in both cases it is the rhetoricity of poetry that is used to sublate and transfer disharmony in the text:

> — This conflict between the general form of a proposition and the unity of the Notion which destroys it is similar to the conflict that occurs in rhythm between metre and accent. Rhythm results from the floating centre and unification of the two. (Hegel 1977: 61)

Both poet and philosopher, however, are aware that language has a 'counter-spirit' or 'counter-thrust' whose force cannot simply be absorbed within the ideal transparency of a logical sequence of signification:

> So, too, in the philosophical proposition the identification of Subject and Predicate is not meant to destroy the difference between them, which the form of the proposition expresses; their unity, rather, is meant to emerge as a harmony. (Hegel 1977: 61)

In this way violence can once again be internalized and represented through the pacifying spectacle of the *Aufhebung* at work.

The epitaph and phenomenology, despite claims in Wordsworth's case to the contrary, are not then the product of a free exchange between reader and text, but of an internally generated system of rules whose coherence depends upon the interplay of 'metre' and 'accent'. Despite a belief in the universalizing emotion of grief, the grave's 'pathos' or 'harmony', we might say, is made the product of the epitaph's 'totalizing claim over its own proper scansion'.[16] But such a text cannot resist indefinitely its necessary resubmission to the reader. Eventually it will be found exposed within a field of exterior and hostile rhetoricity. This is why Wordsworth, in the second essay, continually insists that an epitaph *should* bring us into:

> closer communion with those primary sensations of the heart, which are the vital springs of sublime and pathetic composition, in this and in every other kind. And, as from these primary sensations such composition speaks, so, unless correspondent ones listen promptly and submissively in the inner cell of the mind to whom it is addressed, the voice cannot be heard: its highest powers are wasted. (Wordsworth 1974: 70)

Under the 'all-uniting' receptacle of the dead, the role of the sympathetic reader becomes identical to that of the epitaph, we become the agents of a general act of resurrection, against the violations of time, history and material differences. Thus, by the time of the third essay, *ethical* interpretation is played off against the potential of language to disguise thought, to act as a 'counter-spirit' 'to subvert, to lay waste, to vitiate and to dissolve' (Wordsworth 1974: 85). For Wordsworth, we could say that the infinitization of theory has become absolutely necessary in order to arrest the historical, semiotic flux in which romantic poetry is caught.[17] The organic system of the graveyard always requires an additional point outside its totality and eventually the instability of this framework will pass into the body of the established church. Thus, in the *Excursion*, true evaluation against the 'sharp contradictions' and 'bitter language' of secular understanding is outfaced by the power of the *word*, which:

> ...to guard against the shocks,
> The fluctuation and decay of things,
> Embodied and established those high truths
> In solemn institutions...(*Excursion*, V, 998-1001)

For Wordsworth (as with Coleridge), the all-comprehending body of the Anglican church becomes the strongest contender for the production of an absolute harmony between loss and gain. But it is interesting to speculate a little further on the persistence of stone as the metaphorical recording surface upon which the ideal text and its reading are formed. Why can romanticism no longer trust in the silence of the dead as the work's 'hidden reserve'?

Part of the problem lies in the epitaphs' literal proximity to the bodies of the dead, 'its need to pillage the grave in order to be written' as Karen Sanchez-Eppler puts it in a recent article (1988: 422). Like the grave, poetic language suffers from violent contradiction and the threat of dissolution. The tomb, in Derrida's gloss of Hegel, performs a double function, at once *averting* the gaze from the persistence of the body—the recalcitrant matter of its decay—and *advertising* the continuation of its spirit elsewhere (Derrida 1982: 82). The corpse, however, is indismissable, and, in a certain sense, parodies any attempt on the part of ontology to employ death as a reassuring *other* within the dialectic of immortality. Thus, whilst Wordsworth makes claims to have united life and death by insisting on the fluidity of their boundaries, the reality of the disintegration of bodies stands in constant and mocking opposition to the possibilities of linguistic 'incarnation'. The outcome of this metaphor, beyond mutilation, is that in making the substitution of 'thought' for the dead body as the object in need of the clothing of words as flesh—words that can as easily become a 'poisoned vestment' (Wordsworth 1974: 84-5)—the incarnation of thought is subjected to the same doubleness that we encountered *in* the literal grave. It suffers the same ill-effects—via the parasitic work of decomposition—that belongs as properly to the biological body.

V

Linguistic, aesthetic and ethical systems are all endangered by the return of the body as unregulated organic matter. But the work of the system is always directed towards the accommodation of its disruptions; indeed part of its success depends upon how well the parasite can be included as a functional element within its machinery.[18] Following Wordsworth, Ruskin, in a chapter central to the design of *The Stones of Venice* (1853) (Ruskin 1903-1912), performs just this function by admitting decomposition as an essential part of living form:

> ...imperfection is in some sort essential to all that we know of life. It is the sign of life of a mortal body, that is to say, of a state of progress and change. Nothing that lives is, or can be, rigidly perfect; part of it is decaying, part nascent. (Ruskin 1904, X: 203)

Like Wordsworth there is here a tendency to domesticate decay, so that, along with death, it can itself be incorporated within the 'fine gradations by which one thing passes away into another'.[19] The passing away of biological form is used by Ruskin as a principle of natural variation, submitting a larger structure—such as the Gothic in church architecture—to a temporary disorder, one that is 'without the slightest loss either to its unity or majesty': 'such daring interruptions of the formal plan would rather give additional interest to its symmetry than injure it' (X: 212).

Turning to his section on the 'Grotesque Renaissance' however, we find Ruskin expressing a much more anxious tone. It is here, in describing the architectural features of the church of Santa Maria Formosa, that a renewed inquiry into the nature of beauty, death and preservation begins. Having outlined the vision of St. Mary the beautiful, of the place 'where the white cloud rested', Ruskin advises his fictional onlooker to 'look at the head that is carved on the base of the tower...A head,—huge, inhuman and monstrous,—leering in bestial degradation, too foul to be either pictured or described, or to be beheld for more than an instant' (XI: 144-5). This head joins many others worked into the stones of Venice whose 'expression of sneering mockery' (XI: 145) mocks the formal decorum of the early Renaissance. A typically overwrought pattern of subordinate clauses culminates in the decadent kick of the following description: 'the *teeth* are represented as *decayed*' (IX: 162). For Ruskin it is an excess that must be distinguished from the 'legitimate' grotesque. In *The Stones of Venice* this latter form is composed of two elements, 'one ludicrous, the other fearful' such that neither is allowed to exclude some element of the other: 'there are few grotesques so utterly playful as to be overcast with no shade of fearfulness, and few so fearful as absolutely to exclude all ideas of jest' (XI: 151). The 'noble' grotesque '*plays* with *terror*' (XI: 166) in the same sense as the Kantian Sublime, and likewise it is an essentially judicial machine imposed on the workings of the unconscious; for it to function correctly, the artist, we are told, must 'know(s) the depth of all at which he seems to mock' (XI: 167). But it is here, in the unconscious, that the production of cartoon images threatens to overstep the boundaries of reason. It works as the third element, the degenerate species of grotesque in which 'men...indulge themselves in unnecessary play':

> Incapable of true imagination, it will seek to supply its place by exaggerations, incoherences, and monstrosities; and the form of the grotesque to which it gives rise will be an incongruous chain of hackneyed graces, idly thrown together,—pettiness or sublimities, not of its own invention, associated in forms which will be absurd without being fantastic, and monstrous without being terrible. (Ruskin 1904, XI: 161)

Disgust in Ruskin's text always seems to invade the space between, on the one hand 'the love of God' and on the other 'the fear of...Death' (XI: 163). The funeral darkness of *The Stones of Venice* hides a greater fear than that included under the regulative 'terribleness of sublimity' (XI: 165)—and this entails the slow implosions of the body *after* death.

Years later, the poet Rilke will also visit Santa Maria Formosa. Unlike Ruskin, however, his gaze settles not on sculpted monstrosities but on the commemorative tablets inscribed on the church walls, notably the one that reads (in translation): 'I lived for others while life lasted; now, after death,/I have not perished, but in cold marble I live for myself...' (Rilke 1987: 153 & 319). In the first of the *Duino Elegies* Rilke recalls this visit (line 67); his desire is to beautify loss, specifically to 'remove the appearance/of injustice' about the death of the young (68–9). The opening passage expands on this idea:

> Voices. Voices. Listen, my heart, as only
> saints have listened: until the gigantic call lifted them
> off the ground; yet they kept on, impossibly,
> kneeling and didn't notice at all:
> so complete was their listening... ('The First Elegy', 56–60)

Where sublation occurs between lines 57–8 ('*da ßsie der reisige Ruf/aufhob vom Boden*'), it is because Rilke — more so than Wordsworth or Ruskin — can stage death apparently without any rem(a)inder of its material form. In this Rilke is perhaps the most thoroughly romantic of all writers and in the letters and poetry the continual theme of 'inwardness' joins with an attempt to purge language of everything involved in thinking of death as 'an excess of meaning'.[20] Rilke would italicize every word in this last phrase since his project, as de Man observes, is to free lexis 'from any empirical or transcendent veracity that might conflict with its principle of constitution' (de Man 1979: 48). If the *logos is* subject to decay, then Rilke will perform a different game, a poetic in excess of meaning itself. Death instead becomes a purely linguistic event in which absence takes the place of the impatient — Orphic — desire for presence. But this is clearly impossible — and not only for the reasons that de Man gives. The grotesque is an excess that no form of representation can, by its very nature, hope to contain. If language has its origin in the body then no amount of semantic askesis can free its voice from a cancer of the larynx.

VI

> The interest of philosophy resides in the fact that, in opposition to science or common sense, it must positively envisage the waste products of intellectual appropriation. Nevertheless, it most often envisages these waste products only in abstract forms of totality (nothingness, infinity, the absolute), to which it itself cannot give a positive content; it can thus freely proceed in speculations that more or less have a goal, all things considered, the *sufficient* identification of an endless world with a finite world, an unknowable (noumenal) world with the known (phenomenal) world.[21]

Where Bataille writes in brackets, 'nothingness, infinity, the absolute', we could also add 'language' — the purified region Rilke has in mind when attempting to remove the trace of sadness from the *punctum* of death. At issue in all the systems we have examined is the need to 'appropriate' excess — to produce a stable object against the 'liberating impulses' of heterogeneity. Thus we find Hegel and Wordsworth at work in the graveyard *because* their libidinal interests lie in the irruption and control of excremental forces — death, mutilation, sacrifice. But what is lifted into the higher region always bares the memory of this original heterology. If, then, spirit and decay share the common character of the *foreign body*, and both are returned to the elementary rhythm of appropriation and excretion, 'a burst of laughter' may be 'the only imaginable and definitely terminal result'. In the following paragraph Bataille continues:

> Excretion is not simply a middle term between two appropriations... The inability to consider in this latter case decay as an end in itself is the result not precisely of the human viewpoint but of the specifically intellectual viewpoint (to the extent that this viewpoint is in practice subordinate to a process of appropriation).[22]

This is where Bataille joins with Deleuze and Lyotard in wishing to open thought to the provocation of *the event*; an incommensurability that surpasses the limits. But the threat of appropriation remains, however, always ready to reinscribe a violent heterology such as the rotting corpse within some form of identificatory synthesis (the 'intellectual viewpoint'). For Lyotard, alarmed by the idea that so-called 'pure' intensities may in turn become reductive, it is a matter of refashioning Kant, identifying the *différend* with the effects of the postmodern Sublime. Thus, in facing the possibilities of chaos, disorder and fragmentation, all predicates of the decomposing body and of what is foreign to the compositional work of the speculative, it is not the case that we have done away with 'reflective judgement'. Instead we are asked to consider the effects of a difference beyond 'the plane of re-presentation' — delivering the system over to what exceeds its 'horizon'.[23] In this way, Kant's faculty of the understanding is remodelled on pragmatic, non-univocal grounds. Thought continues, but in the recognition that its figuration is grounded upon a paradox, an unpresentable abyss that is only — to adopt a Derridian motif — *quasi-transcendental*.

Once again, however, in glossing the force of the grotesque with the work of the Sublime, there is always the possibility of 'non-philosophy' marking a return to romantic modes of appropriation. Bataille, however, would introduce a more permanent subversion within the text of econo-mimesis. Throughout his work the call is for warfare on, not a reification of, the self and it is here that phenomenology passes into the more basic phenomena of hallucination and delirium. Between angels and opium, through shit and sacrifice, the intense nervous states of romantic experience are the really primary condition. Stripped of shape and form, of metaphor itself, it resists habitual codes of representation. But if nothing is given except in this equivocal fashion, are we labouring to open or to close the book? According to Derrida and Lyotard the task may well lie beyond us. For Deleuze and Bataille it is right here. Who is to say when romantic desire passes into romantic totality?

Notes

1. For a more extensive discussion of 'Tithonus' and death in romantic poetry see Ward (1986).
2. This notion from Deleuze and Guattari's *Anti-Oedipus* (1984), is put forward as a force of pure multiplicity, 'irreducible to any sort of unity'. The allegorical machine in *A Zed and Two Noughts* is a technical machine in the strict sense of the word in that it is geared towards combining heterogeneous parts into a structural whole. With its breakdown, however, the recording process opens up to a moment of anti-production; it becomes, in Deleuze and Guattari's elusive sense, a 'body without organs' — a disjunctive plain, or surface, on which desire is reinvested as pure

intensity, scrambling the restrictive codes of representation. See Deleuze and Guattari (1984: 10).
3. Georges Bataille, 'The Practice of Joy Before Death', in Bataille (1985: 238).
4. See Lyotard (1978: 45).
5. See Lyotard (1988: 13): 'my prose tried to destroy or deconstruct the presentation of any theatrical representaton whatsoever, with the goal of inscribing the passage of intensities directly in the prose without any mediation at all. This project was quite naive and a little compulsive'.
6. Friedrich Schlegel, 'On the Combinatory Spirit'; quoted in Lacoue-Labarthe and Nancy (1988: 119).
7. See Blanchot (1969), 'L'Athenaeum', pp. 515-27.
8. Preface to *The Excursion* (1814), in Wordsworth (1946, 5: 3; lines 28-9).
9. Wordsworth, 'Preface to Poems (1815)', in Wordsworth (1974, 3: 36-7).
10. Wordsworth, *Essays, Upon Epitaphs*, No. 3, in Wordsworth (1974, 2: 85).
11. See Larkin, P. (1981: 410): 'The later Wordsworth is not unconcerned with mysterious portents arising within him but the concern is no longer exploratory; he refrains rather from *self-rivalry* in what becomes a refrain to self-filiation. The diffusion of personal identity through time is survived via a disjunction that splits between the foundational and the secondary, and opens up a way of following the self by reinforcing a followable self'. *My emphasis*.
12. Bataille, 'The College of Sociology', in Bataille (1985: 251).
13. Bataille 'The Practice of Joy Before Death'. Ibid., p. 239.
14. See Queneau, R. 'Premieres Confrontations avec Hegel', *Critique*, No. 195-196, (August-September 1973): 694-700 referred to in Melville (1986: 71).
15. For partial translations, and as a useful introduction to Bataille's text in its relation to postructuralist theory, I am indebted to Melville (1986: 71-83).
16. The phrase is Melville's (1986: 70).
17. See Klancher (1987: 139).
18. For more on the theory of the parasite and the included/excluded third see Serres (1982).
19. Wordsworth, *Guide to the Lakes*, (1974, 2: 210).
20. See Rilke's 'Letter to Lotte Hepner, November 8, 1915', in Rilke (1987: 340).
21. Bataille, 'The Use Value of D.A.F. De Sade', in Bataille (1985: 96).
22. Ibid., p. 99.
23. See Kant (1973: 606). For a more extensive discussion of the link between Kant and Lyotard see Watson (1988: 189).

Bibliography

Bataille, G. (1970), 'Hegel, la Mort et la sacrifice', in *Oevres Completes*, Paris, Gallimard, 12 vols, 12: 326-345.
Bataille, G. (1985), *Visions of Excess: Selected Writings, 1927-1939*, (tr. and ed. Allan Stoekl), Minneapolis, University of Minnesota Press.
Blanchot, M. (1969), *L'Entretien Infini*, Paris, Gallimard.
Bloom et al., (ed.) (1979), *Deconstruction and Criticism*, London, Routledge and Kegan Paul.
Deleuze, G. and Guattari, F. (1984), *Anti-Oedipus: Capitalism and Schizophrenia*, (tr. Robert Hurley, Mark Seem, and Helen R. Lane), London, The Athlone Press.
Derrida, J. (1978), 'From Restricted to General Economy: A Hegelianism without Reserve', in *Writing and Difference*, (tr. Alan Bass), London, Routledge and Kegan Paul.
Derrida, J. (1982), 'The Pit and the Pyramid: Introduction to Hegel's Semiology', in *Margins of Philosophy*, (tr. Alan Bass), Chicago, Chicago University Press.

Hegel, G.W.F. (1977), *The Phenomenology of Spirit*, (tr. A.V. Miller), Oxford, Oxford University Press.
Kant, I. (1973), *Critique of Pure Reason*, (tr. Norman Kemp Smith), New York, Macmillan.
Klancher, J. (1987), *The Making Of English Reading Audiences, 1790-1832*, Madison, University of Wisconsin Press.
Lacoue-Labarthe, P. and Nancy, J. (1988), *The Literary Absolute*, (tr. P. Barnard and C. Lester), New York, State University of New York Press.
Larkin, P. (1981), 'Wordsworth's "After-Sojourn": Revision and Unself-Rivalry in the later Poetry', in *Studies In Romanticism*, 20: 409-437.
Lyotard, J.F. (1974) *Economie Libidinale*, Paris, Editions de Minuit.
Lyotard, J.F. (1978) 'Notes on the Return and Kapital', (tr. R. McKeon), *Semiotexte* 3,(1): 44-53.
Lyotard, J.F. (1984), *The Postmodern Condition: a Report on Knowledge*, (tr. G. Bennington and B. Massumi), Manchester, Manchester University Press.
Lyotard, J.F. (1985), *Just Gaming*, (tr. Wlad Godzich), Minneapolis, University of Minnesota Press.
Lyotard, J.F. (1988), *Peregrinations: Law, Form, Event*, New York, Columbia University Press.
de Man, P. (1979), *Allegories of Reading: Figural Language in Rousseau, Nietzsche, Rilke and Proust*, New Haven, Yale University Press.
Melville, S. (1986), *Philosophy Beside Itself: On Deconstruction and Modernism*, Manchester, Manchester University Press.
Rilke, R.M. (1987), *The Selected Poetry of Rainer Maria Rilke*, (tr. S. Mitchell), London, Pan Books.
Ruskin, J. (1903-1912), *The Complete Works*, (ed. E.T. Cook), 38 vols, London, George Allen.
Sanchez-Eppler, K. (1988) 'Decomposing: Wordsworth's Poetry of Epitaph and English Burial Reform', *Nineteenth Century Literature*, 42: 415-431.
Serres, M. (1982), *The Parasite*, (tr. L.R. Schebr), Baltimore, Johns Hopkins University Press.
Tennyson, A. (1987), *The Poems of Tennyson*, (ed. C. Ricks), 3 vols, London, Longmans.
Ward, G. (1986), 'Dying to Write: Maurice Blanchot and Tennyson's "Tithonus"', in *Critical Inquiry*, 12:4: 672-687.
Watson, S.H. (1988), 'The Adventures of the Narrative: Lyotard and the Passage of the Phantasm', in Silverman H.J. (ed.), *Philosophy and Non-Philosophy Since Merleau-Ponty*, London, Routledge.
Wordsworth, W. (1946), *The Poetical Works of William Wordsworth*, (ed. E. de Selincourt), 5 vols, Oxford, Oxford University Press.
Wordsworth, W. (1974), *The Prose Works of William Wordsworth*, (ed. W.J.B. Owen), 3 vols, Oxford, Oxford University Press.

2 Is Emily Brontë a Woman?: Feminity, Feminism and the Paranoid Critical Subject

Emma Francis

The critical history of Emily Brontë's poetry is a history of evasion. The vast body of work which advertises its subject as 'Emily Brontë' is, in fact, almost wholly engaged with *Wuthering Heights* (1847) (Brontë 1965). Where her poetry *is* read, the cacophany of other poetic voices almost invariably invoked when speaking of her work — ranging through the canon of male romanticism and its antecedents such as Milton — is at its loudest. That these comparisons function not to elucidate her poetics, but to avoid encountering them, became abundantly clear in 1986 when Robert K. Wallace published *Emily Brontë and Beethoven*. Wallace manages to go one better than the usual account of Brontë as an honorary male romantic a decade or more after the event. His variation of the theme — that Brontë was crucially influenced by her knowledge of the 'Byronic' life and works of Beethoven — is argued out within a structure which alternates discussion of Brontë's work with analysis of three of Beethoven's piano sonatas. This effectively drowns out Brontë for at least half the book, in a grotesque reification of the dynamic more generally at work in readings of her relation to romanticism.

I do not believe that the problem is that critics are incapable of understanding the issues Brontë is exploring in her poetry. For example, J. Hillis Miller's essay on *Wuthering Heights* in *Fiction and Repetition* (1982) is a sophisticated discussion of the way the novel frenetically generates more and more signs out of its sparse archetypes which, paradoxically, drives the possibility of establishing a central referent for them all, further and further away. The reader becomes as confused and disorientated in her search for a coherent interpretation of the narrative as Lockwood, when he is tormented by the 'swarms of Catherines' he sees after examining the first Cathy's alternative signatures graffitied on the windowsill at Wuthering Heights, and by the ever multiplying sermons of the Reverend Jabes Branderham he dreams of when he tries to sleep after reading her diary (Brontë 1965: 61–73). As I will argue later, this seems to me to be one of the main dynamics the poetry is engaged with. In a book concerned with narrative, it would not, of course, be necessary for Miller to make reference to the poetry at all. But he does invoke it, not to draw this parallel but to deny it. He claims that

> Brontë's problem, once she had agreed with her sisters to try her hand at a novel

was to bend the vision she had been more directly and privately expressing in the Gondal poems to the conventions of nineteenth century fiction ... (Miller 1982: 46)

That 'vision' cannot be expressed directly or privately and in the attempt to do so becomes distorted and refracted by the conventions of the medium it unsuccessfully attempts to represent itself in; is a form of stress which is extremely urgent in the poetry. It seems extraordinary that Miller makes his argument for the stress attached to the process of representation in *Wuthering Heights* by a comparison which (fallaciously) denies this stress in the poetry, when an affirmation of it would have substantiated his thesis even more effectively.

Similarly, an essay by Lawrence Starzyk, 'The Faith of Emily Brontë's Mortality Creed' (Starzyk 1973: 295-305),[1] which makes a virtue of the contradictions in Brontë's vision and analyses them in terms of her radical theology, chooses to do this by discussion of one of the few poems where identity, representation and argument are comparatively unified — *No Coward Soul is Mine* (Brontë 1985). Starzyk's point is much more clearly made in two other poems about religious experience, *The Prisoner* and *The Philosopher* (Brontë 1985) which I will consider below. Like Miller, he refuses to encounter his own view of Brontë at the point in her texts where the justification for it is being generated.

I have considered these two writers in the same space as the more outrageous instances of critical bad faith in order to give some idea of the force of the readerly paranoia Brontë's poetry seems to generate. I want to investigate why this might be the case in two ways. First, as a test case, I will give an account of the problems I encountered in my own reading of her poetry; my work on Brontë forms part of a project on nineteenth-century women's poetry. In previous work I had managed to identify a poetics of power and transgression in the poetry of women like Felicia Hemans (1793-1835), Letitia Landon (1802-1838) and Christina Rossetti (1830-1894). They were recuperable for a constructive political reading despite having been encumbered by two very unhelpful critical conventions. They have been read by traditional criticism as most charmingly willing to accept a subordinate poetic role, writing conventional and innocuous lyrics about flowers and piety, leaving the struggle with the collapse of teleology and the philosophical quandary of the relation between subject and object to the Big Boys.[2] Latterly, the reading of them produced by certain feminist critics, under the influence of Lacanian theories of women's problematic entry into and hold upon language, surprises itself with the fact that they managed to write at all.[3] In the face of the hugely prolific output of, in particular, Hemans and Landon who managed to support themselves and their families from their poetry, such accounts, for me, became incomprehensible. I also realized that their assiduous accession to aesthetic restraint — in relation to the forms of poetic language it was permissible for nineteenth-century women to use (which I will discuss below) and, thus, the positions it was possible for them to take up in the political and philosophical debates happening within nineteenth-century aesthetics — results in a repetition of the contradictions upon which those limits were based, which throws them into crisis.

This form of poetic (and political) triumph emerges from a writing and a reading which begins and ends firmly inside the gendered constraints of nineteenth-century poetics. But as I turned to Brontë, here at last, I thought, was a woman whose poetry deals with transgression in such an explicit way that I could not help but produce a rousing hymn of celebration to a woman's achievement, taking control of poetic language to articulate a programme of liberation. But it was precisely in terms of Brontë as a *woman* that I encountered problems in my analysis. The readings of her outlined above function around a refusal of Brontë as being what she is. In the readings of her in relation to the male romantics, there is a refusal that she is a Victorian. In the disproportionate emphasis on *Wuthering Heights* and the avoidance of her poetics at the point where they are most apparent, there is a refusal that she is a poet. As I began to investigate her poetics I experienced the temptation of a similar refusal — of Emily Brontë as a woman. This was not only because of her differences from the poetics of other nineteenth-century women. The terms of the debate about transgression her work led me into, seemed to contain no room for any account of feminity.[4] I will refer to the terms of Georges Bataille's (1973) discussion of Emily Brontë in *Literature and Evil* as representative of the tradition of theorizing transgression Brontë seems to relate to most, but which excludes some of the most crucial aspects of her poetry. Bataille's account brings to light the problems of Brontë's position as the 'avant-gardist' amongst nineteenth-century women poets and the price attached to the radical respectability she has retained among feminist and non-feminist critics.

Second, I will look in detail at *The Prisoner* and *The Philosopher*. It is from a stanza of *The Prisoner* that Bataille demonstrates his maxim 'Eroticism is the approval of life up until death'. (Bataille 1973: 4):

> Yet I would lose no sting, would wish no torture less;
> The more the anguish racks, the earlier it will bless;
> And robed in fires of hell or bright with heavenly shine,
> If it but herald death, the vision is divine! (stanza 18)

This account of desire, as the desire for the ultimate expenditure of identity in death certainly has some purchase on the poem. But the way in which this view of ecstasy as a kind of collapse is framed, by the context of political oppression it is situated in within the poem, reproduces the strategy present in many of the poems: the identities and moral categories which have been collapsed are redistinguished and redeployed. *The Prisoner* ends with the assertion that the disempowerment of the prisoner's oppressors is the result of (their perception of) an 'overruling' by heaven. This resurrects the recuperative dialectic Bataille celebrates Brontë for refusing. The point of excess, where 'life and death, the real and the imaginary, the past and the future, the communicable and the incommunicable' (Bataille 1973: 15 quoting Breton 1972: 123) and all other oppositional categories spill over into and erase each other, is alongside the reassertion of the power of these oppositions.

When we appreciate the way in which these two accounts of power interact with, and actually depend upon, each other in Brontë's poetics, we are getting close to understanding the issues at stake in the refusal she generates in us.

Is Emily Brontë a Woman?

Contrary to the view unproblematically assumed by traditional twentieth-century criticism and theorized by feminist critics such as Margaret Homans (1980),[5] nineteenth-century women were not under psychic or cultural prohibition against the use of poetic language *per se*. What *was* demanded of them was that they use a particular form of it — the language of the Beautiful. The aesthetic split between the Sublime and the Beautiful was formally theorized by Edmund Burke (1958) in *A Philosophical Enquiry into the Origins of Our Ideas of the Sublime and the Beautiful*, and had a huge purchase on English poetry throughout the nineteenth century. The prohibition nineteenth-century women poets were under was against the use of the language of the Sublime, which the male romantics used. The vast amount of poetry written by women in the nineteenth century exploring this aesthetic of the Beautiful was not just suffered, it was enormously popular and received a good deal of contemporary critical acclaim. For the most part, the only objections raised against the poetry are at the points when it transgresses the boundaries of the Beautiful. An explicitly gendered account of power is inscribed across this aesthetic demarcation. Power is produced in the Sublime (gendered male) and becomes dispersed in the Beautiful (gendered female). It is produced by the Sublime experience of threatened privation or death. The Beautiful cannot comprehend power because it is a structure of plenitude which does not have this threat of lack inscribed within it (Burke 1958: 54–71). Thus Brontë, who consistently refuses to write within the aesthetics of the Beautiful, places herself in a unique, and apparently attractively decisive, relation to the power up for grabs in nineteenth-century poetics.

It is largely on the basis of this ostensible lack of relation to the aesthetic of the Beautiful and her engagement with the Sublime structure of empowerment that Emily Brontë has retained her reputation as one woman who is unfettered by the 'masculinist' poetics which many feminist critics have seen as a force of symbolic prohibition on the production of other nineteenth-century women poets. Paradoxically, this has lead to a discussion of Brontë's transgressiveness in terms of parallels which have been drawn between her work and the male romantics. It is at this intersection that Bataille situates her triumph:

> Reproduction and death condition the immortal renewal of life; they condition the instant which is always new. That is why we can only have a tragic view of the enchantment of life, but that is also why tragedy is the symbol of enchantment. The entire romantic movement may have heralded this, but that late masterpiece, *Wuthering Heights*, heralds it most humanely. (Bataille 1973: 11)

Bataille also reminds us that she 'certainly read Byron' (Bataille 1973: 17). To situate my discussion of Brontë's radicalism within the terms of these poetics of transgression is to enter territory where my specifically feminist engagement with the poems, which attempts to speak about Brontë's radicalism in the same space as that of the other nineteenth-century women I am reading, becomes very difficult. Brontë's 'triumph' identified from this perspective is precisely the strategy refused by the other women who interrogate and redefine the limits of their aesthetic permission from within the confines of the Beautiful. I thus forego the possibility of establishing any kind of relation between Brontë's 'feminist' or even 'feminine' poetics and those of almost all other nineteenth-century women poets who refuse strategies of overt transgression, and who will, in this logic, be rendered negligible. Brontë's radicalism will be seen as a function of her *lack of* or difference from 'femininity'.

The dangers of this are highlighted by the striking similarity between Bataille's portrait of Brontë and that always drawn by traditional criticism of her, which has a large stake in disguising her radicalism. Bataille focuses on her 'courage', 'reserve' and 'devotion' (Bataille 1973: 1):

> She lived in a sort of silence which, it seemed, only literature could disrupt. The morning she died, after a brief lung illness, she got up at the usual time, joining her family without uttering a word and expired before midday, without even going back to bed. She had not wanted to see a doctor. (Bataille 1973: 1)

This discussion of lack of Victorian womanly vulnerability is accompanied in Bataille, as in traditional criticism, by an emphasis on the extremely sublimated nature of her 'passion':

> For though Emily Brontë, despite her beauty, appears to have had no experience of love she had an anguished knowledge of passion... keeping her moral purity intact, she had a profound experience of the abyss of evil. (Bataille 1973: 3)

It hardly needs to be pointed out that this is in complete contrast with the other writers discussed in Bataille's volume, whose implication in the most violent and transgressive forms of sexual practice is located by Bataille at the same point as the emanation of their transgressive philosophy and textual strategy. It is through an analysis of Brontë that Bataille concludes that 'Evil... is not only the dream of the wicked: it is to some extent the dream of the good' (Bataille 1973: 18). This involves him in the alignment of Brontë with Catherine (as against Heathcliff) who he defines as

> absolutely moral. She is so moral that she dies of not being able to detach herself from the man she loved when she was a child. But although she knows that Evil is deep within him, she loves him to the point of saying 'I am Heathcliff'. (Bataille 1973: 8)

This form of goodness, so overdetermined that it can comprehend evil, Bataille terms 'hypermorality' (Bataille 1973: 10). But it is Heathcliff who craves death in order to repair his attachment to Catherine. In chapter 29 he makes it his business to mutilate Cathy's coffin so that when he is buried next to her their two bodies will mingle in decomposition.

What is at stake in this most uncharacteristic demarcation of identities on Bataille's part is a refusal of feminity and feminine sexuality as non-transgressive. The patriarchal psychic formations implicated in this refusal are too obvious to merit discussion. The point is that she is placed by Bataille in the same isolation from the mass of nineteenth-century women poets as traditional criticism has always placed her, even if he does it for the opposite reason; the wish to recuperate, rather than deny her transgressiveness. It is significant that in this essay Bataille repairs his link with surrealism, which he had broken away from several decades before, in the invocation of Breton's *Second Surrealist*

Manifesto (1972). His quarrel with Breton had been that some surrealist accounts imply that transgression comes about for the individual on a psychic level, detached from social reality, rather than, as Bataille was anxious to emphasize, at the point where 'individual' psychic forces break down into the corporate movement of the 'Popular Front in the streets' (Bataille 1985: 161–168). The following passage comes from the same essay Bataille quotes to elucidate Brontë's conceptualization of the 'point . . . where life and death, the real and the imaginary' etc collapse into each other:

> What could those people who are still concerned about the position they occupy *in the world* expect from the Surrealist experiment? (It is) in this mental site, from which one can no longer set forth except for oneself on a dangerous but, we think, a supreme feat of reconnaissance. (Breton 1972: 124)

I cannot help feeling that by re-establishing the proximity of this text to his own work Bataille is gesturing towards a source of justification for his isolationist strategy. To make Brontë's transgressiveness a function of her uniqueness in this way, is to make it a function of her a-sexualism in both senses. Bataille's approach refuses her transgressiveness at the same point as traditional criticism does: her femininity. The transgressive moments which draw me to Brontë's texts, on closer examination repel me, as seemingly incompatible with identifying her in any meaningful way as a woman.

The Prisoner
The Prisoner (Brontë 1985) is curiously conscious of this dilemma. The woman who experiences what, I would agree with Bataille, is the most intense instance of this ecstasy within the poetry, is a 'marble' (if not plaster) saint, akin to the de-sexualized Emily Brontë thought capable of conceiving her:

> The captive raised her head; it was as soft and mild
> As sculptured marble saint or slumbering unweaned child.
> It was so soft and mild, it was so sweet and fair
> Pain could not trace a line nor grief a shadow there. (stanza 7)

The contradiction implicit in this description, that she is both 'soft' and 'hard', is multiplied by the fact that this celebration of her inviolacy comes precisely at the point at which she has been violated:

> The captive raised her hand and pressed it to her brow:
> 'I have been struck', she said, 'and I am suffering now'. (stanza 8)

Readers of *The Prisoner*, from Charlotte Brontë (who separated the first three stanzas from the rest of the poem in its 1850 edition) onwards, have been unable to comprehend the apparent disjuncture between different parts of the poem. I want to consider this phenomenon not as a manifestation of some kind of 'failure' but as central to its strategy. The initial encounter between the speaker and the prisoner establishes the dynamic of his relation to her as one of misrecognition. This lack of encounter occurs throughout the poem. The first three stanzas stand in problematic relation to the rest of the poem. They occur chronologically after, not before the narrative of the prisoner, making it impossible to read the beginning of the poem until we have read the end. The experience it describes seems to bear some relation to the prisoner's ecstasy. It looks to the coming of a 'Wanderer' who is invisible and invulnerable to hostile gazes, as the prisoner's 'messenger of hope' is. But this is not stated explicitly. Disparities in the language used to describe the two experiences throw into doubt whether they are the same. Within stanzas 13–18, the most frequently anthologized because the most seemingly unified section of the poem, are the most acute instances of lack of encounter, this time between experience and its representation. The transition between stanzas 13 and 14 signals that a representation of the ecstatic experience is about to be given: 'visions rise and fall that kill me with desire — /Desire for . . .'. But in stanza 14 the language of the collapse of identity we expect *is* employed, but to describe what the ecstatic experience *is not*. The desire invoked by the 'visions' is 'for nothing known in [the prisoner's] maturer years'. The remaining three lines of the stanza are given over to describing the condition of these 'maturer years', where the prisoner has insisted the experience cannot be situated. But it is at this moment when it is denied that all the elements of ecstasy occur. Time is disrupted and collapsed. Although the 'maturer years' are in the future, what will happen in them is spoken of in terms of history not prophecy: 'when joy *grew* mad with awe'. This reversal is then reversed again as the future, which is expressing itself as the past, doubles itself by looking towards a further future: 'at counting future tears'. The stanza then throws itself back to the (future) past: 'When, if my spirit's sky was full of flashes warm,/I knew not whence they came, from sun or thunder storm'. The breakdown of the boundary between interiority and exteriority of 'spirit's sky', and of demarcations in the natural world in the confusion of 'sun' and 'thunder storm' is made even more significant by the fact that the experience they are thrown into conflict by, the 'flashes warm', is expressed in a form which inverts the conventional order of noun and adjective.

Having (not quite) avoided representing ecstatic experience in this curious way, the prisoner's narrative picks up the description of the prelude to the experience and continues with it for the next two stanzas. The next point of disjuncture comes on the (second) point where the description tries to move into a representation of ecstasy, at the end of stanza 16:

> My outward sense is gone, my inward essence feels:
> Its wings are almost free — its home, its harbour found;
> Measuring the gulf it stoops and dares the final bound.

The battle between the imagery of liberation — 'Its wings are almost free', 'it dares' — and that of restriction — 'Its harbour found', 'it stoops' — culminates at the end of the stanza, where language is 'bound' inside the stanza, denied entry into the territory of the ecstatic experience which occurs, completely unrepresented, between stanzas 16 and 17. Representation comes back into operation at the point where the recession of ecstasy induces pain.

I do not believe that this avoidance of representing ecstatic experience should be seen as either aesthetic or ethical failure on Brontë's part. *The Prisoner* does not avoid encountering ecstasy. What it does is to deploy the experience and its representation separately. This interrogates, in an extraordinary anticipation of the avant-gardist dilemma, the political purchase of ecstatic experience.

Although this moment of ecstasy is situated at the point of the collapse of identity, encountering it in its represented form means that identity and agency are re-activated as we read the experience. The poem throws the act of reading into sharp relief; in both the emphasis on the lack of full encounter between the prisoner and the speaker persona, and in the problematic mis-reading we are forced to employ in order to reconstruct the ecstatic experience. Bataille's reading of Brontë's transgressiveness is achieved at the cost of de-sexualizing her in a way which, I have argued, is indistinguishable from the strategy of the most reactionary accounts of her. This is not the inevitable consequence of reading her accounts of the collapse of identity, but some politically charged consequence *is* inevitable. We can now begin to understand the relation of the first three stanzas to the rest of the poem. They explore, from within the text, what happens when the ecstatic experience is *read*. Affected by the prisoner's account of her liberation, the speaker of the poem attempts to enter into it himself. That he has misread it becomes apparent in his failure to reproduce the terms the prisoner represented it in. The prisoner's 'messenger' 'comes with western winds', 'evening's wandering airs' and 'that clear dusk of heaven that brings the thickest stars' (stanza 13). It is unclear whether it is the determining movement of these elements which brings the 'messenger', or whether his coming is coincidentally simultaneous with their coming. In the first speaker's perception there is none of this indeterminacy: 'The little lamp burns straight; its rays shoot strong and far/I trim it well to be the Wanderer's guiding star' (stanza 2). There is no doubt here that the material will determine the immaterial. The natural has also become transformed into the artificial. The substantiality of the 'thickest stars' has become transformed into 'lamp', the singular mimic of a star. Whereas the prisoner's stars thicken and burn of their own volition — they 'take a tender fire' — this severely edited version of them in the first speaker's narrative is mutilated further as he 'trims' the lamp. The first speaker situates the coming of his 'Wanderer' at the point when 'all (except himself) are laid asleep' despite the fact that the prisoner is identified with sleep by his admission — he calls her a 'slumbering unweaned child' and her own 'mute music soothes my breast, unuttered harmony/That I could never *dream* till earth is lost to me'. The 'Wanderer' is identified in more personified terms than the 'messenger' as the presence of the capital letter in his name implies. The prisoner's 'messenger' is mentioned once and then disappears in favour of the depersonalized 'visions'. The 'Wanderer' is retained in the first speaker's account and by the third stanza he has become an 'angel'. The transformation of the prisoner's experience, from the desire for the 'visions' of stanzas 13–16, to the desire for the 'Death' they will 'herald' in stanza 18, also fails to happen in the first speaker's account. He identifies his encounter with the 'Wanderer' or 'angel' wholly with the 'Cheerful', 'soft', pleasurable, interior he looks to draw him into. Violence and pain are identified with the outside, the 'wildering drifts' and 'groaning trees' tormented by the 'breeze'. The prisoner's account not only destroys the demarcation between inside and outside, but the 'visions' bring with them enough pain to 'kill', seemingly by means of the violence they have taken possession of from the 'winds' and 'stars', which are rendered 'pensive' and 'tender', more passive, by the visions' passage through them.

The political effect this (mis-) reading of the prisoner's ecstatic experience has is to activate an explicit master/slave dialectic. The ending of the poem, which propels us back to its opening, asserts the breakdown of the speaker's power over the prisoner. In the first three stanzas we find the speaker conscious of specific social oppression, paradoxically from those his language identifies as his social inferiors:

> Frown my haughty sire, chide, my angry dame;
> Set yourselves to spy, threaten me with shame;
> But neither sire nor dame, nor prying serf shall know
> What angel nightly tracks that waste of winter snow. (stanza 3)

The triumph of the prisoner is to construct liberation out of her oppression, to exchange 'short life' for 'eternal liberty'. The experience of her observer demonstrates that the attempt to reproduce the latter half of the equation involves invoking the former: the attempt to transgress involves simultaneously a deeper entry into the economy which resists transgression. At this point where the (inevitable) interaction of identity and its collapse produces paranoia, I will begin my discussion of *The Philosopher* (Brontë 1985), which deals with this structure even more explicitly.

The Philosopher

> There is indeed, etymologically, a close relationship between paranoia and ecstasy. If ecstasy is to be outside of oneself, then paranoia is to be literally beside oneself: *para* (alongside, beyond) + *noos*, *nous* (mind). In a sense paranoia can be understood as ecstasy experienced from 'within', ecstasy which still fears the loss of self, which has to be 'beside itself' but also has a desperate need to maintain the boundaries of it self's territories. (Wiliams 1989: 14)

If 'ecstasy' signifies the process of going beyond the self and the economy which sustains it, then paranoia is the process of (mis-) recognizing, with distress, that transgression. It is the inability to fully relinquish an identity which is collapsing. It is the disruption brought about within the economy ecstatic experience transcends, generated by the attempt to read that experience from a point of view still within that economy. It is the highly-stressed political articulation of ecstatic experience:

> O for the time when I shall sleep
> Without identity—
> And never care how rain may steep
> Or snow may cover me. (stanza 2)

Before he utters it, the poem has interpreted the philosopher's expression of desire for the ecstatic collapse of identity as the function of his paranoia. Whilst the philosopher is contemplating the physical suffering he could escape by death, the physical reality he separates himself from is wholly benign and pleasurable:

> Enough of Thought, Philosopher;
> Too long hast thou been dreaming
> Unlightened in this chamber drear
> While summer's sun is beaming—... (stanza 1)

This mis-recognition signals that the philosopher is in the same problematic 'paranoid' relation to ecstatic experience as the speaker in *The Prisoner*. His 'sad refrain' sets up insurmountable barriers to reaching ecstasy. If

> No promised Heaven these wild Desires
> Could all or half fulfil—
> No threatened Hell with quenchless fires,
> Subdue this quenchless will! (stanza 3)

it is impossible to imagine how identity *is* to be extinguished. The philosopher's appeal to a language of transcendence, to express the urgency of his plea, back-fires on him. The categories of Heaven and Hell have failed, but he can find no new language to replace them which could conceptualize a greater power to erase the need for 'fulfilment' and 'subdual'. Neither does he erase their authority. This is not a demonstrable atheism; the 'promise' and 'threat' of Heaven and Hell are not rendered negligible within the logic of the stanza. The literal meaning of these lines is that, due to the lack of any representative proof of the possibility of an economy beyond Heaven and Hell, the subsistence of identity, which is the inevitable consequence of it, will continue. Any other reading which would see this stanza as looking towards (the possibility of) an alternative economy, depends upon a preconception of that economy's existence and constitution. This mis-match between what we and the philosopher feel the stanza should say and what it actually does say is registered by the overdeterminedly or doubly poetic nature of the two stanzas. In *The Prisoner*, the problem of how to represent ecstatic experience is dealt with by deploying the experience and its representation in different places. In these two stanzas of *The Philosopher* the problem is much more urgent. Not only is there a complete failure to represent ecstasy, but the enormous stress generated by trying to represent it creates the need for language to signal itself as present and pre-eminent, by italicizing itself. Similarly, the first speaker's appeal to the philosopher in stanza 1 'what sad refrain/concludes thy musings once again?' invites and expects the repetition of a pre-existent linguistic pattern. These poems seem to allow no escape from the argument that the attempt to represent the collapse of identity is militated against by the process of representation itself.

But as the poem continues, the possibility of encountering, through representation, even the economy of fixed identities disappears. The philosopher recalls his encounter with 'A Spirit' who seems to suggest some way out of this bleak situation. He appeared in a very specific spatial and temporal position, 'I saw a Spirit standing, man/Where thou dost stand an hour ago', (stanza 7). Yet when the philosopher attempts to search for him within this economy of identifiable time and space he finds that the spirit is no longer there:

> —And even for that Spirit, Seer,
> I've watched and sought my lifetime long;
> Sought Him in Heaven, Hell, Earth and Air,
> An endless search and always wrong! (stanza 10)

This desperate searching around definable space and time activates the limitless — 'endless' and 'always'. The philosopher appeals to the spirit as an alternative to the need for the erasure of identity:

> Had I but seen his glorious eye
> Once light the clouds that 'wilder me,
> I ne'er had raised this coward cry
> To cease to think and cease to be. (stanza 11)

But the very condition and motivation of the philosopher's appeal is that the spirit is part of the economy where identity collapses, he is both present and absent, reachable and unreachable in the structure of the poem. The philosopher's search within the economy of identity activates the categories of its dissolution. As was the case in *The Prisoner*, the (partial) representation the poem makes of the possibility of this collapse is thus dependent on the activity of the economy which refuses it. The philosopher attributes to the spirit the power of a transformatory gaze. In fact the poem argues that in spite of himself, the philosopher's gaze is transformative. Under pressure of it, the spirit shifts from one economy to another. But this power is dependent upon the philosopher at each stage mis-recognizing the economy he is within. He is perpetually 'beside himself', failing to comprehend and encounter where he is.

This 'paranoia' is fundamental to the strategy of the poem as a whole. Unlike *The Prisoner* which was split between two voices, *The Philosopher* has a triple articulation. We have extremely sparse information about the first speaker. He is identified directly twice by the philosopher, in stanzas 7 and 10, on both occasions immediately after an identification of the spirit. The syntax of the first identification allows for the designation 'Man' to be a qualification of the ontology of the spirit: 'I saw a Spirit standing, Man,' (stanza 7). The fact that he has the closest spatial and temporal contact with the elusive spirit adds to the suggestion that they are identical. The second address identifies him as 'Seer'. Because of the semantic similarity of this category with that of philosopher, a similar collapse occurs between the philosopher and the one to whom he expresses his alienation. So, in a sense, the collapse of identity the philosopher longs for is already happening, and is a symptom of the strength of his despair of it.

Poetics, Politics and Paranoia

The study of transgression happening in these two poems is more complex than Bataille suggests. Alongside an expression of the desire for the collapse of identity, Brontë places an account of the paranoia — the distress registered at this collapse — which is the inevitable consequence of encountering it. In a sense, Brontë is giving us an account of what happens when we try to read her, inside her poems.

In the light of this analysis it becomes possible to see why all readers of Brontë, including me, have experienced such a strong temptation to refuse her poetry. My readerly paranoia, my temptation to make Brontë into a 'special case' because she challenged a category I was determined to invoke in relation to her, arose through trying to place her as a *woman* in the face of her repudiation of the poetics other nineteenth-century women poets unanimously embrace, and (consequently) the undesirably misogynist conceptualizations of transgression I was forced into. These problems seemed to be unique to the particular context of my reading. But uncovering this dynamic of the production of paranoia which is so central to the poems, indicates the link of my specific problems with those of the other readers of Brontë I cited at the beginning of this paper. It seems that the stronger the temptation Brontë produces to try and identify a particular formation her poetry offers us, and the stronger the critical good faith we are prepared to employ in this attempt, the more the poetry confounds us. But looking closely at, in particular, *The Philosopher* has made me realize how vital it is that I do not abandon her, that I do not deny that she is a woman. In this poem it is at the point where the process of mis-reading is at its most acute that what is being searched for emerges. The desired collapse of identity is articulated by the philosopher's cry of despair of it ever being possible. Translated back onto my reading of Brontë, this means that I do not need to be haunted by her image as a male Romantic, developing a poetics which repudiates femininity.

From a methodological point of view, I also find this concept of reading as a form of paranoia extremely attractive. It seems to me to be a very productive way to conceive the strategy I, as a feminist critic, want to bring to the texts I am working on. A central problem in feminist readings of texts from previous historical periods is that they either place twentieth-century political problems and structures of thought onto texts to which in various ways they are not appropriate, or, alternatively, they attempt to let the text determine its own terms of discussion, which is impossible; but even if it were not, it removes the focus of the reading from the political urgency which originally stimulated it. If, as a feminist critic, I admit myself as terminally paranoid — that is, in distress at the way in which the political questions and demands I carry are being undermined and reformulated by the texts as I am reading them — I will be simultaneously encountering both my own motivation for entering these texts *and* the way the uniqueness of each text can sustain and enrich this motivation.

This paranoia, this point of crisis in reading which I believe is potential in all texts, but which is inescapable in Brontë's poetry, is an agony which is wholly productive. If Miller, Starzyk, all the other critics of Brontë and my own reading of her would enter into it fully, we would experience fully the power of the political vision we must never be ashamed to own in our relation to the text. But we must also not be afraid to see collapse, in order to have it returned to us in forms we could never imagine without this violence.

Notes

1. This is the only extended discussion of Emily Brontë, in the periodical *Victorian Poetry*, which indicates the strength of the refusal to engage with her as a Victorian, generated by her association with romanticism.
2. See, for example, Elizabeth Jennings' 'Introduction' to *A Choice of Christina Rossetti's Verse*, Faber (1970): 'Christina was the least intellectual of the family of two girls and two boys ... Her subjects were limited, it is true, but she never made the mistake of writing beyond the limits of her experience' (pp. 11-12).
3. This assumption has been axiomatic since the onset of feminist work on nineteenth-century women's texts. Both Sandra Gilbert and Susan Gubar's *The Madwoman in the Attic*, Yale University Press (1979), and Margaret Homans' *Women Writers and*

Poetic Identity, Princeton University Press (1980), take it as read that women are psychically and culturally prohibited from using poetic language. This assumption has remained so inviolate that in 1987 Jan Montefiore could devote her chapter on Christina Rossetti, in *Feminism and Poetry*, to a Lacanian reading of the sonnet sequence *Monna Innominata*, arguing that the text expresses the poet's inability to overcome symbolic prohibition in the structure of poetic language.
4. In *Gender and Genius*, The Women's Press (1989), Christine Battersby has pointed out the problems clustered around the use of the term 'femininity' in nineteenth-century aesthetics. Standing in for a particular condition of consciousness and language the romantics sought to achieve in their poetry, it in fact excludes women (as biological and historical subjects) from itself. I am attempting to reclaim this term, using it to signify not just the biological category of 'woman', but at the point in my argument where I attempt to align this category with an account of language which will represent *and* transgress it.
5. See note 3. above.

Bibliography

Bataille, G. (1973), 'Emily Bronte', *Literature and Evil*, 3-17, (tr. Hamilton, A.), London, Calder and Boyars.
Bataille, G. (1985), 'The Popular Front in the Streets', *Visions of Excess*, 161-168, (tr. Stoekl, A.), Manchester, Manchester University Press.
Battersby, C. (1989), *Gender and Genius: Towards a Feminist Aesthetic*, London, The Women's Press.
Breton, A. (1972), 'Second Surrealist Manifesto' (1930), *Manifestos of Surrealism*, (tr. Seaver, R. and Lane, H.R.), Ann Arbor, University of Michigan Press.
Bronte, E.J. (1846a), 'No Coward Soul Is Mine', in Bronte (1985): 172-3.
Bronte, E.J. (1846b), 'The Prisoner', in Bronte (1985): 170-2.
Bronte, E.J. (1846c), 'The Philosopher', in Bronte (1985): 161-2.
Brontë, E.J. (1965), *Wuthering Heights* (1847), (ed. Daiches, D.) Harmondsworth, Penguin.
Brontë, E.J. (1985), *Selected Brontë Poems*, (ed. Chitham, E. and Winnifrith, T.), Oxford, Basil Blackwell.
Burke, E. (1958), *A Philosophical Inquiry into the Origins of Our Ideas of the Sublime and the Beautiful* (1757), (ed. Boulton, J.T.), Oxford, Basil Blackwell.
Gilbert, S. and Gubar, S. (1979), *The Madwoman in the Attic: The Woman Writer and the Nineteenth-Century Literary Imagination*, New Haven, University of Yale Press.
Homans, M. (1980), *Women Writers and Poetic Identity: Dorothy Wordsworth, Emily Brontë and Emily Dickinson*, Princeton (N.J.), Princeton University Press.
Jennings, E. (1970), 'Introduction' to *A Choice of Christina Rossetti's Verse*, London, Faber and Faber.
Miller, J.H. (1982), *Fiction and Repetition*, Oxford, Basil Blackwell.
Montefiore, J. (1987), *Feminism and Poetry*, London, Pandora Press.
Starzyk, L. (1973), 'The Faith of Emily Brontë's Mortality Creed', *Victorian Poetry*, 11, 295-305.
Wallace, K. (1986), *Emily Brontë and Beethoven*, Athens, Georgia University Press.
Williams, L.R. (1989), 'Submission and Reading: Feminine Masochism and Feminist Criticism', *New Formations 7: Modernism and Masochism*, 11-17.

3 'What language can utter the feeling': Identity in the Poetry of Emily Brontë

Kathryn Burlinson

'No coward soul is mine' proclaims the speaker of Emily Brontë's 1846 lyric which takes this line as its title; 'No trembler in the world's storm-troubled sphere'.[1] Such courageous assertions accord with the popular conception of Emily Brontë as wild girl of the moors, unafraid to separate fighting dogs with her bare hands, battling against elements and elegance alike. Brontë myths have notoriously overshadowed Brontë texts, yet in Emily Brontë's poetry there are instances where poetic voices wilfully speak out against convention and constraint, giving some credence to the literary myth-makers. In 'Often rebuked, yet always back returning' (H: 255),[2] the speaker naïvely yet proudly defies religious, historical and literary tradition, asserting independence of spirit and refusing guidance out with the self:

> I'll walk, but not in old heroic traces,
> And not in paths of high morality,
> And not among the half-distinguished faces
> The clouded forms of long-past history. (stanza 1)
>
> I'll walk where mine own nature would be leading:
> It vexes me to choose another guide... (stanza 4)

Yet alongside such unequivocal affirmations run other, far less assured, figurations of the self; figurations that problematize the issue of 'mine own nature' and propose a model of identity that is unstable, divided, and temporally indeterminate. The making of the self is a constant preoccupation in Brontë's lyric verse, as it is in *Wuthering Heights* (Brontë 1967). Leo Bersani's observation on the novel that 'the question is not so much what to be as how to be' might equally be applied to the poetry (Bersani 1978: 190).

In this focus on subjectivity, Brontë may be seen to have much in common with her romantic fore-fathers, and certainly Wordsworthian and Byronic ideologies of the self are noticeable in her work. But Brontë also exhibits a post-romantic (and Victorian) preoccupation with the legacy of romanticism, where doubts about the self and its potentiality underpin poetic articulation.[3] Transcendent subjectivity may still be desired in Brontë's writing, but the impossibility of this project is repeatedly figured. There is a troubled recognition that the high romantic dream of obliterating the distinction between subject and object necessarily defeats itself, for the negation of difference is also the negation of the self. As Catherine Belsey (1986: 68) has put it, 'the obliteration of the object implies the fading of the subject' for the self ceases to be when it has no other against which to define itself. A similar recognition occurs in 'I'm happiest when most away' of 1838 (H: 220), where imaginative apprehension of a state outside the constraints of self-consciousness simultaneously anticipates the dissolution of the self. Union with 'infinite immensity' only takes place 'When I am not and none beside'.

Historically situated between the political and aesthetic idealism of romanticism and the emergence and consolidation of Victorian cultural identity,[4] Brontë's poetic texts are the site of a struggle in which self-representation is fraught with doubt and difficulty. A number of lyrics discussed here focus on locating the self in language and in time; others explicitly address self-division and yearn for its cessation. One such is 'Enough of Thought, Philosopher' of 1845 (H: 220), a dialogue in which one speaker challenges the 'sad refrain' of a 'Philosopher', whose recurrent 'musings' on quotidian existence, as Stevie Davies (1983: 86) has observed, amount to an unqualified death-wish:

> O for the time when I shall sleep
> Without identity,
> And never care how rain may steep
> Or snow may cover me!
>
> No promised Heaven, these wild Desires
> Could all or half fulfil;
> No threatened Hell, with quenchless fires,
> Subdue this quenchless will! (stanzas 2 and 3)

The next stanza establishes the link between the philosopher's death-drive and the experience of self-division, as the self is split into conflicting forces. Sacrilegiously, the philosopher claims that 'Three Gods within this little frame/Are warring night and day'. This blasphemous parallel to the Holy Trinity goes beyond a simple dualism of the self, and proposes a model of identity which denies unity within. Though the lyric's other speaker then recalls a vision in which a 'Spirit' unified three divergent streams (or selves), the philosopher's search for such an experience of subjective totality is described as 'an endless search and always wrong!' Scepticism about the existence of a unifying agent blends with yearning for such a possibility, as the philosopher replies to the first speaker:

> —And even for that Spirit, Seer,
> I've watched and searched my lifetime long;
> Sought Him in Heaven, Hell, Earth and Air,
> An endless search and always wrong!
>
> Had I but seen his glorious eye
> Once light the clouds that 'wilder me,
> I ne'er had raised this coward cry
> To cease to think and cease to be. (stanzas 10 and 11)

The philosopher cannot find the 'Spirit' or 'Word' which might assure stability, and this produces a despair which is seen to find relief only in release from self-consciousness. Only in death may the warring selves make peace, as all is finally 'lost in one repose'.

'Enough of Thought, Philosopher' is one among a number of Brontë's poems which use dialogue as a way of writing about divisions in the self. But Brontë does not always allow her speakers to remain as distinct as they appear in this poem; not, for example, in the lyric 'In the earth, the earth, thou shalt be laid' (H: 190). Here the stances adopted by the two speakers dissolve, towards the end of the lyric, into a complex interfusion in which absolute positions are difficult to distinguish. The lyric may be read as an internal dialogue that contemplates romantic perspectives on death. Its significance in relation to Brontë's model of identity lies in its inability to maintain stability, even between the seemingly opposed inner voices.

The poem begins with the first speaker gloomily predicting the mortal fate of the other, perceiving the grave as morbid and repellent: 'In the earth, the earth, thou shalt be laid, /A grey stone standing over thee;/Black mould beneath thee spread/And black mould to cover thee'. The second voice then expresses a romantic ideal of death as ultimate mergence with nature: ' "Well, there is rest there, So fast come thy prophecy;/The time when my sunny hair/Shall with grass roots twinèd be" '. An opposition is thus established between the two points of view, with the borderline between life and death appearing more questionable for the second speaker than for the first. Nature's process of absorption and reclamation is simultaneously a process which the second speaker wishes to surrender to, and one that s/he looks forward to being actively involved in.

The first speaker then protests: 'But cold, cold is that resting place/... All who loved thy living face/Will shrink from its gloom and thee'. Yet here the first speaker adopts the discourse of the second in speaking of the grave as a 'resting place'. Although this is a clichéd euphemism, it nonetheless implies some ongoing possibility of consciousness or sentience after death. The oppositions between the two voices, and between life/death begin to be problematized. This kind of impinging of one voice upon another continues through the next stanza, as the second speaker replies: ' "... *here* the world is chill,/And sworn friends fall from me;/But *there*, they'll own me still/And prize my memory" '. It is the second speaker that now insists on division and separation, but s/he inverts the other's perspective in attributing 'chill' to the living world and constancy in relationships to the grave.

In the lyric's penultimate stanza, only one voice remains, and it appears to be that of the first speaker, lamenting the death of the other: 'Farewell, then, all that love,/All that deep sympathy'. The lyric's last stanza, however, ends with the following couplet: 'One heart broke only there —/*That* heart was worthy thee!' This is an odd and equivocal ending, for 'There' appears to refer to the grave, yet hearts conventionally break in the living, not the dead. There is an ambiguity about *which* heart is being referred to, and this raises the question as to who is actually speaking. The assertion in the penultimate stanza is similarly disorienting, as the speaker seems simultaneously to posit absolute truths about the indifference of the universe: '... heaven laughs above/Earth never misses thee', and to undermine these certainties by seeming to speak from a position in which such things are not knowable — ie from this side of death.

The lyric, ultimately, refuses to settle on a stable point of reference. And it illustrates the difficulty of locating any final point of certainty with the self, as internal dialogue becomes increasingly scrambled and confused.

Uncertainty, self-doubt, and self-diffusive energies may be found not only in Brontë's lyric verse but also in the Gondal poems, where the persona of a particular character acts as a mask behind which explorations of identity take place. 'Rosina Alcona to Julius Brenzaida' (H: 222) is concerned with memory; not only the memory of an other but the remembrance of the self's past selves, and in A.G.A. (H: 54–5), it is the multiple shadows and spectres of the unconscious mind which preoccupy the lyric. Often, it is through temporal shifts in Brontë's texts that the flux of subjectivity is registered, as the lyrics slide and skip between different temporal locations. A fairly minor example of this tendency can be seen in 'I am the only being whose doom' of 1837 (H: 36). What is also interesting here is the way in which the text disrupts the reader's position, refusing us the satisfaction of stability at the lyric's end.

In the first part of this poem, the 'I' reflects upon itself, writing itself in negative formulations and speaking of its own insignificance to others:

> I am the only being whose doom
> No tongue would ask, no eye would mourn;
> I never caused a thought of gloom,
> A smile of joy, since I was born. (stanza 1)

A special responsibility is placed upon the reader here for the utterance is dependent upon an addressee, yet the 'I' claims to have no relation with any textual 'other'. But we are not able simply to identify with the speaker's plight. For at the end of the poem, she likens herself to all who are 'hollow, servile, insincere' and confesses to her own 'corruption'. This final stanza confirms what the reader may have felt in stanzas 3 and 4, where the speaker admits, and then immediately denies, the desire for love. Stanza 3 confesses that:

> There have been times I cannot hide,
> There have been times when this was drear,
> When my sad soul forgot its pride
> And longed for one to love me here. (stanza 3)

Though the speaker is looking back in time, we are told that she 'cannot' hide her past desire 'for one to love me here'. The present tense of 'cannot' locates the utterance in this temporal dimension, yet the next stanza banishes not only past feelings but their present acknowledgement:

> But those were in the early glow
> Of feelings since subdued by care;
> And they have died so long ago,
> I hardly now believe they were. (stanza 4)

We cannot share the speaker's tendency to disbelieve, following so recent an admission. The voice of this lyric refuses to speak logically and sequentially about itself, finally throwing all its utterances into question in the final stanza. We cannot force coherence on the text; rather it forces us to accept an unstable, shifting and untrustworthy self.

If lyrics such as 'I am the only being whose doom' force an acceptance of inconsistencies and contradictions in respect of subjectivity, other Brontë poems explore the connected problem of the relationship between ourselves and our language. One such is 'Loud without the wind was roaring' of 1838 (H: 90). This will be quoted in full.

1. Loud without the wind was roaring
   Through the waned autumnal sky;
   Drenching wet, the cold rain pouring
   Spoke of storming winters nigh.

2. All too like that dreary eve
   Sighed within repining grief;
   Sighed at first, but sighed not long—
   Sweet—How softly sweet it came!
   Wild words of an ancient song,
   Undefined, without a name.

3. 'It was spring, for the skylark was singing.'
   Those words, they awakened a spell—
   They unlocked a deep fountain whose springing
   Nor Absence nor Distance can quell.

4. In the gloom of a cloudy November,
   They uttered the music of May;
   They kindled the perishing ember
   Into fervour that could not decay.

5. Awaken on all my dear moorlands
   The wind in its glory and pride!
   O call me from valleys and highlands
   To walk by the hill-river's side!

6. It is swelled with the first snowy weather;
   The rocks they are icy and hoar
   And darker waves round the long heather
   And the fern-leaves are sunny no more.

7. There are no yellow-stars on the mountain,
   The blue-bells have long died away
   From the brink of the moss-bedded fountain,
   From the side of the wintery brae—

8. But lovelier than corn-fields all waving
   In emerald and scarlet and gold
   Are the slopes where the north-wind is raving,
   And the glens where I wandered of old.

9. 'It was morning; the bright sun was beaming.'
   How sweetly that brought back to me
   The time when nor labour nor dreaming
   Broke the sleep of the happy and free.

10. But blithely we rose as the dusk heaven
    Was melting to amber and blue;
    And swift were the wings to our feet given
    While we traversed the meadows of dew,

11. For the moors, for the moors where the short grass
    Like velvet beneath us should lie!
    For the moors, for the moors where each high pass
    Rose sunny against the clear sky!

12. For the moors where the linnet was trilling
    Its song on the old granite stone;
    Where the lark—the wild skylark was filling
    Every breast with delight like its own.

13. What language can utter the feeling
    That rose when, in exile afar,
    On the brow of a lonely hill kneeling
    I saw the brown heath growing there.

14. It was scattered and stunted, and told me
    That soon even that would be gone;
    Its whispered, 'The grim walls enfold me;
    I have bloomed in my last summer's sun.'

15. But not the loved music whose waking
    Makes the soul of the Swiss die away
    Has a spell more adored and heart-breaking
    Than in its half-blighted bells lay.

16. The spirit that bent 'neath its power,
    How it longed, how it burned to be free!
    If I could have wept in that hour
    Those tears had been heaven to me.

17. Well, well, the sad minutes are moving
    Though loaded with trouble and pain;
    And sometime the loved and the loving
    Shall meet on the mountains again.

This text is ostensibly concerned with the speaker's recollections of the natural world. The lyric also raises questions, however, about writing and representation, for example in stanza 13, as the speaker asks 'What language can utter the feeling/That rose when, in exile afar,/On the brow of a lonely hill kneeling/I saw the brown heath growing there'.

This is a question that the text yearns to answer, to this end deploying a range of linguistic strategies throughout the poem, all of which seek, in one way or another, to 'utter the feeling' and establish relation. The question is also, and crucially, concerned with the problem of matching past experience — 'I saw the brown heath growing there' — with present expression. Re-presentation in writing, in respect of nature, the self, and time, is a central problem with which the lyric struggles. Stanza 14 describes the heath's communication with the speaker: 'It was scattered and stunted, and told me/That soon even that would be gone;/Its whispered, "The grim walls enfold me;/I have bloomed in my last summer's sun".' The problem here of course is that words are re-presenting nature, that nature is seen to speak in words. The existence of any 'pre-linguistic', unmediated contact between the speaker and the natural world is lost in the recollection, as words stand in for nature in its absence. Nature's figuration within poetic/linguistic convention is stressed at the very start of the lyric, as the pouring rain of the first stanza '*Spoke* of stormy winters nigh' (my italics). Further, the relation between human and natural realms is baldly exposed as relying on the adoption of simile or metaphor in the opening of stanza 2: 'All too like that dreary eve/Sighed within repining grief;'.

Language as agency is also stressed as the 'words' of a remembered 'song' awaken 'a spell' in the 3rd stanza, unlocking a 'deep fountain' or spontaneous linguistic overflowing which promises to overcome 'Absence' and 'Distance'. But this is a promise that remains unfulfilled, as all that is generated is more language — language which assures that temporal and spatial division is maintained.

As the lyric progresses, the speaker's attempt to recover personal experience is overriden (or re-covered) by the constant production of new texts. In the ninth stanza, the remembered song generates another temporal and linguistic frame — 'that brought back to me' — which then evokes another text — 'The time when nor labour nor dreaming/Broke the sleep of the happy and free'. The pre-lapsarian tone of these lines suddenly gives way to a romance mode as a lovers' narrative is introduced at the beginning of stanza 10: 'But blithely we rose'. The lovers, however, do not reach their destination, though they begin a journey, for by the time we reach stanza 13 it is only the 'I' which remains, and an 'exile[d]' 'I' at that: the affirmation of relation between self and other, which fades, then shifts to an affirmation of relation between self and nature, which is immediately problematized in 'What language can utter the feeling'.

One of the effects of this production of new texts is to render it difficult to locate the speaker in time. The lyric operates within at least three temporal dimensions, three 'layers' of memory, but there is (once again) no fixed point from which the 'I' speaks.

The 'Wild words of an ancient song/Undefined, without a name', come to the speaker as if in a moment of inspiration in the lyric's second stanza, and appear in different guises in the quoted lines of stanzas 3 and 9. We do not learn the origin of this song though it evokes origin in itself, speaking of beginnings — 'spring' and 'morning' — and of an ancient time before linguistic definition — 'Undefined, without a name'. This appears to echo Rousseau's idea that song preceded speech,[5] yet although the lyric strives to recover the 'sweet' moment of hearing the song, this proves as impossible as it would be to discover the original Word, *writing's* mythical inspiration. The quoted lines of stanzas 3 and 9 are of course *remembered*, and do not necessarily correspond to the 'ancient song' itself.

If it is the original Word that is desired, the paradox highlighted in this lyric is that writing moves onwards in its attempt to re-capture. The lyric chases nature yet reveals the impossibility of capturing it in its own time, as language continually imposes *its* terms and *its* time. 'Loud without the wind was roaring' ends with the poem registering the onward march of time in the movement of a line: 'Well, well, the sad minutes are moving,' as it looks forward to the next time — 'sometime' — when, it is promised, a union will take place.

'Loud without the wind was roaring', like the other poems discussed here, illustrates Brontë's interrogation of identity and representation — themes pursued also in *Wuthering Heights*. Brontë's poetry has often been devalued beside the achievement of her novel, but this perspective appears fit for review. The poetry does, however, demand an aesthetics which can allow for fractures and fragmentations, uncertainties and contradictions. In 1976 Robin Grove sounded slightly alarmed when he suggested that in Brontë's verse 'No "self" worth speaking of is, really, engaged' (Grove 1976: 44). Yet by 1983, Stevie

Davies was confidently asserting the 'continuous and irascible self-division' in Brontë's poetry (Davies 1983: 86). I will go further in suggesting that Brontë's explorations of identity and her questioning of the stable subject may be relevant to the discussion not only of romantic and Victorian verse, but also of modernist writing. If the instability of subjectivity is seen as a primary preoccupation of modernism, it is clearly not confined therein. To adopt a teleological perspective is of course problematic, but we might nonetheless feel prompted to re-write the biographical comment made by Brontë's tutor M. Héger: 'She should have been a man — a great navigator' (Gaskell 1975: 230), since from the perspective of the twentieth century, her own navigations appear to have been right on course.

Notes

1. All references to Brontë's poems are to *The Complete Poems of Emily Jane Brontë*, edited by C.W. Hatfield (1941), New York, Columbia University Press; hereafter referred to as H followed by page number, eg 'No coward soul is mine' (H: 243).
2. Hatfield disputes Emily's authorship of this poem, but this has subsequently been contested and it is generally agreed that the poem is Emily's.
3. For a discussion of this tendency in the work of Robert Browning, see Aidan Day's critical commentary in *Browning: Selected Poetry and Prose*, London, Routledge, forthcoming. It might also be argued here that Shelley's verse is troubled by similar preoccupations.
4. Although there is much disagreement about precisely what constitutes the Victorian period, I am taking Victoria's accession to the throne in 1830 as its beginning. The bulk of Brontë's poetry was written between 1838 and 1845.
5. See Rousseau's *Essay on the Origin of Language* (1967), tr. John H. Moran, and Derrida's critique in *Of Grammatology* (1974: 165-268), tr. Gayatri Spivak, Baltimore, Johns Hopkins University Press.

Bibliography

Belsey, C. (1986), 'The Romantic Construction of the Unconscious', in Barker et al., (eds), *Literature, Politics and Theory*, London, Methuen, 57-76.
Bersani, L. (1978), *A Future For Astyanax*, London, Marion Boyars Ltd.
Brontë, E. (1967), *Wuthering Heights*, (ed. David Daiches), Harmondsworth, Penguin.
Davies, S. (1983), *Emily Brontë: The Artist As A Free Woman*, Manchester, Carcanet.
Day, A. (ed.) (forthcoming), *Browning: Selected Poetry and Prose*, London, Routledge.
Derrida, J. (1974), *Of Grammatology*, (tr. Gayatri Spivak), Baltimore, Johns Hopkins University Press.
Gaskell, E. (1975), *The Life Of Charlotte Brontë*, Harmondsworth, Penguin.
Grove, R. (1976), ' "It Would Not Do": Emily Brontë as Poet', in Smith, A. (ed.) (1976), *The Art Of Emily Brontë*, London, Vision Press, 33-67.
Hatfield, C.W. (ed.) (1941), *The Complete Poems of Emily Jane Brontë*, New York, Columbia University Press.
Homans, M. (1980), *Women Writers and Poetic Identity*, Princeton, Princeton University Press.
Rousseau, J. (1967), *Essay On The Origin Of Language*, (tr. John H. Moran), New York, F. Ungar.

4 Epiphany and Subjectivity in Charlotte Brontë's *Villette*
Susan Watkins

The term *epiphany* is probably most closely associated with the work of James Joyce. There has been considerable confusion over the concept and its use, so firstly I would like to establish a working definition of epiphany which will be used throughout this article, and secondly, to link this term with Charlotte Brontë's *Villette* (Bronte: 1985).

In the early part of his literary career James Joyce made a collection of brief prose poems. He called them epiphanies and recorded them in a volume of the same name.[1] Later, Joyce extensively 'borrowed' these scenes for inclusion in his prose fiction.

Epiphany is also well known to Joyce critics as part of Stephen Dedalus' theory of aesthetics in *Stephen Hero* (Joyce 1969) (the preworking of *A Portrait of the Artist as a Young Man*) (Joyce 1987a). Stephen observes a man and a woman talking at night as he walks the streets of Dublin, and the experience affects him profoundly. He evolves his theory of the epiphany to describe moments like these, which he defines as 'a sudden spiritual manifestation, whether in the vulgarity of speech and gesture or in a memorable phrase of the mind itself' (Joyce 1969: 217).

Critics have since associated the term epiphany with other *moments of revelation* in the work of Joyce and other authors, for example the wading girl episode at the end of chapter four of *A Portrait*. Here, Stephen struggles to forge an identity that admits sexuality and emotion, and free himself of the ideological restraints of the Catholic church. Other, similar epiphanies abound in Joyce's work: Gabriel's experience at the end of 'The Dead' (Joyce 1987b) and Stephen's pandybatting, to name but two. What is common to all these experiences is a concern with the construction of character and subjectivity within a text. Such moments act as nodal points for the realization and development of the self.

Major criticism discussing epiphany has confined itself to Joyce and other 'mainstream' moderns like Woolf, James and Eliot. Connections have been made between Wordsworthian *spots of time* experiences and epiphany, but there has been a distinct reluctance to use the term in connection with Victorian authors. Robert Langbaum states sweepingly 'With very few exceptions the epiphanic mode does not appear in fiction until the turn of the century' (Langbaum 1983: 340). I would argue that Charlotte Brontë's *Villette* is one Victorian novel that makes integral use of epiphany in its construction of subjectivity.

Lucy Snowe has two distinct selves in *Villette* and both of them are innate, God-given constants and not social constructs. The first is the independent, self-reliant individual. This self is achieved through the deliberate absence of any ideological influences on Lucy; for example, family, class, religion, or sex. Of most importance is the lack of any family background at all. Lucy's only major reference to her family situation occurs at the beginning of chapter four: 'Miss Marchmont'. In intensely metaphoric language we are told of the loss or estrangement of her family, importantly symbolized through drowning:

> To this hour, when I have the nightmare, it repeats the rush and saltness of briny waves in my throat, and their icy pressure on my lungs. I even know there was a storm, and that not of one hour nor one day. For many days and nights neither sun nor stars appeared; we cast with our own hands the tackling out of the ship; a heavy tempest lay on us; all hope that we should be saved was taken away. (Brontë 1985: 340)

The biblical allusion is important here in creating a non-specific, impersonal effect, and is marked by the change from the first person singular to plural. The casting out of the tackling refers to the disciples throwing out their nets, and the word 'saved' connotes religious redemption as well as denoting escaping death. By clothing any references to family in such religious symbolism our sense of Lucy's actual and emotional isolation is increased.

Neither is any attempt made to indicate the effect of Lucy's class background on her early conception of her self. In *Jane Eyre* (Brontë 1981) we get a strong sense of the effect of the emotionally blundering, 'nouveau riche' Reids on Jane—the sensitive child of 'distressed gentlefolk'. In *Villette* there are no such indications. Although the Brettons are precisely positioned, the formative early influences on Lucy—her family—are not. We can only assume that she is not of the poorest class.

The influences of religion and conceptions of sex are located within the province of the second self, which I will be discussing later.

The construction of the independent, self-reliant individual is also aided by Lucy's remarks characterizing her self, most of which occur in response to the behaviour of others. When faced with the intensely emotional child, Paulina, and her jealously possessive behaviour with her father and John Bretton she remarks 'I, Lucy Snowe, plead guiltless of that curse, an overheated and discursive imagination' (Brontë 1985: 69).

Whether or not these statements are reliable is a question to be discussed later in this article but particularly at the beginning of the novel, Lucy's reaction to the emotion of others adds to the conception of her objective, impersonal self, somehow removed from the influences that affect other people, in short, a 'looker on of life'.

A similar effect is created by her solitude in taking important decisions, which are all matters of caprice, sanctioned by religious guidance—for example the decision to go to London. Faced by a walk home in starlight, the Aurora Borealis has a determining effect:

> A bold thought was sent to my mind; my mind was made strong to receive it. 'Leave this wilderness', it was said to me, 'and go out hence'. 'Where?' was the query. I had not far to look; gazing from this country parish in that flat, rich

middle of England — I mentally saw within reach what I had never yet beheld with my bodily eyes: I saw London. (Brontë 1985: 104)

Like the passage about the loss of the family, this also has a visionary quality. The command of the 'bold thought' suggests a biblical revelation, and the passage makes explicit use of the motif of the solitary pilgrim, friendless and alone apart from God's guidance. We find this solitude again in a passage reflecting upon Lucy's decision to go abroad. Here she rejects the pull of emotional and personal links, as she has none. She also daringly rejects the social ties of allegiance to country, usually a strong emotion for the Victorian imperialist.

The passage where Lucy goes aboard the *Vivid* on her way to Brussels is the 'highpoint' in the novel's construction of the independent, self-reliant self. Lucy is removed from even the commonest human relations. The waiter, who she thinks is her friend because of his kindness to her, sniggers at her over-tipping him. The driver is warned not to 'leave her to the watermen' (Brontë 1985: 110), but instead 'offers [her] up as an oblation' (Brontë 1985: 110) and instantly drives off. The watermen are crude and unhelpful. Once making for the ship, however, Lucy's spirits revive. She finds herself strengthened rather than otherwise by her isolation. On deck, she makes a final assertion of her mental and spiritual independence:

> I feel that, as—
>   Stone walls do not a prison make,
>   Nor iron bars a cage,
> so peril, loneliness, an uncertain future, are not oppressive evils, so long as the frame is healthy and the faculties are employed; so long, especially, as Liberty lends us her wings, and Hope guides us by her star. (Brontë 1985: 117)

The physical isolation of the small boat on the sea thus becomes a symbol of independence and self-reliance.

Lucy's calm, firm, independent self is thus constructed in many ways. She is steadfastly unaffected by the common influences of social interaction that determine others, and shows great independence both in discussing herself and in making decisions. She is a towering individual personality, divorced in all but the most arbitrary ways from connection with the external world.

Running parallel to this personality, however, is the second of Lucy's selves. It is sexual, emotional and ambitious, needing love and a place in the world. It is private, intensely individual, and innate — Lucy's 'true' nature. It is also specifically religious: when Lucy is left completely alone in the rue Fossette over the vacation and suffers a nervous fever that emphasizes the demands of this self she says 'I felt, too, that the trial God had appointed me was gaining its climax, and must now be turned by my own hands, hot, feeble, trembling as they were' (Brontë 1985: 232). This nervous illness results in her visiting a Catholic priest for emotional contact.

If we refer back to the drowning metaphor that veils the loss of Lucy's family, we are reminded that sea symbolism is used explicitly elsewhere in the novel, for example when Lucy is discussing her life with Miss Marchmont, again within chapter four:

> I forgot that there were fields, woods, rivers, seas, an ever-changing sky outside the steam-dimmed lattice of this sick chamber; I was almost content to forget it. All might have mirrored a mermaid. When I closed my eyes I heard a gale, subsiding at last, bearing upon the house-front like a settling swell upon a rock-base. I heard it drawn and withdrawn, far, far off, like a tide retiring from the shore of the upper world—a world so high above that the rush of its largest waves, the dash of its fiercest breakers, could sound in this submarine home, only like murmurs and a lullaby. (Brontë 1985: 254–5)

This is an unthreatening description—the room is 'calm', 'little', and pastel in colour. The pin-cushion is neutralized by its comparison to coral. All is delicate, nothing is harsh. The mirror is described in consciously poetic diction as a 'glass'. It reflects Lucy, not as she is, but as a mermaid, hiding her true identity from her and for her. She is safe from the dangerous attack of the gale—its removal far off emphasizes her security by its distant presence. This passage is both foetal and primeval, but also childlike.

The recurrent use of sea symbolism is important. It appears at crisis points in Lucy's life, and is germane to the construction of the emotional, sexual self in the novel. The sea is a symbol of the tribulations of life and their emotional effects. In these passages we see the self that withdraws from, and fears, emotional engagement yet simultaneously wants and desires it.

This self also appears at other moments of crisis in the novel, namely, in its epiphanies. An important example occurs at the end of chapter twelve, where Lucy is sitting in the allée défendue. She is initially struck by the contrast between the seclusion of the spot—its apparent distance from the city—and its actual nearness. This opposition is seen firstly in terms of nature and art, 'I was sitting on the hidden seat reclaimed from fungi and mould, listening to what seemed the far off sounds of the city' (Brontë 1985: 175); then in terms of time, 'hence it was but five minutes walk to the park, scarce ten to buildings of palatial splendour' (Brontë 1985: 175); and then in terms of space, 'Quite near were side-streets brightly lit, teeming at this moment with life' (Brontë 1985: 175). This experience is not totally subjective, however, the two environments are indeed 'worlds apart'.

Lucy denies that she is thinking about this contrast, but the reflections it produces provoke the emergence of the sexual, emotional self. She becomes strangely receptive to the sight of the moon, the 'object' of the epiphany. In contrast to the perceptual confusion concerning the school and the city, and the unsettled feelings this provokes, the moon is a symbol of constancy in both time and place:

> I had seen that golden sign with the dark globe in its curve leaning back on azure, beside an old thorn at the top of an old field, in old England; in long past days, just as it now leaned back beside a stately spire in this continental capital. (Brontë 1985: 175)

This constant, as the last opposition to a string of shifting, unstable contrasts and 'tricks' of perception, reminds Lucy of the solidity of her past emotional life and the fragmentation of the present. The epiphany concludes with a cry for the lost emotional stability of childhood.

Throughout *Villette* we see the construction of subjectivity as a *constant* occurring in many ways. Lucy's psyche is sharply split into two distinct selves — the self of independence and isolation and the self of emotion and sexuality. This division smacks of an attempt to 'divide and rule' on the part of the narrating voice. The influence of the socialization process on the development of subjectivity is suppressed, and a fundamentally conservative notion of a God-given, innate and unchanging self is constructed. Possible ideological influences are ignored or truncated, and the emotional personality is 'disguised' by the use of the sea metaphor.

However, in many ways this notion of the construction of subjectivity in *Villette* is insufficient. Frequently the two selves do not remain so sharply differentiated. In many passages where the split is apparent one of the selves tries to maintain the 'upper hand' and position its opposite as an 'other' to be observed and commented on. For example, at the end of the epiphany previously discussed, when Lucy compares her childhood emotional stability with her current situation, she continues 'About the present, it was better to be stoical; about the future — such a future as mine — to be dead. And in catalepsy and a dead trance I studiously held the quick of my nature' (Brontë 1985: 175). Here is an apparently straightforward division between the 'quick' of Lucy's 'nature' (the emotional self) and the isolationist 'I' who represses it. This is one of the first uses of physical violence as a metaphor for conscious repression.

But as we read on things become more complicated. Up to this point, narrator and focalizer have been closely aligned — 'overcome' by recollected emotion — but now the narrator reasserts her distance from the experience, with the words 'At this time, I well remember whatever could excite — certain accidents of the weather, for instance' (Brontë 1985: 175). 'Certain' and 'for instance' suggest a cooler, less emotional, more conversational register; and 'At this time' and 'I well remember' introduce a temporal distance. These accidents of weather are feared because they 'woke the being I was always lulling, and stirred up a craving cry I could not satisfy' (Brontë 1985: 175). The identity split is introduced again here but the 'I' is identified with the narrator, while the focalizer is now solely the emotional personality, described in bestial terms. Because the split between both personalities is now sanctioned by the narrator's distance, the power of the emotional personality is allowed greater freedom than before, and cannot be satisfied. The story then moves again from the general to the specific, 'One night' (Brontë 1985: 176), with a corresponding diminution of distance, and confusion of the two personalities, thus adding sympathy to the emotional self, who now becomes 'I' and not an inanimate 'being', and who is not responsible for her strange actions, 'too resistless was the delight of staying with the wild hour ... too terribly glorious, the spectacle of clouds split and pierced by white and blinding bolts' (Brontë 1985: 176). We can see that the *distance* between the two selves is variable, as is the *power* of each self, which waxes and wanes correspondingly.

The concluding comment of this episode returns us to the metaphor of physical violence for emotional and sexual repression:

> This longing, and all of a similar kind, it was necessary to knock on the head, after the manner of Jael to Sisera, driving a nail through their temples. Unlike Sisera, they did not die, they were but transiently stunned, and at intervals they would turn on the nail with a rebellious wrench: then did the temples bleed, and the brain thrill to its core. (Brontë 1985: 176)

Both selves now inhabit the focalizer, and are personified as Jael and Sisera, thus provided with a complete identity each, allowing the narrator a spurious independence. They fight for total control of Lucy, but neither wins. The violence of the first self is insufficient to contain the second, which gains a masochistic pleasure from the struggle, thus subverting, though not destroying it. This is a simultaneously destructive yet enlivening recurring metaphor of sado-masochistic violence.

In this epiphany, then, we see the impossibility of pinning down and separating the two selves intermingled within Lucy Snowe, which are constantly overtaking each other's territory, and are fundamentally shifting and unstable. The emergence of the emotional self which undercuts the other self's apparent disclaimers of its presence is focused around the moments of epiphany in the novel, for example in the vision of the Aurora Borealis already mentioned. This passage is overtly concerned to present Lucy's solitude and independence in decision-making. The idea of going to London is passively registered, 'A bold thought was sent to my mind; my mind was made strong to receive it' (Brontë 1985: 104). The reader, however, is aware that this 'biblical revelation' is provoked by the excitement resulting from a moonlight walk and the sudden manifestation of the Aurora Borealis. It is not God speaking to Lucy, but her second self.

These moments, and there are many of them in the novel, rest on the unreliability of the narrating voice for the suggestion of one self (usually the emotional one) invading the other. The epiphany in the allée défendue is provoked by the contrast between the school's cloistered existence and the excitement of the nearby city. But the narrator says:

> Of this contrast I thought not, however: gay instincts my nature had few; ball or opera I had never seen; and though often I had heard them described, and even wished to see them, it was not the wish of one who hopes to partake a pleasure if she could only reach it—who feels fitted to shine in some bright distant sphere, could she but thither win her way; it was no yearning to attain, no hunger to taste; only the calm desire to look on a new thing. (Brontë 1985: 175)

Lucy does indeed protest too much! The suggestion of emotional longing is present in the words 'yearning' and 'hunger', which echo the voracious imagery used elsewhere to indicate the emotional self. The passage's success rests on our distrust of the narrator, which relies on the recurrence of such imagery.

Frequently this judgement of the narrator works retrospectively. On a first reading we may accept remarks about other people's 'overheated imaginations' and our awareness of the existence of an emotional self increases gradually along with our sympathy and involvement with Lucy. A re-reading offers a very different perspective, where the linear development of the novel is supplemented by the more 'vertical' lyric qualities of imagery and symbolism. This is obviously a characteristic common to reading generally, but it is particularly prominent in *Villette*. To generalize, we can identify the independent, isolated self with the plot development of the novel and the emotional and sexual self with its recurrent symbolic patterns.

The hidden sexual power of the emotional self in these symbolic patterns is clarified by even a rudimentary psychoanalytic approach. If we reconsider some of the passages already discussed, we can see an initial concern with repressing sexual demands, though these are often couched in emotional terms. For example, the passage using the sea symbol to describe Lucy's life with Miss Marchmont ends in this way:

> I forgot that there were fields, woods, rivers, seas, an ever-changing sky outside the steam-dimmed lattice of this sick chamber; I was almost content to forget it. *All within me became narrowed to my lot.* (my emphasis) (Brontë 1985: 97)

Here, the comparison of the sick-*chamber* to the female genitals is emphasized by the last sentence, which suggests conscious repression of emotion displacing the *unconscious* repression of physical desire.

A similar example occurs in the epiphany in the 'forbidden alley', itself another potent symbol of repressed female sexuality:

> About the present, it was better to be stoical; about the future — such a future as mine — to be dead. *And in catalepsy and a dead trance I studiously held the quick of my nature* (my emphasis). (Brontë 1985: 175)

This example is a more specific rendition of the conscious, independent self preventing unconscious sexual desire from 'coming to life', again making use of the metaphor of physical violence. The word 'nature' often stands for something else in Brontë's work, and here has the effect of suggesting the more acceptable *emotion* rather than sexuality.

Later on in the epiphany the metaphors of physical violence evoked to repress emotion in fact suggest penetration and sexual release:

> I could not go in: too resistless was the delight of staying with the wild hour, black and full of thunder, pealing out such an ode as language never delivered to man — too terribly glorious, the spectacle of clouds, split and pierced by white and blinding bolts. (Brontë 1985: 176)

The idea of sexual climax as being 'beyond words' is important here in suggesting that sexuality is 'behind' much of the overt content of the novel.

The Jael and Sisera simile has already been discussed in terms of the pleasure gained from the attempt to repress emotion. It only remains to point out that this is sexual pleasure: the conscious, independent self paradoxically tries to repress sexuality through an act of violence that the unconscious desire compares to the sexual act, gaining a masochistic release.

The sexual self in the novel emerges in various unexpected ways as a result of repression. We have already seen sexuality disguised as emotion, and sadomasochism underlying violently repressive metaphors. Elsewhere the novel suggests voyeurism and auto-eroticism. The passage already quoted (see p. 51 — Brontë 1985: 232) shows the religious source of the emotional self is explicitly auto-erotic, 'I felt, too, that the trial God had appointed me was gaining its climax, and must now be turned by my own hands, hot, feeble, trembling as they were' (Brontë 1985: 232). Lucy's voyeurism is apparent early on in the novel, in her reactions to the relationship of Paulina and her father. Although the narrator's expressions of distance from the imaginative emotion of Paulina are important in constructing Lucy's independent, isolated self, we also detect the envy undercutting these statements, which allows her emotions a place, and establishes a connection between Paulina and Lucy. The vicariousness of Lucy's experience is directly expressed in the following comment, 'He kissed her. I wished she would utter some hysterical cry, so that I might get relief and be at ease' (Brontë 1985: 71). The 'hysterical cry' would stimulate sexual release in Lucy.

What is clearly apparent from these quotations is the presence of not only the emotional self in the province of the independent, isolated self; but also the presence of sexuality within *that* self, though it is not explicitly acknowledged as such by the narrator. The complications of subjectivity are thus greater than would at first appear.

This is nowhere more apparent than in the passage discussed earlier where Lucy wakes up in the Brettons' house and compares her room to a 'cave in the sea'. This simile again makes implicit reference to the female genitals, and the whole passage is concerned with suppressing sexual threat, whether from inside the self—the red satin pin-cushion, a symbol of sexual excitement, is neutralized by comparing it to coral—or outside—the gale. More important, however, is Lucy's attempt to lose personal identity, firstly by comparing her reflection in the glass to a mermaid. This is interesting because it suggests a non-recognition of the self-image that shows how deeply traumatized Lucy is, and is reminiscent of Lacan's mirror-stage (1977: 1-7). In refusing the habitual image of her 'self' Lucy evokes fantasy as a means of escaping the symbolic matrix in which, according to Lacan, the self is objectivised as an alienated 'subject'. The regression to this 'pre-mirror stage' continues in the second metaphor of the 'submarine home' with waves breaking on the surface far above.

Interestingly enough, some critics have discussed epiphany in terms of Freud's *oceanic feeling*, which they describe as a longing for a return to the safety of the pre-oedipal phase. Huck Gutman calls it 'the requited desire of the ego for a loss of itself, for its undifferentiated merge into the cosmos' (Gutman 1988: 116), and Rosemarie A. Battaglia refers to a 'parental embrace which overcomes feelings of infantile helplessness' (Battaglia 1988: 144).

In *Villette* Lucy's subjectivity is built on the forcible separation of her two selves, the first a calm, independent, isolated one, and the second the emotional, sexual self. These are so forced apart because of the fundamentally conservative construction of subjectivity in the novel—the resistance to socialization and ideology as influencing character. The view of self is that it is innate, inborn and God-given, and it is easier to position emotion, sexual feeling and a spiritual/religious sensitivity as *constants* and not social *constructs*, than the influences of family, or class for example.

The importance of epiphany in the novel is as a focus of moments of self-awareness that highlight the inevitable failure of this attempt to keep the two selves separate. Because of the 'welling-up' of emotion through symbols and metaphors that centre on the epiphanies in the novel (though they are not confined to them), the division between the two selves and the 'balance of power' is never firm, but constantly shifting, waxing and waning. The use of unreliable narration and sexual symbolism underlying the emotional self further destabilizes the conservative construction of subjectivity, to offer a reading of it that admits the possibility of change within the self, and therefore the possibility of 'nurture' affecting 'nature'. Epiphany thus has an integral part to play in acting as a nodal point for the dialogue about subjectivity in *Villette*.

Notes

1. The complete *epiphanies* are available in Scholes and Kain (1965). A useful discussion of this material and also of criticism on epiphany can be found in Beja (1983).

Bibliography

Battaglia, R. (1988), 'Stages of Desire in Joyce', in Scott, B.K. (ed.) (1988), *New Alliances in Joyce Studies: When its Aped to Foul a Delfian*, London, Associated University Presses, 37–47.
Beja, M. (1983), 'Epiphany and The Epiphanies', in Bowen, Z. and Carens, J.F. (eds) (1983), *A Companion to Joyce Studies*, Westport, Greenwood, 707–725.
Brontë, C. (1981), *Jane Eyre* (edited and introduced by Q.D. Leavis), Harmondsworth, Penguin.
Brontë, C. (1985), *Villette* (Lilly, M. (ed.) and introduced by Tony Tanner), Harmondsworth, Penguin.
Gutman, H. (1988), 'Rousseau's Confessions: A Technology of the Self', in Martin. L.H., Gutman, H. and Hutton, P.H. (eds) (1988), *Technologies of The Self: A Seminar with Michel Foucault*, London, Tavistock Publications, 99–120.
Joyce, J. (1969), *Stephen Hero* (edited and introduced by T. Spencer, second edition revised with a foreword by J.J. Slocum and H. Cahoon), London, Cape.
Joyce, J. (1987a), *A Portrait of the Artist as a Young Man*, London, Grafton.
Joyce, J. (1987b), 'The Dead', in *Dubliners*, London, Grafton, 160–201.
Lacan, J. (1977), *Ecrits: A Selection* (tr. by Alan Sheridan), London, Tavistock Publications.
Langbaum, R. (1983), 'The Epiphanic Mode in Wordsworth and Modern Literature', *New Literary History*, 14: 335–358.
Scholes, R. and Kain, R.M. (1965), *The Workshop of Dedalus: James Joyce and the Raw Materials for 'A Portrait of the Artist as a Young Man'*, Evanston, Illinois, Northwestern University Press.

5 'They suck us dry': A Study of Late Nineteenth-century Projections of Vampiric Women

Sian Macfie

Bram Stoker's *Dracula* (1897) is not the first, but is nonetheless the most famous, literary exploration of the vampire theme. The blood-drinking, undead, Eastern Count with his pointed teeth, livid skin and crimson lips constitutes what the twentieth-century reader perceives to be the archetypal vampire. The blood-sucking kiss is evidently a sexual affair and Dracula chooses young virgins for his prey. The vampire myth portrays the female victim of the vampire's bite as being sensual and libidinous: she has in some sense 'invited' the assault, just as in popular mythology the victim of rape is said to have 'provoked' the attack:

> There was undoubtedly something, long and black, bending over the half-reclining white figure...and something raised a head, and from where I was I could see a white face and red, gleaming eyes... Her lips were parted, and she was breathing not softly as usual with her but in long heavy gasps... she put her hand up to her throat again and moaned. (Stoker 1897: 93–4)

Folklore holds that the woman transmogrifies into a vampire in order to retain her youth and beauty. In Stoker's tale, the female vampire's victims are primarily young children, thus inverting the cultural ideal of the maternal woman:

> We saw a white figure advance—a dim white figure, which held something dark at its breast... was bent down over what we saw to be a fair-haired child... We could see that the lips were crimson with fresh blood, and that the stream had trickled over her chin and stained... (Stoker 1897: 215)

The notion of the vampiric woman was not, however, simply confined to literature and mythology. In his 1889 anthropological study *Obeah: Witchcraft in the West Indies* Hesketh Bell speaks of the prevalence of black magic rites and the incidence of female vampirism amongst West Indian women:

> ...loogaroos are human beings, generally old women, who have made a pact with the devil, by which, in exchange for some occult power, they have bound themselves to provide a certain quantity of human blood every night during their lifetime for the delectation of the arch fiend. (Bell 1889: 166)

The high public profile of occult groups practising the Black Mass, a parody of the sacramental transubstantiation of wine into blood, heightened anxieties concerning apostolic women.

In addition to superstitious ideas of women's involvement in black magic and vampirism, the late nineteenth century was also increasingly preoccupied with the idea of female sexuality and its perceived relation to vampirism. In 1897 Philip Burne-Jones exhibited his painting 'The Vampire' in which he depicts a vampire-woman descending upon her victim, a man who lies sleeping on a couch as if exhausted with love-making.[1] Burne-Jones' painting draws upon late nineteenth-century notions of the libidinous woman as vampire. In 1892, in his *Psychopathia Sexualis*, R. Von Krafft-Ebing describes the case of a nymphomaniac female patient suffering from the condition of blood-fetishism. Her lover:

> ...first had to make a cut in his arm. Then she would suck the wound, and during the act become violently excited sexually. This case recalls the widespread legend of the vampires, the origin of which may perhaps be referred to such sadistic facts. It has its origin in the myth of the *lamiae* and *marmolykes*, blood-sucking women. (Krafft-Ebing 1892: 87)

In his 1895 text *The Female Offender* co-written with W. Ferrero, Caesar Lombroso, a well respected criminologist, describes the female nymphomaniac's lust for biting and sucking blood:

> Nymphomania transforms the most timid girl into a shameless bacchante. She tries to attract every man she sees, displaying sometimes violence, and sometimes the most refined coquetry. She often suffers from an intense thirst, a dry mouth, a fetid breath, and a tendency to bite everybody she meets, as if affected with hydrophobia. (Lombroso and Ferrero 1895: 296)

The notion of the vampiric woman also came to be culturally associated, in the period 1880–1900, with the idea of the woman suffering from sexually transmitted disease. The notion of vampirism as a venereal disease was exploited by the painter Félicien Rops. In his 1892 picture 'Mors Syphilitica' he draws upon the contemporary concern regarding the spread of syphilis through the mixing of blood and bodily fluids during sexual intercourse. In his picture he depicts a naked woman with red lips, the suggestion of vampire teeth and bat-like wings. Commentators such as Frederick Lowndes in his 1886 study *Prostitution and Venereal Disease* spoke of the syphilitic epidemic:

> There is literally no comparison between the amount of disease propagated by one man, however vicious, and by one prostitute... there is scarcely any limit to the number of men whom one prostitute may infect, and, should any of them be married men, the disease may also spread to their wives and unborn children. (Lowndes 1886: 18–19)

Public anxiety reached its height concerning the spread of syphilis amongst the military. In *The Social Evil with Suggestions for its Suppression and Revelations of the Working of the Contagious Diseases Acts* by 'an ex-Constable' (1883) the author explains how the promiscuous woman, or the prostitute seemed to directly threaten Britain's imperialist aspirations:

> The ravages...arising from a considerable percentage of soldiers and sailors contracting a specific disease...So great was the suffering, that at times, among the combined fleets as many hands as would suffice to man an Ironclad were invalids, from causes attributable to that malady. (Anon. 1883: 2)

It was not, however, simply women's sexuality that came to be equated with vampirism. Rather, the female body itself came to be associated with the 'curse' of vampirism. It was believed that women were particularly prone to what was termed 'moral madness' on account of the debilitating effects of the menstrual cycle. In his work *Dictionary of Psychological Medicine* Daniel Hack Tuke (1892) declared, 'The menstrual function can...create a mental condition varying from...a simple moral malaise...to actual insanity' (p. 803). In speaking of 'The frequent deficiency of the corpuscular richness of the blood met with in the first stages of insanity' (Tuke 1892: 140) he drew a direct link between moral insanity and anaemia. It was believed that an anaemic woman suffering from moral madness could be driven to attempt to replenish her supply of blood lost in the menstrual flow. Indeed, a painting by Joseph-Ferdinand Gueldry entitled 'The Blood Drinkers', depicts just such a group of blood-sipping invalid women. In *Transfusion: its History, Indications and Modes of Application*, Jennings (1883) controversially recommends the transfusion of animal blood to cure female anaemia, suggesting that: 'direct transfusions of moderate quantities of arterial blood from the carotid of a lamb into the veins of a human subject might exert a beneficial influence upon the constitutional symptoms in various forms of anaemia' (Jennings 1883: 39). His descriptions of how the transfusion of human blood could be used to reanimate women who had haemorrhaged in childbirth also roused deep-seated social anxieties:

> It is in obstetric practice that the operation is most frequently demanded...there are many [cases] where the patients were positively *in articulo mortis* when the operation was commenced—cases in which the fresh lease of life can be fairly attributed to transfusion. (Jennings 1883: 3–4)

Once again, therefore, the function or dysfunction of the female body was juxtaposed with notions of the perceived threat of vampirism.

At the close of the nineteenth century, notions of the close connection between the female and the vampiric were largely based upon a sense of women's association with blood. However, the idea of female vampirism also came to be understood in a more figurative sense. In addition to the idea of the literal contagion of the blood, vampirism came to be associatively linked with the notion of a moral contagion and especially with the 'contamination' of lesbianism. Henry Havelock Ellis (1897: 100) asserted that 'homosexuality... occurs with special frequency in women of high intelligence who...influence others'. The notion of vampirism also came to be used metaphorically to refer to a social phenomenon, the 'psychic sponge'. The psychic sponge was understood to be a woman who was perceived to be a drain on the energy, and emotional and intellectual resources of her companions. In 1896, in the journal *Borderland*, Franz Hartmann spoke of female vampiric sponges who:

> ...unconsciously vampirize every sensitive person with whom they come in contact, and they instinctively seek out such persons...I know of an old lady, a vampire, who thus ruined the health of a lot of robust servant girls, whom she took

into her service and made them sleep in her room. They were all in good health when they entered, but soon they began to sicken, they became emaciated and consumptive and had to leave the service. (Hartmann 1896: 354)

A new category of vampire fiction and art developed in the 1880's and 1890's in which this theme of the woman who sapped health and strength was examined. *The Parasite* (1891) by Arthur Conan Doyle is a tale about the shadowy Miss Penelosa who sets out to destroy the career, home life and mind of Professor Gilroy. *Vampires* by Julien Gordon (1891), the pseudonymous Julie Grinnell Cruger, is the story of the draining of a young man's energy by his wife and mother-in-law. Mary Elizabeth Braddon's story 'Good Lady Ducayne' (1896) details the enervating effect of an elderly lady upon her young female employee. Artists also experimented with the theme of a symbolic vampirism that did not involve the sucking of blood. Edvard Munch's woodcut and lithograph 'Vampire' (1895/1902) is an expressionistic portrayal of this psychological form of vampirism whilst Walter Crane's woodcut of 1886 depicts a type of social vampirism, the vampire of capitalism.

In the latter part of the nineteenth century there were thus two main literary versions of the vampiric woman: supernatural fantasy texts focused on the woman as physical blood-sucker whilst realistic, psychological novels presented women as metaphorically draining the resources of individuals and society. One of the most interesting of the *fin-de-siècle* vampire tales is Florence Marryat's *The Blood of the Vampire* (1897). Florence Marryat, (1838–1899), was the daughter of Captain Frederick Marryat, the author of *The Children of the New Forest* and other adventure stories for children. Florence was a journalist and was for a time editor of *London Society* but she was primarily known as a sensation novelist. She was a popular and prolific writer, producing some fifty-seven novels, many of them triple-decker. She formed her own theatre company and achieved some celebrity as an actress, director and writer of dramatic and musical entertainments. During the latter part of the century, she became involved in the spiritualist movement. *The Blood of the Vampire* is particularly fascinating because it is, in a sense, a generic hybrid in that it examines the question of vampirism from both the literal and the figurative angles: Mrs Brandt is presented as a physical drinker of blood whilst her daughter, Harriet, and Harriet's adoptive mother, the Baroness Gobelli, are projected as metaphoric vampires. Harriet, we are informed, saps the emotional, and Gobelli, the financial resources of unwitting victims. Marryat's text is, therefore, of interest on account of the manner in which it stands uneasily balanced between the fantastic and the realistic; between the supernatural and the social or psychological; between the religious and the scientific economy of ideas. The fact that the author elects to project not one but three women as vampires, primarily on account of their perceived sexuality and racial characteristics, renders this text a particularly interesting example of the genre on account of the insights which it offers into late nineteenth-century stereotypes of race, gendered identity and female sexuality.

Unlike earlier supernatural tales where vampirism is portrayed as an affliction of the soul requiring exorcism by a member of the clergy, Marryat's text medicalizes vampirism; it is the physician, Doctor Phillips, who 'diagnoses' the vampiric condition. Doctor Phillips asserts that he works not with belief or superstition but with empirically observable scientific facts. He maintains that he is a rationalist and a realist and insists upon the fact that 'we medical men know' (Marryat 1897: 125). He is adamant that the diagnoses that he makes are verifiable as 'the truth, medically and scientifically' (Marryat 1897: 298).

In the case of Mrs Brandt, Doctor Phillips diagnoses a case of blood-sucking vampirism: 'she thirsted for blood, she loved the sight and smell of it' (Marryat 1897: 122). However, when Phillips goes on to associate Mrs Brandt's mixed race status with her alleged vampirism, describing her as a 'bloodthirsty half-caste' (Marryat 1897: 123) it becomes apparent that his diagnosis is based less upon advances in medical pathology than upon his own prejudiced belief that inter-racial liaisons are in some sense aberrant. According to the Doctor's eugenecist definition, the mixed-race woman, suffering from an insufficiency of 'good' (white) blood, is driven by a frenzy of haematomania to attempt to overcome her racial hybridity.

The Doctor is a firm believer in the evolutionary model. He affirms the law of genetic predetermination maintaining that 'we medical men know the consequences of heredity' (Marryat 1897: 125). The 'blood of the vampire' of the title is thus, according to the Doctor's philosophy, not simply the blood that is imbibed by Mrs Brandt but also the blood of heredity by means of which genetic taints are passed along the female line. Thus, the Doctor asserts that it is unavoidable that Mrs Brandt's daughter should have 'inherited the vampire's blood' (Marryat 1897: 296).

Where Doctor Phillips approaches Mrs Brandt's case as a pathologist treating a bodily dysfunction, he views his role with Harriet as being that of an 'Alienist' (a mental pathologist), attempting to cure a disease of the mind. Her complaint, he declares, is that of psychic or mental vampirism:

> The natures of persons differ very widely. There are some born into this world... who *draw* from their neighbours, sometimes making large demands upon their vitality—sapping their physical strength, and feeding upon them, as it were, until they are perfectly exhausted... This proclivity has been breath of its victims. (Marryat 1897: 297)

Whereas in his diagnosis of Mrs Brandt the Doctor associates mixed race with blood-sucking vampirism, in Harriet's case Doctor Phillips links psychic vampirism with liberated female sexuality. It is, according to Phillips: 'her wide mouth and blood-red lips... the way in which she uses her eyes... her... sensual disposition' that guarantees his diagnosis (Marryat 1897: 139).

The Doctor's diagnoses of vampirism in the case of both mother and daughter are, thus, clearly motivated by racist and misogynist attitudes. What is most extraordinary about *The Blood of the Vampire* is the way in which the narrator's voice colludes in the promulgation of these prejudiced views. Indeed, Phillips' diagnoses are openly endorsed: 'Doctor Phillips was innocent of having misjudged, or slandered anyone' (Marryat 1897: 294). The narrative is most concerned with elucidating the reasons for the projection of Harriet as a psychic vampire. Her desire for intense friendships with women is portrayed as a sign of a 'drawing nature'. Close female bonding and lesbianism are conflated with notions of the unhealthy draining of female vitality:

> There was an attraction about the girl, which Mrs Pullen acknowledged, without wishing to give in to. She could not keep her eyes off her! She seemed to hypnotize

her as the snake is said to hypnotize the bird, but it was an unpleasant feeling, as if the next moment, the smouldering fire would burst forth into flame and overwhelm her. (Marryat 1897: 50)

Harriet is not, however, easily classifiable as a lesbian; she also experiences strong heterosexual urges. The narrative voice juxtaposes notions of female (hetero) sexuality with ideas of the woman as vamp, as bestial predator upon men and insists that Harriet's 'hungry, yearning look was more accentuated than before — it seemed as if she were on the alert, watching for something, like a panther awaiting the advent of its prey'. (Marryat 1897: 65). In the same way that notions of mixed race are conflated with ideas of vampirism as an attempt to attain racial purity, so in the case of Harriet's sexuality it is implied that psychic vampirism is the attempt to resolve the split between the human and the animal and to attain generic purity. It is further implied that psychic vampirism must also be regarded as the attempt to escape the ambiguity of the bisexual state, and attain a 'pure' and monolithic sexuality.

The narrator's voice thus embraces the doctor's stereotype of the sadistic and sensual mixed-race woman and accepts the equation of liberated female sexuality with vampirism, whether of the physical or metaphoric variety. In addition to the projection of Mrs Brandt and Harriet as vampiric women, Marryat also elects to present Harriet's adoptive mother, the Baroness Gobelli, as a vampire in the figurative sense. Where the projection of Mrs Brandt's and Harriet's vampirism is predominately rooted in racial and sexual tensions, the portrayal of Madame Gobelli as a vampire most evidently springs from class anxieties. Before marrying the Baron, she was employed as a cook and her lack of breeding is revealed in her unfeminine appetite. She is, we are told, 'a very coarse feeder, scattering her food over her plate and not infrequently over the table cloth as well' (Marryat 1897: 4). The narrative voice equates Gobelli's low class origins with social vampirism; to be working class is to be vampiric upon those who form the professional classes or who belong, through heredity, to the aristocracy:

> 'You may have money, I know — and a goodish lot, I fancy'... exclaimed the Baroness, who immediately thought what a good thing it would be if Miss Brandt could be persuaded to sink her capital in the boot trade. (Marryat 1897: 64)

The Baroness is presented as a type of 'androgen' and her 'unfeminine' forays into the commercial world of business and finance are projected as a vampiric sapping of male potency. To be incompletely feminine is to be thrust into vampirism in the attempt to attain a single, preferably male, gendered identity.

The narrator colludes with the 'scientist', Doctor Phillips, in the conflation of the non-Aryan, the lesbian, the working-class and the 'masculine' female with the vampire woman. In contradistinction to this, the narrative voice establishes three 'acceptable' modes of feminity for a 'normal' woman. Margaret is the paragon of 'feminine' virtue; she sublimates her personal desire into the duty of motherhood. Elinor, though less highly praised, is nonetheless heralded as an example to other women; she has subsumed her own identity within that of her husband. The nuns at the convent have devoted their whole lives to prayer and to the service of God.

However, despite the overt espousal of the voice of 'reason', the narrative is unable to suppress opposing voices. At the heart of the novel there is a contest for meaning; the very structure of the text is based upon this fundamental dichotomy. The first of the dissenting voices is in fact that of Margaret who challenges the Doctor's view of 'normal' subjectivity: 'Are you not a little prejudiced, dear Doctor?' (Marryat 1897: 120). Ralph suggests that the physician's problem may be a little more serious: 'Phillips you must be mad!' (Marryat 1897: 142). The most significant critique of the scientist's 'rationality' is, however, presented by the artist, Anthony Pennell, an intellectual and idealist. As a socialist and reformer, Pennell seeks to expose the white, patriarchal bourgeois interests that are served by the hegemonic system that demands conformity to the 'norm':

> Anthony Pennell was a Socialist in the best and truest sense of the word ... He made a large income by his popular writings and the greater part of it went to relieve the wants of his humble friends ... But his Socialism went further and higher than this. Money was not the only thing which his fellow creatures required — they wanted love, sympathy, kindness and consideration — and these he gave also ... He ... waged a perpetual warfare against the tyranny of men over women; the ill-treatment of children; and the barbarities practised upon dumb animals. (Marryat 1897: 265–6)

The 'official' narrative is, thus, unable to repress the voice of Pennell, a novelist, who speaks out against the demonization of women who are black, working-class, lesbian, non-feminine. Pennell's words echo through the subtext like the voice of the novel's unconscious. His voice subverts that of the scientist and that of the narrator who mimics the scientist. Marryat the novelist is thus ironically undercut by the fictional author who is her own creation.

In the light of this radical uncertainty regarding the issue of female gendered identity and sexuality that underlies *The Blood of the Vampire* it is interesting to note that Marryat wrote the novel after having been herself accused of being a psychic vampire. In her semi-autobiographical text *There is no Death* (1891) she quotes William Fletcher whose description of her is later echoed by the Doctor's characterization of Harriet in the novel:

> You are a Child of Destiny ... Your life is fuller of tragedies that any life I ever read yet ... You draw people to you, and live upon their life; and when they have no more to give, nor you to demand, the liking fades on both sides. It must be so, because the spirit requires food the same as the body; and when the store is exhausted, the affection is starved out, and the persons pass out of your life ... More than that, if you continue to cling to those whose spiritual system you have exhausted, they would poison you, instead of nourishing you. You may not like it, but those you value most you should oftenest part with ... Constant intercourse may be fatal to your dearest affections. You draw so much on others, you *empty* them, and they have nothing more to give you ... All people are not born under a fate, but you were, and you can do very little to change it ... (Marryat 1891: 238–40)

It appears that Marryat interpreted this as being linked to what she perceived as her failure as a mother: she suffered from a number of miscarriages and premature births and it seems she believed that her body was in some way poisoning the progeny that she carried. Her projection of Harriet as a vampire, on account of her sapping of the vitality of new-born babies, is particularly interesting in the light of Marryat's sense that she had herself vampirically drained her own child, Florence:

> [I] had been the cause of the untimely death of her body... It was a warning to me (as it should be to all mothers) not to take the solemn responsibility of maternity upon themselves, without being prepared to sacrifice their own feelings for the sake of their children. (Marryat 1891: 107)

The death of her second daughter was also, to some extent, associatively linked with notions of vampirism: 'My beloved girl, who died in child-birth... from blood-poisoning which (as everybody knows) is most contagious, especially for women in the same condition' (Marryat 1894: 237). The fact that unresolved grief over the deaths of these daughters should have led Marryat to an embrace of the Spiritualist Church in an attempt to draw emotional strength from the spirits is of particular moment in the light of the fact that in the novel she projects Gobelli as a vampire precisely on account of her involvement in spiritualism and her ability to draw psychic force from the dead. Marryat's two accounts of her involvement in the spiritualist movement, *There is no Death* (1891) and *The Spirit World* (1894), bear witness to the author's complex and ambivalent response to the spiritualist endeavour. She believed that the seance was an arena in which power was vampirically transferred between medium and spirit; the medium would acquire spiritual force, the spirit would be endowed with the physical power necessary to materialize. Troubling doubts and anxieties were raised by the notion that the medium would, as it were, vampirically draw the spirits of the dead into her own consciousness: 'Remember what the word 'medium' signifies—a channel through which the spiritual waters are conveyed to your lips... The spirits of the departed pass into... the medium' (Marryat 1894: 293). The transfer of force was such that while the medium drew psychic strength from the spirits, the dead would drain physical substance from the medium:

> 'You see,' said Miss Showers 'Florence [a spirit]... I can detach certain particles from her organism for my own use... I can take them from her (as you see I do) in order to render my invisible body visible to you.' (Marryat 1891: 153-4)

The seance was, thus, the discursive space in which the 'egos' of living and dead would disturbingly fuse. The horror of the vampiric encounter, the dissolution of the boundary between self and other, was the very tenet upon which the spiritualist enterprise was founded. However, perhaps the most troubling aspect of the spiritualist seance for Marryat was the fact that it facilitated the unleashing of female desire. Marryat's projection of Harriet as a vampire on account of her perceived lesbian tendencies assumes a new significance in the light of the author's descriptions of her own intimate encounters with mediums such as the adolescent Rosina Showers. In the following extract Marryat describes how the spirits encouraged her to draw (sexual) energy from the entranced figure of the young medium:

> The two [spirits] led me between them to the sofa on which Miss Showers was lying. They passed my hand all over her head and body... her heart appeared to

have become proportionately increased. When my hand was placed upon it, it was leaping up and down violently, and felt like a rabbit or some other live animal bounding in her bosom. (Marryat 1891: 152)

In the light of Marryat's conflation of female sexuality with vampirism in her novel, it is interesting to see the terms in which she describes an encounter between herself and a male spirit in her spiritualist text: 'I turned my head, and there stood a dark figure beside the bed... Upon this, the figure rose in the air until it hung suspended, face downward, over the bed. In this position it looked like a huge bat with outspread wings' (Marryat 1891: 90).

It is clear that Marryat was suffering from deep-seated anxieties regarding the issue of female gendered identity and particularly of female sexuality and that her writing of *The Blood of the Vampire* must to some extent be regarded as the playing out of these tensions. In the light of her conflation of ideas of female sexuality and spirituality with the notion of vampirism, it is interesting to note that in the 1880s and 1890s women's obsession with the spiritual was paradoxically thought to be occasioned by an excess of physicality, by an excess of blood. The Christian Literature Society in 1893 declared that the spread of spiritualism could be halted by the application of leeches to drain excess blood from the veins of the mediums: 'Some affliction of the brain which in its severer form causes insanity may... occasion spectral illusions... illusions were caused by too much blood. When some was withdrawn by the application of leeches the illusions began to fade' (Murdoch 1893: 7-8).

Marryat's equivocal response to the women she projects as vampires can be read as a symptom of her radical uncertainty regarding the place of the physical and of the spiritual in the female subject. *The Blood of the Vampire* forms a link in the history of the proliferation of late nineteenth-century projections of vampiric women by novelists, physicians, priests and criminologists. This proliferation betokens a *fin-de-siècle* crisis in the definition of 'femininity' where the hegemonic response to the emergence of new modes of female subjectivity—to the rise of the 1890s cult of the 'New Woman'—was to demonize her, to classify her as sick, as evil, as vampiric.

Notes

1. Paintings referred to in this article are reproduced in Dijkstra, B. (1986), *Idols of Perversity*, London, Oxford University Press.

Bibliography

Anonymous (1883), *The Social Evil with Suggestions for its Suppression, and Revelations of the Working of the Contagious Diseases Acts* (by an ex-constable of the Devonport division), Bristol, W.H. Morrish.
Bell, H. (1889), *Obeah: Witchcraft in the West Indies*, London, Sampson Low, Marston Searle and Rivington.
Braddon, M.E. (1896), 'Good Lady Ducayne', *The Strand Magazine*, Vol. XI (Feb 1896): 185-199.
Doyle, A.C. (1891), *The Parasite*, London, Smith, Elder and Co.
Ellis, H.H. (1897), *Studies in the Psychology of Sex, Vol. I, Sexual Inversion*, London and Watford, University of London Press.

Gordon, J. (1891), *Vampires*, London, New York, Melbourne and Sydney, Ward Lock, Bowden and Co.
Hartmann, F. (1896), *Borderland*, Vol. III(3) (July 1896): 353–358.
Jennings, C.E. (1883), *Transfusion: Its History, Indications, and Modes of Application*, London, Bailliere, Tindall and Co.
Krafft-Ebing, R. von (1892), *Psychopathia Sexualis, with Especial Reference to Contrary Sexual Instinct: A Medico-Legal Study* (tr. Charles Gilbert Chaddock), Philadelphia and London, The F.A. Davis Co.
Lombroso, C. and Ferrero, W. (1895), *The Female Offender* London, T. Fisher Unwin.
Lowndes, F. (1886), *Prostitution and Venereal Diseases in Liverpool*, London, J. and A. Churchill.
Marryat, F. (1891), *There is No Death*, London, Kegan Paul Trench Trubner and Co.
Marryat, F. (1894), *The Spirit World*, London, F.V. White and Co.
Marryat, F. (1897), *The Blood of the Vampire*, London, Hutchinson and Co.
Murdoch, J. (1893), *Theosophy Exposed or Mrs Besant and Her Guru, An Appeal to Educated Hindus*, Madras, The Christian Literature Society.
Stoker, B. (1897), *Dracula, A Tale*, Westminster, Archibald Constable and Co.
Tuke, D.H. (1892), *A Dictionary of Psychological Medicine with the Symptoms, Treatment and Pathology of Insanity and the Law of Lunacy in Great Britain and Ireland*, London, J. and A. Churchill.

6 Wallace Stevens: An Exemplary Subject

Carolyn Masel

It is difficult for the student of Wallace Stevens to avoid sometimes feeling like one of his mythical characters, a figure he took from Emerson: the scholar of one candle. One persists, in the midst of obscurity, single-minded, yet feeble in solitude. Occasionally, 'the mind is like a hall in which thought is like a voice speaking' (Stevens 1957: 168): knowledge of a presence seems imminent. But on bad days, the whole oeuvre may come to resemble a hall of mirrors, reflecting (or distorting?) one's own meanings, musing the obscure. Few poets have remained so tantalizingly elusive; few poets have made their readers feel so alone.

For few poets have remained so doggedly impersonal. The fiction 'Stevens' remains unknowable, being too abstracted, too diffuse in the poetry to be said to constitute a 'subject'. Stevens himself attributed authorship to something called 'Mind' or 'mind'—significantly without pronoun, abstracted and unpossessed. Though his poetry is rich with idiolect, unmistakable as a signature, his subjectivity remains hidden from us. Selfhood is simply not on, nor in, the line. Whatever else poetry was for Stevens, it was not lyric self-expression. What he proferred in his *Collected Poems* (henceforth CP—1954) was not a self, nor a life, but a life of the mind: a secondary construct, derived from an empirical self, but separate from it. And this secondary self is only deducible from the kinds and forms of thought that he proffers as exemplary. This 'Stevens' is recognizable as a set of recurring preoccupations (such as the relation between imagination and reality), and a set of recurring strategies (such as the ousting of authority). The composing consciousness seems habitually allusive, with a favourite body of authors and texts; and it tended, after a period of experiment, to frame its thoughts in blank *terza rima*, whose three lines may come to bear the structural weight of the three terms of a syllogism, and which we have come to think of as a characteristic stanza shape, one intrinsic to the signature, 'Wallace Stevens'.

Many of Stevens' poems are impersonal in kind, and utilize impersonal structures. Many are third person past tense narratives: histories, parables and anecdotes. In such poems, impersonality is frequently enlisted in the service of pathos—as in these two examples, from 'Anglais Mort à Florence' and 'Less and Less Human, O Savage Spirit':

> A little less returned for him each spring.
> Music began to fail him. Brahms, although
> His dark familiar, often walked apart.

> His spirit grew uncertain of delight,
> Certain of its uncertainty, in which
> That dark companion left him unconsoled
>
> For a self returning mostly memory.
> Only last year he said that the naked moon
> Was not the moon he used to see, to feel
>
> (In the pale coherences of moon and mood
> When he was young), naked and alien,
> More leanly shining from a lankier sky.
>
> ---
>
> It is the human that is the alien,
> The human that has no cousin in the moon.
>
> It is the human that demands his speech
> From beasts or from the incommunicable mass.
>
> If there must be a god in the house, let him be one
> That will not hear us when we speak: a coolness,
>
> A vermilioned nothingness, any stick of the mass
> Of which we are too distantly a part.

We might describe both of these poems as poems of yearning, the one informed by a despairing nostalgia, and the other by a yearning for the numinous. But in neither poem is subjectivity valued in itself. Rather, the representation of subjectivity—of lyric experience—is subordinated to the representation of the aesthetic response to lyric experience. The merely personal is sacrificed to the aesthetic requirements of the publicly constructed self, which, if it suffer, must experience a representative and exemplary suffering.

But the absence of subjectivity may itself be an indication of a kind of subjectivity. For such an absence may be read as the product of an aesthetic response to a series of perceived problems surrounding the representation of selfhood in poetry.

Some of these problems would seem endemic to the impulse to be representative, to speak on another's behalf. The problem of the role of the poet—to put the matter crudely—is one that is inevitably faced by, though not peculiar to, the writer of odes; for an ode, being 'a celebratory poem written in elevated language upon an occasion of public importance' (Fry 1980: 4–5), is the most thoroughly decorous, conservative and self-consciously 'poetic' of all kinds. Any claim on the part of the speaker of an ode to speak representatively must rest on her ability to maintain a formal decorum. One critic, Paul Fry, has remarked, 'Considered as an entertainment, the ode is not a sleight of hand but a performance on the high wire, not an illusion but an enchantment—or incantation' (Fry 1980: 9). But ever since the eighteenth century, this decorum has been problematized in various ways and the resulting crucial questions about poetic vocation, including anxieties about the provenance as well as the province of poetry, are intertwined with questions about one's right to represent another. Despite Wordsworth's description of the poet as 'a man speaking to men', odes tend to isolate their speakers, enforcing a lonely virtuosity. It is this which distinguishes their invocations from those of their cousins, the writers of hymns.[1]

We can see Stevens' links with the perennially difficult tradition of the ode in any number of poems, including 'The Idea of Order at Key West', *Notes towards a Supreme Fiction* and *An Ordinary Evening in New Haven*, from the latter of which I have chosen this example (canto IX, CP 471):

> We keep coming back and coming back
> To the real: to the hotel instead of the hymns
> That fall upon it out of the wind. We seek
>
> The poem of pure reality, untouched
> By trope or deviation, straight to the word,
> Straight to the transfixing object, to the object
>
> At the exactest point at which it is itself,
> Transfixing by being purely what it is,
> A view of New Haven, say, through the certain eye,
>
> The eye made clear of uncertainty, with the sight
> Of simple seeing, without reflection. We seek
> Nothing beyond reality. Within it,
>
> Everything, the spirit's alchemicana
> Included, the spirit that goes roundabout
> And through included, not merely the visible,
>
> The solid, but the movable, the moment,
> The coming on of feasts and the habits of saints,
> The pattern of the heavens and high, night air.

Perhaps the first thing we notice about this canto is how unstable, how slippery it is: the enjambed lines bespeak constant movement, a restless mind, the sheer quickness needed to name the elusive 'real'. Nor can the reader understand what it is that 'we' seek except from moment to moment, as Stevens names it more nearly. The shared purpose implicit in a 'we' grammar is confirmed by the use of an impersonal generalization: '*the* certain eye'. Since 'a view of New Haven' is merely an example of what might be seen with certainty, we might expect 'A view of New Haven, say, through *a* certain eye'; but '*the* certain eye' suggests that the eye becomes, in its certainty, single, whole, representatively communal. Similarly, 'reality' is a useful term in its singularity; Stevens does not imply that there can be different certainties for different eyes. At the same time, the impersonality, or, more accurately, the non-identity, of the communal self is emphasized since New Haven may be seen *through* the certain eye, but not *by* it. The eye — despite the inevitable pun of 'eye' and 'I' — is not a metonymy for a seeing self, but remains an agency merely.

The other set of problems about subjectivity which seems particularly pertinent in relation to Stevens is the *symboliste* legacy, especially the concept of 'pure poetry', and its corollary, poetic autonomy. The French symbolists' *poésie pure* had its source in Poe's essay, 'The Poetic Principle'. For him, poetry was a 'purely' aesthetic medium, explicitly divorced from both intellect and morality. It required intensity which Poe thought could be achieved by a heightened lyricism; 'a pure poetry' was intended to have the same effect upon its audience as music, a complete enchantment. Baudelaire, Mallarmé and Valéry were all interested in Poe's theory and practice. Each adapted Poe's practice of a lyricism in which the denotative meanings were, as much as possible, suppressed, while the connotative meanings were emphasized. Baudelaire, rephrasing Poe, extended the idea of poetic purity to include poetic autonomy: 'The goal of poetry is of the same nature as its principle, and it should have nothing in view but itself'.[2]

Stevens' interest in 'pure poetry' is most apparent in the 1930s. In an essay of 1937, 'The Irrational Element in Poetry', he says:

> It may be that my subject expressed with greater nicety is the irrational manifestations of the irrational element in poetry; for if the irrational element is merely poetic energy, it is to be found wherever poetry is to be found. One such manifestation is the disclosure of the individuality of the poet. It is unlikely that this disclosure is ever visible as plainly to anyone as to the poet himself.

And a little later in the same essay:

> It is conceivable that a poet may arise of such scope that he can set the abstraction on which so much depends to music. In the meantime we have to live by the literature we have or are able to produce. (Stevens 1957: 219, 222)

However, it is in a later war-time poem, 'The Creations of Sound' (Stevens 1954: 310–11), that he sets out to explore the differences between music, poetic language and speech. Stevens does not seek, in this poem, to sever speech and writing, but makes, on the contrary, a fundamental claim for speech. However, at the same time, he takes the very radical step of separating speech from self-presence; for, by the terms of this poem, poetic speech does not originate within the self, nor is it spoken by the self.[3] Self-presence and authority are indeed to be eschewed, according to this poem, which may sound unnervingly familiar to postmodernist ears:

> If the poetry of X was music,
> So that it came to him of its own,
> Without understanding, out of the wall
>
> Or in the ceiling, in sounds not chosen,
> Or chosen quickly, in a freedom
> That was their element, we should not know
>
> That X is an obstruction, a man
> Too exactly himself, and that there are words
> Better without an author, without a poet,
>
> Or having a separate author, a different poet,
> An accretion from ourselves, intelligent
> Beyond intelligence, an artificial man
>
> At a distance, a secondary expositor,
> A being of sound, whom one does not approach
> Through any exaggeration. From him, we collect. (stanzas 1–5)

In this first part of the poem Stevens is explicitly arguing that the poetry of X —whoever X is—is not music, in contrast to his own mellifluous rhetoric. We note the improvisational feel of the series of subordinate clauses of the first two stanzas, with their hypnotic repetitions, which seem so much like a musical elaboration of the algebraic proposition, 'If the poetry of X was music...'. But the poetry of X lacks 'the abstraction on which so much depends', an essential transcendental power. His words remain self-expression, and it is by his failure that an aesthetic, even an ethos, of the *proper* relation between poet and poem becomes known.

Critics have suggested several possible identities for X. Gerald Bruns thinks that either Mallarmé or William Carlos Williams could be the kind of poet that Stevens wished to specify (Bruns 1985: 35), while Harold Bloom identifies X as T.S. Eliot (Bloom 1977: 151-2, 277ff, 321).[4] But to assert this is, surely, to make the poem more of a reactionary piece than one intuitively feels it to be. Underlying the individual criticism of X and his claims, surely Stevens is arguing that *no* poetry can attain the formal condition of music. Pure poetry is a prescriptive rather than a descriptive term. Stevens may be putting his own capacity for melody-making on the line, in implicit competition with X, but he argues that words are an unsatisfying medium insofar as they retain a connection with their human origin. Words and poems ought to seem to have originated from an other than human source, or if that cannot be managed, their source should at least seem to be someone other than their real originator. To posit that X is Eliot is to miss the significance of X as an abstract figure. In an algebraic expression X stands for a representation of a non-specific value or identity. And this seems to be precisely what X is doing in the poem: acting as a substitution—manifesting Stevens' insistence on an abstract, generalized figure, rather than a specific identity. There is perhaps something high-minded about this—as if to suggest that not even for the purpose of refutation ought 'a man too exactly himself' be represented. Indeed, the bardic X has been separated from the general run of humanity that is represented in the poem by an 'us' grammar. The claim is made that if poetry is to represent anything of 'us', then the transcendence of the personality of the poet is imperative.

The whole of Stevens' preferred aesthetic of abstraction is constructed from the generality of 'words'. The 'artificial man' is, at least, 'a being of sound', but it is ambiguous as to whether he is shaped by, or is a source of, sound. We may note also Stevens' play with the 'x' sound in the poem—in 'the man too e*x*actly himself' and in the 'secondary e*x*positor' whom 'one does not approach/ Through any e*x*aggeration'. Stevens is objecting to a conception of poetry as a kind of melodrama, or monodrama. Indeed, the exaggerated gestures of the noble theatre of self are nicely deflated by the short, sharp sentence, 'From him, we collect'. Demotic, democratic, this slangy, gangsterly affirmation actually signals a reversal of 'our' status in relation to the true poet: approaching him is no longer to be thought of, for he has become an originary figure, a collective entity from whom we collect ourselves.

Having numbered himself among 'us', the speaker's next gesture is to dissociate himself from 'us' temporarily. 'We' becomes 'you', and 'you' takes orders from an implicit 'I':

> Tell X that speech is not dirty silence
> Clarified. It is silence made still dirtier.
> It is more than an imitation for the ear. (stanza 6)

What does this change of grammar signify? Who is the implicit 'you' that the speaker addresses? In the kind of reading advocated by David Walker in his book *The Transparent Lyric* (1984), the 'you' would be the reader or readers, an explicit invitation to join in a debate. But another reading is possible—one which does not involve an external referent. In this reading, the imperative signals the splitting of the self into a speaking 'I' and an attentive 'you', *as if the process of accretion had been completed, and a 'secondary expositor' created*. It is this 'artificial man/At a distance' who is being entrusted with the speaker's message to X. The message itself is obscure, if not obscurantist—as if to prove the point that saying something does not make clear an unheard meaning. Speech, being 'more than an imitation for the ear', is not merely a vocalized realization of imagined speech for the satisfaction of the physical ear, nor does the listening ear merely imitate what is spoken. Rather, Stevens contends that both speaking and listening are bound up with the life of the imagination, which is not predicated upon any circumstantial identity.

The following stanza renews the charges against X, and the force of the apostrophe weakens and fades. The speaker's counter-affirmation once more takes priority:

> He lacks this venerable complication.
> His poems are not of the second part of life.
> They do not make the visible a little hard
>
> To see, nor reverberating, eke out the mind
> On peculiar horns, themselves eked out
> By the spontaneous particulars of sound. (stanzas 6–7)

And the last stanza is a triumphant proclamation; the dialectical structure of refutation and counter-affirmation is continued, but the argument proper is over:

> We do not say ourselves like that in poems.
> We say ourselves in syllables that rise
> From the floor, rising in speech we do not speak.

Is Stevens recommending here a poetry which aspires not to the illusion of someone speaking but to the formal condition of music? In that 'we say ourselves in syllables'—'words' and 'sounds', in that the physical or vehicular aspect of language is emphasized over the denotative—this would seem to be the case. But considered as a lyric poem, 'The Creations of Sound' seems quite distinctly speakerly. Part of this speakerly quality must derive from the poem's logical method, and the use of a philosophical diction ('If the poetry of X was music... we should not know that...'). Philosophical discourse and debate are predicated on a belief in the capacity of language to be denotative, which belief is shared by users of the spoken word. The apprehension of spoken or written language differs in this important respect from the apprehension of music, whose significance is of a different order.

But the triumph of this last stanza is a logical triumph: the paradox of 'speech we do not speak' achieved as the ultimate extension of the logical method. It is in this stanza that Stevens raises the question of agency. For the fact that the syllables rise 'in speech we do not speak' does not necessarily mean that they are unspoken, but that they are unspoken by us. Who, then, is the agent of poetic speech, 'intelligent beyond intelligence'? And is it our syllables or ourselves who are 'rising in speech we do not speak'? Ultimately, Stevens asserts, the agent of poetic speech is a mystery: indeed, it appears to operate in a closely analogous way to that of the *logos*—always bearing in mind that to create an analogy for the *logos* is to effect a substitution. The syllables of poetry do not originate in 'us', but 'rise from the floor'—yet 'we say ourselves' in them. Self-transcendence is not possible through composing poetry, Stevens suggests: instead, 'our' transcendence may be accomplished by 'our' being spoken—*uttered*—by another.

The deferral of power that is represented by the final lines of 'The Creations of Sound' is replicated in many other poems—the most famous being at the end of *Notes toward a Supreme Fiction* (CP 406)—where 'you' retains her otherness, thereby perpetuating, through the desire that she elicits, the process of poetry:

X

Fat girl, terrestrial, my summer, my night,
How is it I find you in difference, see you there
In a moving contour, a change not quite completed?...

* * *

They will get it straight one day at the Sorbonne.
We shall return at twilight from the lecture
Pleased that the irrational is rational,

Until flicked by feeling, in a gildered street,
I call you by name, my green, my fluent mundo.
You will have stopped revolving except in crystal.

My interest is not so much in the nature of the figures deferred to as in the way they operate as occasions of deferral. For these chimeric figures, who are found throughout Stevens' *oeuvre*, together signal a strategy of deferral that we come to think of as being characteristic of 'Stevens'. And my concern here is the ways in which those occasions of deferral are indicated by Stevens' pronoun usage.

There is a sense in which every use of a pronoun other than 'I' or 'we' constitutes a minimal gesture of deferral, since every such use is an admission of alterity. It is the kind and degree of alterity ceded by the speaking self that is variable. As to the kind of alterity, we can say that the pronoun determines our stance toward the figure it donates. A pronoun positions its referent and ourselves in relation to each other. We can begin to frame a series of paradigms: generally speaking, 'he', 'she', 'it' and 'they' are viewed in profile; 'you' (singular and plural) are addressed *face à face*; 'we' face in the same direction as does the speaker. These paradigms are, of course, reductive; they are also fallible. Nevertheless, they do illuminate a number of possible ways in which self and other mutually compose each other by defining each other as relative entities. Pronouns, moreover, being substitutes for a name or names, can be said to lack completion. They may even lend themselves to undoing

Adam's task of naming—as they do in *Notes*, where, at the end of the poem, the speaker has yet to name his Muse. Stevens' characteristic usage of pronouns as instruments of deferral is, as I have suggested, part of a much larger strategy of deferral. This larger pattern manifests itself in Stevens' interest in prayer, in apostrophe and invocation—in short, in the rhetoric of deferential address—and also in Stevens' interest in the Sublime, which is the mode or genre in which deferral is necessary to transcendence.

One poem offers itself as a particularly good test case for assessing the consequences of this practice. 'The Idea of Order at Key West' (Stevens 1954: 128-30), is one of Stevens' most popular poems and is very frequently explicated. Most of its readers have focused on the ideas about creativity that are expounded within it, seeking to elucidate the idea of order of which it is apparently an epiphany. Harold Bloom has ably pin-pointed the difficulties in the poem's logic. It is slippery and inconclusive about the aesthetics it professes, and these are not always consistent with the aesthetics that it manifests. This is by no means always a fault in Stevens, as Bloom himself acknowledges:

> Stevens writes a poetry centered on the *aporia* between rhetoric as persuasion and rhetoric as a system of tropes, and in a curious way this centering became a guarantee of his poetic importance. (Bloom 1977: 105)

Nevertheless, Bloom who thinks it the finest poem in *Ideas of Order* and finer than any poem in *Harmonium*, considers its faults to be grave ones:

> ...the Key West poem has its desperate equivocations and its unresolvable difficulties, more perhaps than even so strong a poem can sustain. In some respects, it is an impossible text to interpret and its rhetoric may be at variance with its deepest intentionalities. (Bloom 1977: 93)

According to Bloom, the two chief problems are 'nearly antithetical to each other': 'The poem affirms a transcendental poetic spirit yet cannot locate it, and the poem also remains uneasily aware about the veritable ocean...' (Bloom 1977: 104). I want to suggest that these problems might be less antithetical than Bloom has claimed; that is, I want to suggest that they share a common source in the poem's central strategy and that this strategy is one in which Stevens' choice of pronouns is crucially implicated.

The poem begins as a narrative, a recounted history, as person and tense indicate:

> She sang beyond the genius of the sea.
> The water never formed to mind or voice,
> Like a body wholly body, fluttering
> Its empty sleeves; and yet its mimic motion
> Made constant cry, caused constantly a cry,
> That was not ours although we understood,
> Inhuman, of the veritable ocean. (Stevens 1954: 128)

Can we disentangle the syntax here—reassign the clauses to their subjects, reckon what belongs to the ocean, and to her, and to ourselves? The poem's metaphysical mode invites us to do so, yet we are distracted in our task by the poem's rhetoric: its rhythms smooth or disturbed, its repetitions blurring distinctions, its melopoeia. Clearly, there is a gap between its rhetoric and its argument — between the precision and clarity that are needed for the proper presentation of an aesthetic and the desire to enchant the intellect. Bloom, who draws our attention to this gap, is nevertheless moved by the poem's mellifluence.[5]

The poem's rhetoric is opaque, rather like a filter of the senses. We are conscious of the poem as *voice*, as a vocal and aural performance. But we do not hear 'her'. Only the fact of her singing is reported to us; only the fact of her singing — not her song — has any significance for us. While this may guarantee, in a sense, her otherness, it also alerts us to our dependence on the poem (and not her song) as a medium of revelation.

Stevens' use of the rhetoric of 'pure poetry' here amounts to a critique of the aim of the symbolistes to produce an autonomous poetry. The essence of Stevens' critique is neither ontological nor linguistic; it is moral. For Stevens, in contrast to Poe, did not divide an aesthetic realm from an ethical one, but employed this unworldliest of styles in a poem which seeks to elucidate the function of poetry. 'Our' witness is necessary if 'she' is to fulfil her mediating function, which means that 'her' role, though 'she' have nothing to do with 'us', is nevertheless social, relative.

Who is 'she' in the context of the poem? No proper name, or other noun, is supplied as a referent. This means that 'she' and 'her' are not merely words substituting for other words; instead, 'she' is all her identity. Nevertheless, like all pronouns, reiteration serves to reinforce our sense of a persistent referent. Then there is the matter of gender: the significance of Stevens having specified otherness as 'she'. Stevens' use of 'she' evokes — if it no longer invokes — a patriarchal strategy of reading which is integral to many aspects of 'literary tradition', particularly in this case the tradition of the ode. In 1934, when the poem was written, 'she' was — as, for that matter, 'she' is now — *more gendered* than 'he'. A 'he'-grammar was the third person normative expression of experience — male experience being the predominant form of accredited literary experience — and unless indicated otherwise, the poem's speaker was generally masculine. 'She', it seems, was differentiated from 'he' like Eve from Adam's rib. The literary culture that informs 'The Idea of Order at Key West' dictates that the speaker be masculine; the use of the gendered pronoun 'she' may be read as setting the seal on her otherness.

Since 'she' in the poem has no specific identity, it is perhaps remarkable that this 'purely' linguistic construct 'she' — this partial indicator of gendered human otherness — should have so great a power to evoke a literary tradition. For it would seem that the use of 'she' is sufficient to place the poem as a special kind of sea-shore lyric, evoking a tradition which includes Arnold's 'Dover Beach', (Arnold 1965: 239), Whitman's sea-shore lyrics 'As I Ebb'd with the Ocean of Life' and 'Out of the Cradle Endlessly Rocking' (Whitman 1921: 290), and extends beyond formal poetry to include Stephen Dedalus' epiphany at the end of *A Portrait of the Artist as a Young Man*. Bloom (1977), reading the poem back against 'As I Ebb'd . . .', sees 'her' as a variation of the American muse-as-mother. Whitman, as Bloom observes, 'found the muse his mother to be his oceanic sense and . . . identified his father with the shore'. Hence, 'to sing beyond the genius of the sea is to defy the poetics of Whitman' (Bloom 1977: 98). Yet the singer is also 'very Shelleyan and has the same relation to the world she makes as Shelley's Emilia has to 'Love's rare Universe' in *Epipsychidion* (Bloom 1977: 102). Furthermore, Stevens' 'she' has something in common with Wordsworth's 'Solitary Reaper', 'a girl who sang as if her song could have no ending' (Bloom 1977: 103). Bloom is nonetheless very vague about what 'she' actually depicts. His statement, 'At Key West, the idea of order is incarnated by one singing woman "striding there alone"...' seems clear enough; yet he has referred to her on another occasion as 'the singing girl', and on another three occasions as 'the girl at Key West', a phrase which, on reiteration, comes to sound somewhat gnomic (Bloom 1977: 88, 94, 95, 96). This continual slippage, this oscillation between 'woman' and 'girl' should perhaps make us wary of the sheer number of specific texts which, Bloom claims, inform Stevens' use of the word 'she' here. Bloom's reading of Stevens' sources — if that is what they are — points to the female of 'The Idea of Order at Key West' as an archetype: figural (capable of 'striding there alone'), yet so abstract as almost to constitute perhaps a *topos*, or a feminine principle. At one point Bloom comes close to acknowledging that which Stevens is *not* doing in relation to 'her' — composing a self — but at the last minute he veers away from this acknowledgement, instead laying her lack of selfhood as a charge against Stevens.[6]

While on the subject of gender, it seems worth mentioning Frank Lentricchia's early reading of the poem in *The Gaiety of Language* (1968). In the light of his informed and persuasive accounts of the French symbolistes, Lentricchia's readings seem somewhat reactionary, as if denying the associative ways of meaning that the symbolistes promoted. Instead, we have the inflexibility of New Criticism, which Lentricchia has subsequently renounced.[7] While we can admire his insistence on rigorous logic, the meanings that he ascribes to Stevens' lines being consistent seem massively overdetermined if not wrong-headed. In the matter of gender we can see this very clearly. Here is the poem's triumphant climax, and his response to it:

> It was her voice that made
> The sky acutest at its vanishing.
> She measured to the hour its solitude.
> She was the single artificer of the world
> In which she sang. And when she sang, the sea,
> Whatever self it had, became the self
> That was her song, for she was the maker. Then we,
> As we beheld her striding there alone,
> Knew there never was a world for her
> Except the one she sang and, singing, made. (Stevens 1954: 129)

As I see it, the main thrust of the passage is the notion that the world she made and ordered was not the world of the sea. She failed conspicuously to do that, and she failed because she had to: the imagination can have no intercourse with reality — the sexual image of impotence is as appropriate to Stevens' poetic as the potent sexual image is for romantic theory. This is his philosophical world view, but he yet feels that the woman has become too much an escapist of the imagination, as she focuses at the horizon where the world seems to end, too willingly a solipsist who disregards the hard particulars of experience which he believes must be the ground of a vital poetry. (Lentricchia 1968: 185).

I am not at all sure that sexual imagery is pertinent here, and I find the association of the feminine with impotence gratuitous and somewhat ludicrous.[8] The notion of male potency as a metaphor for creative power is certainly one that informs many romantic texts. Stevens, as Lentricchia is aware, saw the poet as the inheritor of the romantics in precisely this respect, writing on the subject in 1943 (Stevens 1951: 37–67). What strikes us about Stevens' presentation of 'the figure of youth as virile poet' is its conservatism. He is easily recognizable, a stock figure from the romantic repertoire. However, to say that Stevens adopts virility as a metaphor for creative power does not make 'her' a symbol of impotence.

If the meaning of Stevens' 'she' seems problematic, his use of the pronoun 'we' is even more so. Who, indeed, are 'we'? There is no sure answer. It would seem that 'we' has a shifting status. 'We' for Bloom signifies the speaker and Ramon Fernandez (the companion revealed late in the poem); yet he remarks, somewhat strangely, that:

> Stevens is not quite in solitude as he listens to the girl at Key West, though we don't know that until rather late in the poem, just as we are startled to find late in *Tintern Abbey* that Wordsworth is accompanied by Dorothy. (Bloom 1977: 96)

This strikes me as simply inaccurate; the use of a 'we' grammar in the first stanza suggests strongly that the speaker was accompanied, although the identity of his companion is not revealed until late in the poem. So late, indeed, that by the time he *is* named, we might not expect anyone to be named at all. Rather, taking as our model Stevens' usage of 'she', we might expect 'we' to have the same generalizing status: to signify 'I and someone else'. And in fact 'we' does not necessarily include Ramon Fernandez: he can be considered merely someone to whom the speaker calls to interpret 'our' common experience.

There is also the question of whether or not the 'we' here may represent a gesture of inclusion of the reader. This seems feasible insofar as the speaker gives us directions not merely for interpreting, but actually for *experiencing* her song:

> The song and water were not medleyed sound
> Even if what she sang was what she heard,
> Since what she sang was uttered word by word.
> It may be that in all her phrases stirred
> The grinding water and the gasping wind;
> But it was she and not the sea we heard. (Stevens 1954: 128)

This inclusiveness of the reader in 'we' — if that is what is intended — seems to be of a most authoritarian kind. Stevens is not so much inviting his readers to share an experience of epiphany as informing us that 'we' once experienced such an epiphany: that 'we understood,/Inhuman, of the veritable ocean'. It is not as if we had the experience but missed the meaning. Rather, the poem's task is to persuade us to recognize Stevens' account of it as ours: to let the fact of the poem speak on our behalf. There is, however, nothing persuasive about Stevens' use of a 'we' grammar; he simply claims, and proclaims, 'us'. He assumes our complicity, foisting an experience, a history, upon us. 'We', after all, rhymes with 'she' and 'sea'.

Having presented the case for 'we' including the reader as convincingly as I can, I must say that *I* am not wholly convinced that it is so. The problem with such an interpretation, it seems to me, is that in implicating the words and the reader in an actual social contract, it invokes, in fact, reality as a model. Do we really undergo, or believe we have undergone, the experience that is being attested to on our behalf? Surely we are not required to do so. Stevens' use of a 'we' grammar can better be explained in structuralist terms, which delimit a different usage, or usages, of the pronoun from its usage in common speech. In 'The Idea of Order at Key West', 'we' would appear to encompass a number of significances which are not always consistent with one another. 'We' may signify 'the reader and the speaker', or 'Ramon Fernandez and the speaker' — two specific readings which are not compatible — or it may signify all of humanity. 'We' is a floating signifier, whose conflicting significations render it radically unstable, and whose usage is thus permeated with a feeling of unease.

The scheme of relations between 'her', 'ourselves' and 'the ocean' is set out in the first stanza of the poem. This presentation is, as I have indicated, crucial to the poem as a whole since the transcendent spirit which Bloom claims 'Stevens affirms but fails to locate', must be sought in the arrangement of the three entities, in their dispositions toward one another. Pronouns are in this sense like chess pieces: their names define their relations with one another. What Stevens does with these intrinsically relational words is to undercut their localizing quality, and the effect is rather as if the chessboard itself were being pulled out of shape. 'The genius of the sea', that famously American spirit of place, is evoked in order to place her singing 'beyond' it. It would seem that her song is not rooted in a *genius loci* after all; yet there is a sense in which her song encompasses that spirit by singing beyond its boundaries. It is, however, impossible to locate 'her' precisely in relation to the sea and, subsequently, in relation to 'us'.

If, as I have suggested, the pronoun 'we' does not necessarily include Ramon Fernandez, could it be possible that Ramon Fernandez, subject of the truly startling late apostrophe, is merely a name to conjure with?

> Ramon Fernandez, tell me, if you know,
> Why, when the singing ended and we turned
> Toward the town, tell why the glassy lights,
> The lights in the fishing boats at anchor there,
> As the night descended, tilting in the air,
> Mastered the night and portioned out the sea,
> Fixing emblazoned zones and fiery poles,
> Arranging, deepening, enchanting night.
>
> Oh! Blessed rage for order, pale Ramon,
> The maker's rage to order words of the sea,
> Words of the fragrant portals, dimly-starred,
> And of ourselves and of our origins,
> In ghostlier demarcations, keener sounds. (Stevens 1954: 130)

My sense is that that palpable strangeness of this apostrophic finale has been consistently underplayed by critics. Harold Bloom (1977: 96) and Eleanor Cook (1988: 119, 130-4) account for it by reading the strangeness of

Wordsworth's apostrophe to (of?) Dorothy in *Tintern Abbey* as a precedent, which has the effect of neutralizing somewhat the oddness of the Stevens poem. Bloom, in addition, undoes the bond between the two stanzas that is created by their both being cast as address, by calling the last stanza the 'coda' (Bloom 1977: 103). Jonathan Culler, in his excellent essay 'Apostrophe', has argued that the avoidance or glossing over of the inherent strangeness of apostrophe is always the case amongst critics and, in a sense, an inherent danger of the critical enterprise (Culler 1977: 59–69). I shall be referring to his specific arguments a little later, but first it needs to be said that the case is complicated by 'Ramon Fernandez' being the name of an actual person. In a letter of 1947, Stevens wrote:

> ... the name of Ramon Fernandez is arbitrary. I used two every-day names. As I might have expected, they turned out to be an actual name.

And he mentioned the matter again in a letter of 1953:

> Ramon Fernandez was not intended to be anyone at all. I chose two every-day Spanish names. I knew of Ramon Fernandez, the critic, and had read some of his criticisms but I did not have him in mind. (Stevens 1966: 798, 798n)

Bloom is, I think, right to be chary of taking these comments at face value:

> ... in spite of some grumpy letters he was a modern French critic whom Stevens had certainly read. As a formalist Fernandez had much in common with Stevens, but *The Idea of Order at Key West* is a High Romantic poem, and Fernandez was anti-Romantic, being in this a Gallic equivalent of Eliot or Tate. (Bloom 1977: 102)

Bloom makes the actuality of Fernandez relevant, interpreting the relationship between poet and critic (hardly surprisingly) as a combative one, one out of which he can make a distinction between a rage *for* order and a rage *to* order that will sustain his own dichotomizing method: 'With the last full stanza, Ramon Fernandez as anti-Romantic inquisitor enters the poem, but only to be admonished' (Bloom 1977: 96). In fact, it is the poem's speaker who is the inquisitor here since it is he who summons Fernandez and calls him to account: 'Ramon Fernandez, tell me, if you know. . . .' In Bloom's agonistic reading the imperative is a challenge. Presumably Ramon Fernandez does *not* know why a pattern of order crystallized at that particular moment of time; his idea of order is inadequate to such events.

However, it is possible to hear these lines quite differently. Stevens himself does not mention that the actual Fernandez is French; what is important to him about the name is its Spanishness. Indeed, the names that together compose the name 'Ramon Fernandez' are hardly 'two every-day names'—one learns to be most wary of Stevens when he professes ordinariness. Totally unexpected as they are, they arrive with a verbal flourish, with the bravura of the professional conjuror. However, though they are surprising, they are not exactly exotic—for a generic, or every-day Ramon Fernandez would more likely be a native of Florida (itself a Spanish name) than a European Spaniard (or Frenchman). His name, so florid perhaps to Connecticut ears, would sound ordinary (rather than ornate) to his own.

Could Ramon Fernandez be a spirit—or even a genius—of Key West? How long does it take for the language of an originally foreign, imperial power (Spain) to be able to represent the language of *genius loci* (Florida)? In any case, Stevens specifies 'Key West' rather than 'Florida' in the title, so it seems very unlikely indeed that Ramon Fernandez could signify anything at once so specific and so abstract as a 'spirit of place', or 'naturalized Europe'.

Nevertheless, this elusive and surely (somehow) local figure is invoked, called into being, very much as if he were an accountable authority. It is, however, this very accountability that Stevens problematizes: 'tell me, *if you know*'. Unlike Bloom, my sense is not that Ramon Fernandez is being invoked only to be refuted; rather, it seems that Stevens takes certain steps to de-authorize the identity he invokes. And ultimately the *explanation* of epiphany that the speaker demands of Fernandez is seen to be less important than the sheer affirmation of the perceived pattern as a miracle. Beside the perception of an order, Ramon pales. The poem's final stanza is not a 'coda', but the culmination of a kind of narrative; the bursting forth 'Oh! Blessed rage for order, pale Ramon' has been prepared for. It represents the triumph of rhetoric (where rhetoric is the conveyor of feeling) over logic and argument: blessed rage for order over order itself.

In a classical sense, Stevens' address to Ramon Fernandez is clearly an apostrophe, a startlingly late calling out to a heretofore absent listener, a *pro tem* audience who fades into the background, quickly overwhelmed by the recounting of the epiphany itself; the question 'tell me ... why ...' becomes swamped in the particulars of the event. We only hear of Fernandez again to see how distant he has become: 'pale Ramon', distant as the moon, and, as such, a suitable object toward which to direct one's final triumphant utterance.

Culler suggests that we might identify apostrophe with 'lyric itself' (Culler 1977: 60), and in 'The Idea of Order at Key West' such an identification seems to be invited by the change from a 'we' to an 'I' grammar at the moment of apostrophe: 'Ramon Fernandez, tell me, if you know'. It seems that the speaker sheds the communal authority afforded him as a spokesperson at the moment he is transformed into a lyric 'I'. This is, once again, to limit the authority of Fernandez since he is not asked to 'tell *us*', as a priestly figure would be expected to do. It may be argued that the change to an 'I' grammar merely signals that Ramon Fernandez has, up until this point, been the speaker's companion, part of the 'we' on whose behalf the speaker speaks. However, in the last lines of the poem the speaker assumes once more his public mantle when he speaks of 'ourselves' and of 'our origins'. Since he is addressing distant 'pale Ramon' at this point, it seems to me highly unlikely that the final 'we' could also include the addressee.

However, as we have seen, Stevens calls on Ramon Fernandez as an authority, which is a characteristic strategy—one might say, *the* characteristic strategy—of *invocation*. To invoke an authority is to be authorized; invocation is a self-empowering gesture achieved by means of an act of deference. But an authentic authority must last, according to Fry (1980: 11): his/her/its presence must be sufficiently palpable to act as a source of power. Ramon Fernandez is not. Indeed, Stevens explicitly undermines his authority by being equivocal about his knowledge, even as he holds him accountable. In a move which came to be characteristic of Stevens, the speaker de-authorizes his addressee in order to authorize himself.

'The Idea of Order at Key West' leaves us with a series of questions about the relations of the identities represented by pronouns to one another—questions which are, in essence, political. The explanation that the speaker seeks from Ramon Fernandez would appear to concern a second event—subsequent to the recognitions that crystallized while beholding her 'striding there alone', and very possibly as a consequence of them. Does the authority of Ramon Fernandez as interpreter surpass that of the female figure in the poem as a creative artist? Stevens suggests not, since he renders the former's authority questionable. Nevertheless, the mere fact that Fernandez is called upon raises the question. Without going so far as Lentricchia (1968: 185), who takes the view that Stevens turns against the solipsism that 'she' represents at the end of the poem—that his attitude toward her solipsism is, ultimately, 'ironic'—I should say that the apostrophe to Ramon Fernandez has the effect of destabilizing not only the poem's decorum (as do all apostrophes) but her status as supreme figure as well.

Does Stevens endorse her solipsism? The rhapsodic tone of the poem as a whole would suggest so. Stevens seems to treat her as an allegorical figure, to advocate the creative procedures which she exemplifies. However, he avoids confronting directly the implicit comparison between her creative act and his own, and this may come to seem like an evasion. 'She' may be 'the single artificer of the world in which she sang', but 'we' do not exist there. 'She' did not create 'us' for 'she' is separate from 'us', as 'we beh[o]ld her striding there alone'.

Is the use of a third person pronoun simply a device for avoiding having to proclaim solipsism, as it were, on one's own behalf? What, indeed, is Stevens' rationale for the act of deferral? These questions become even more pressing when we consider that it is a rare poem of Stevens that locates an 'I' firmly at the centre of the perceived world. What advantages might a third person treatment have over a first person treatment? At the simplest level, one thing it seems to me that it might do would be to take the pressure off poetic form, which, in a third person treatment, does not have a special status as lyric self-expression. To work this way—by anecdote, instance and allegory—is to disengage the self of the speaking subject from the exemplary centre. What the speaker *says* (or the writing itself) can then be used either to endorse or to undermine the values for which such a centre stands. The converse could equally be argued: ie that the practice of deferral, and in particular the use of a third person pronoun to delimit the identity deferred to, results in *increased* pressure on poetic form, which will always have a moral weight, an import as rhetoric. When, in addition, the figure at the centre represents a value, and that value is a creative aesthetic of solipsism, certain fundamental contradictions are inevitable. The imagination of the speaking subject, in including a concept of solipsistic otherness, is itself non-solipsistic; indeed, it is manifestly dialogic.

Notes

1. Fry (1980: 7) observes that:
   Like the hymns, the ode or 'hymn exempore' longs for participation in the it never participates communally, never willingly supplies a congregation with common prayer because it is bent on recovering a priestly role that is not pastoral but hermetic.

2. Quoted in Preminger (1974: 682). For a detailed account of the poetic theory of each of Poe, Baudelaire, Mallarmé and Valéry, see Lentricchia 1968: 28-38.
3. Indeed, it is arguable that Stevens' working definition of 'poetic speech' conforms closely to Derrida's definition of writing.
4. By 1944, when 'The Creations of Sound' was written, X had already appeared in an early poem, 'Anecdote of Canna', and in another poem, 'Extracts from Addresses to the Academy of Fine Ideas'. In 1918 when 'Anecdote of Canna' was first published, Eliot had not yet alienated Stevens by his orthodox Christianity, nor had he yet upstaged him — which happened when *The Waste Lane* was published nine months before *Harmonium*. And Eliot had not yet written 'Tradition and the Individual Talent', with its famous dictum of impersonality: 'Poetry is not a turning loose of emotion, but an escape from emotion; it is not the expression of personality, but an escape from personality' (Eliot 1951: 21). In 'Anecdote of Canna', then, it is unlikely that X could be Eliot. However, in 'Extracts from Addresses to the Academy of Fine Ideas', III (1940), the connection with Eliot is unmistakable, given that *Old Possum's Book of Practical Cats* had been published the year before.
5. Bloom 1977: 97: 'Is there a better first line, or a better first stanza, in all of Stevens?'
6. His criticisms are made in relation to the poem's triumphant climax (stanza 11 34-43):

> This stanza is the poem's attempted sublimation of its deepest intentions or desires for utterance, and like all such metaphors it 'fails'. This is not poetical failue so much as it is argumentative or topical failure, for the sublimating metaphor tries to emphasize the resemblance between inner voice and outer ocean, at the expense of the dissimilarity. Stevens perspectivizes desperately, in the Nietzschean manner, to evade the fiction of the human self. Did the sea become the singer's self, when it 'became the self/That was her song'? Whitman hovers overtly here, as he has been hovering covertly throughout the poem. What song can the woman be singing if it is not a song of herself? (Bloom 1977: 102)

The answer to Bloom's question must be *any* song; we do not know what she sang. It seems to me that, far from 'perspectivizing desperately', Stevens has deliberately distinguished between herself and her song. The song is *itself*, emptied of 'her' identity.

7. See especially *After the New Criticism* (1980) and *Ariel and the Police* (1988).
8. But for an exploration of one aspect of the history of the normative state of Western culture, whereby feminine impotence is taken to be a corollary of masculine potency, see Battersby 1989.
9. *La Florida*, the land of flowers, was so named by the Spanish conquistador, Juan Ponce de Léon, who, while searching for the fountain of eternal youth in 1513, was driven by a storm upon the coast. Report has it that he gave this name to the land partly because of its wealth of flowers and partly because it was Easter when he discovered it. Easter, *Pascua de la Resurrección* is also sometimes called *Pascua Florida*, because in Spain flowers generally come up at this time. (de la Vega 1951: xxi, 8, 8n).

Bibliography

Arnold, Matthew (1965), *The Poems of Matthew Arnold*, (ed. Kenneth Allott), London, Longman.
Battersby, Christine (1989), *Gender and Genius: Toward a Feminist Aesthetics*, London, The Women's Press.
Bloom, Harold (1977), *Wallace Stevens: The Poems of Our Climate*, Ithaca and London, Cornell University Press.

Bruns, Gerald L. (1985), 'Stevens without Epistemology', *Wallace Stevens: The Poetics of Modernism*, (ed. Albert Gelpi), Cambridge, Cambridge University Press.
Cook, Eleanor (1988), *Poetry, Word-Play and Word-War in Wallace Stevens*, New Jersey, Princeton University Press.
Culler, Jonathan (1977), 'Apostrophe', *Diacritics* 7 (Winter), 59–69.
Eliot, T.S. (1951), *Selected Essays*, (Third edition), London, Faber.
Fry, Paul H. (1980), *The Poet's Calling in the English Ode*, New Haven, Yale University Press.
Joyce, James (1977), *The Portrait of the Artist as a Young Man*, London, Grafton.
Lentricchia, Frank (1968), *The Gaiety of Language: An Essay on the Radical Poetics of W.B. Yeats and Wallace Stevens*, Berkeley and Los Angeles, University of California Press.
Lentricchia, Frank (1980), *After the New Criticism*, Chicago, University of Chicago Press.
Lentricchia Frank (1988), *Ariel and the Police: Michel Foucault, William James, Wallace Stevens*, Brighton, Harvester Press.
Preminger, A. (ed.) (1974), *The Princeton Encyclopaedia of Poetry and Poetics*, New Jersey, Princeton University Press.
Stevens, Wallace (1951), 'The Figure of Youth as Virile Poet' (1943), *The Necessary Angel: Essays on Reality and the Imagination*, New York, Knopf, 37–67.
Stevens, Wallace (1954), *Collected Poems*, New York, Knopf.
Stevens, Wallace (1957), *Opus Posthumous*, (ed. Samuel French Morse), New York, Knopf.
Stevens, Wallace (1966), *Letters of Wallace Stevens*, (ed. Holly Stevens), New York, Knopf.
de la Vega, Garcilaso (1951), *The Florida of the Inca*, (tr. and ed. John Grier Varner and Jeanette Johnson Varner), London, Nelson.
Walker, David (1984), *The Transparent Lyric: Reading and Meaning in the Poetry of Stevens and Williams*, New Jersey, Princeton University Press.
Whitman, Walt (1921), *Leaves of Grass*, New York, The Modern Library.

7 The Ideological Eye-witness: An Examination of the Eye-witness in Two Works by George Orwell

Peter Marks

The resilient myth of George Orwell as a blunt, contentious, but fundamentally honest writer draws much of its force from Orwell's position as an eye-witness to crucial events or significant situations. Whether as down-and-outer in London, imperial policeman in Burma, militia man in Spain, or investigative reporter in northern England, Orwell had seen for himself many of the things he would later describe. This fact, coupled with a spare prose style—a style too readily accepted as guileless—gave to much of Orwell's writing the quality of reality, faithfully captured. Modern critical debate, however, has called into question the capacity of the author to depict reality, objectively or otherwise; the terms themselves—'author', 'depiction', 'reality' and 'objectivity', are viewed with varying degrees of scepticism. The role and status of the eye-witness, the 'I' in literature, are under scrutiny.

This has always been true in the proper arena for the eye-witness, the court of law. In court, the eye-witness is not to be trusted. Or, at very least, not to be trusted completely, or immediately. Although the claim to have seen an event, to be in possession of evidence, suggests a grasp of reality, the inherent subjectivity of the first-hand account is manifest. In a court of law the eye-witness is liable to rigorous questioning. Both the bona fides, the 'character', of the eye-witness, and the validity of the account itself must be established. And there is always the threat of other evidence, other eye-witnesses.

In literature the situation is different. Since the narrator, the 'I' of the work, exists only as words on paper, the establishing of the 'character' of the eye-witness must itself be confined to the text. More importantly, all the 'evidence' presented has been selected and arranged by the author with a particular verdict in mind. The trial, it would seem, is rigged. Yet, in terms of the courtroom analogy, the reader operates as a jury, weighing evidence, accepting and rejecting as seems fit. Literature fundamentally differs from law in that, potentially, there are as many verdicts as there are readers.

The role and status of the eye-witness have a particular relevance for Orwell criticism. A recurring element in analyses of his work is the conflation of the writer and his writings. Bernard Crick has noted 'astonishing agreement... that [Orwell's] work can only be understood by characterizing the man' (Crick

1982: 39). The confusion of writer and writings is heightened in those works purporting to give first-hand accounts of events or situations. Is the narrator of such pieces, the 'I' from whose viewpoint the narrative unfolds, to be taken as Orwell? If so, what effect might this have on any interpretation of the 'evidence' put forward? This problem is especially important in Orwell's case, for he is one of those intriguing writers able to draw vilification or praise from either political wing. To compound these difficulties, before the publication of *Animal Farm* in 1945, only five years before his death, Orwell was a well-considered but relatively minor writer. The received Orwell is a multifaceted, and in many ways posthumous, creation. Nevertheless, the problem of disentangling Orwell from his work remains; the writer may be 'dead', in Barthes' terms (Barthes 1977: 142–8), but is still capable of haunting the text. Examining two short, early pieces by Orwell allows for the consideration of these questions and problems.

'A Hanging' (1970a) and 'Shooting an Elephant' (1970b) occupy the ambiguous space at the intersection of fiction and non-fiction. Both can operate successfully as fictional short stories. Nevertheless, in the index to *The Collected Essays, Journalism and Letters of George Orwell*, both are categorized as 'non-literary' events in Orwell's life; 'shoots an elephant' and 'participates in hanging' are given equivalent status with 'street fighting in Barcelona' and the rather less momentous 'buys chessmen and mends a fuse'. There is no corroborating evidence that these events occurred, the respective index references pointing solely to these works. Clearly, the editors of the collection accept Orwell's role in these events, and consequently consider 'A Hanging' and 'Shooting an Elephant' to be first-hand accounts. Analysis of each piece questions this simplistic assumption. Orwell uses the perspective and persona of the eye-witness, the 'I', as a rhetorical device, both for structural and ideological purposes.

'A Hanging' is one of Orwell's earliest published works. In fact, it pre-dates 'Orwell'. Eric A. Blair, under whose name the piece first appeared in 1931, was not to adopt a pseudonym for more than a year after its publication. It is commonly interpreted as a simple morality tale, in which a British imperial functionary in Burma comes to realize the 'unspeakable wrongness' of capital punishment. At the hanging of a Hindu prisoner for an unspecified crime, the narrator observes the condemned man avoiding a puddle on his path to the gallows. The prisoner's unconscious signal of his essential humanity triggers a revelation in the narrator's mind, for 'till that moment I had never realized what it is to destroy a healthy, conscious life' (Orwell 1970a: 68). Despite this illumination, the execution takes place. In the aftermath the narrator's own perceptions are drowned in social ritual: 'We all drank together, native and European alike, quite amicably. The dead man was a hundred yards away' (Orwell 1970a: 71).

Surprisingly, given the narrator's role as both eye-witness and (apparently) as sole perceiver of the moral implications of the hanging, he is delineated only sketchily. The first person pronoun 'I' occurs only half a dozen times in relation to the narrator. Instead, he is subsumed repeatedly in a number of groups. Initially he is merely one of the imperial officials and local operatives overseeing the execution. The first reference to him as an individual is oblique — a dog bounds into the gallows procession, races up to the condemned man, and licks him playfully. After it is caught the dog is restrained by having the narrator's handkerchief linked through its collar. Soon after, the narrator experiences epiphany at the puddle, the revelation causing him to consider the implications of the hanging. Yet he does so within the context of a larger group. The prisoner, until now segregated from those carrying out his execution, is included by the narrator: 'he and we were a party of men together...and in two minutes, with a sudden snap, one of us would be gone — one mind less, one world less' (Orwell 1970a: 68–9). The sense of community, however, is fleeting. Once on the scaffold the prisoner's rhythmic chant, as he steels himself for execution, elicits the confession from the narrator that 'the same thought was in all our minds: oh, kill him quickly, get it over, stop that abominable noise' (Orwell 1970a: 69). Briefly included in a broad humanity, the prisoner is summarily dispatched. The execution is carried out. Momentarily, and obliquely again, the narrator is individualized. In the immediate aftermath of the hanging, he notes that '[t]he prisoner had vanished, and the rope was twisting on itself. I let go of the dog' (Orwell 1970a: 70). Yet it is as part of the imperial administration that the narrator views the corpse, adopting an institutional aloofness to the body. As they leave the gallows yard, a crude joke relaxes tension, and again the narrator flashes into view: 'I found that I was laughing quite loudly. Everyone was laughing' (Orwell 1970a: 71). The process of momentary individualization, followed immediately by subsumption in a group, is repeated.

The narrator's lack of self-definition, his constant and changing inclusion within a variety of groups (British imperial officials, all men, those guiltily socializing after the execution) might be taken to suggest a common humanity, and therefore to reinforce the immorality of extinguishing a life. Yet the narrator himself defines each group, designating who is and is not a member. The most obvious instances concern the prisoner whose position in relation to the human, social world is dictated by the narrator's perceptions, seemingly at the narrator's whim. Even in the moment when he appears to be included most fully, one of 'a party of men together', the prisoner's exclusion is imminent, for 'in two minutes, with a sudden snap, one of us would be gone'. The narrator has, in a sense, already rationalized the condemned man out of existence. The subsequent passionless description of the corpse is, in these terms, understandable. The man who so recently was another mind, another world, ultimately is described by the narrator as being 'dead as a stone'. The brutal dehumanizing effect of this simile reinforces the extent to which the sensibilities of the narrator control the portrayal of characters and events. He functions as a mechanism of inclusion and exclusion, and therefore of legitimacy. The subjectivity of the self, inherent in the role of eye-witness, overwhelms the apparent objectivity of the description.

The narrator's degree of control is recognizable in the depiction of other characters. Although only five pages long, a number of those involved in 'A Hanging' are portrayed. The only character apart from the narrator who certainly is British is the superintendent of the jail. Like the narrator, only lightly sketched, he is formal, but seemingly little else. Still, he does show a sense of decency, albeit macabre, in allowing the condemned man time to chant upon the scaffold. Local characters are also delineated, but repeatedly in negative terms: the prisoner is puny and sports 'the moustache of a comic man on the films' (Orwell 1970a: 67); the head jailer, 'a fat Dravidian', is characterized as garrulous and sycophantic; the hangman has a 'servile crouch'

(Orwell 1970a: 69); a Eurasian jailer is depicted as crudely insensitive to the horror of the situation. The reactions of the local characters are shown as less humane than their imperial masters. These portraits plainly are subjective, and tendentious.

The narrator, then, is both the origin of the perceptions contained in 'A Hanging', and also operates as a structural principle, a mechanism of inclusion and exclusion, defining the boundaries and the members of a variety of groups. Inherent in the latter function, and emphasized by his apparent role as vehicle for the moral argument of the tale, the narrator tends to validate the group of which he is most clearly a member, the imperial British. His very lack of substantiality tends to obscure his position in an imperial administration empowered with the authority to extinguish human life. And his apparently unique recognition of the horror of execution functions to humanize the more general perception of the British. Instead of being the outcome of imperial domination, the 'unspeakable wrongness of cutting short a life' is considered in universal terms. As a consequence, a detailed critique of the power structure involved in the execution is eschewed. The two British characters delineated are shown almost as onlookers, rather than as representatives of the imperial authority administering the hanging. The narrator functions to deflect attention from, rather than to focus attention on, the reality of the situation.

Ironically, despite his pivotal importance in structuring and interpreting events in 'A Hanging', the narrator largely proves inadequate in his key role, that of eye-witness. For, if the immorality of taking life is central to the moral and emotional thrust of the narrative, it is the one thing the narrator does not witness. The grisly moment of execution is portrayed as a magician's trick; the prisoner simply vanishes. The institutionalized coldness with which the narrator observes the dead man operates to neutralize the horror of the situation. Yet one character in 'A Hanging' does experience horror at the taking of life. Immediately the prisoner 'disappears' the dog (let go of by the narrator) runs to the back of the gallows, 'stopped short, barked, and then retreated into a corner of the yard, where it stood among the reeds, looking timorously out at us' (Orwell 1970a: 70).

There are, in fact, two eye-witnesses in 'A Hanging'. The linking of narrator and dog by means of the handkerchief is not accidental; indeed, the clumsiness of the symbolism is striking. Too often, the importance of the dog is overlooked in readings of the piece. Yet it functions strategically within the narrative. The dog's intrusion into the procession to the gallows is the first instance in which the seemingly inevitable flow of the execution is disrupted. Its antics mock the sinister pomp of the humans, their attempts to capture the dog deteriorating into slapstick. The animal's ready acceptance of the inherent humanity of the condemned prisoner pre-figures the narrator's illumination of the worth of life. And the dog's 'humane' reaction to the execution starkly contrasts with the brutish indifference of the other characters. Its perception appears to transcend the shortcomings of those of the humans. The dog's pedigree, 'half Airedale, half pariah' (Orwell 1970a: 69-70), incorporating both colonizer and colonized, insider and outsider, blatantly signals this transcendence. The penny drops with a clang.

This recognition of the symbolic importance of the dog necessarily undercuts those readings of 'A Hanging' founded upon a conception of the piece as a first-hand account. The narrator and the dog both provide evidence, which together amounts to more than the sum of the parts. Neither understands the event in its entirety, but together they offer to the reader a means to understanding. The narrator's ignorance of the wider implications of the situation he supposedly is relating only emphasizes that he, just as much as the dog, is an element in the construction of the narrative. This does not weaken the indictment of capital punishment which remains important to the force of 'A Hanging'. Rather, an understanding of the shortcomings of the narrator as eye-witness reveals complexities often ignored in those analyses which innocently accept the work as non-fiction. The spectre of Orwell need not be invoked, then, to successfully interpret 'A Hanging'. Instead, a recognition of the interaction of man and dog on a less literal level, uncovers resonances that otherwise would be ignored, thereby strengthening its undoubted power.

If the narrator in 'A Hanging' is primarily a spectator, that of 'Shooting an Elephant' is the focal point. Though, again, a middle-ranking imperial official, the narrator of the second piece is a far more complex character and central to the situation he describes. 'Shooting an Elephant' begins: 'In Moulmein, in Lower Burma, I was hated by large numbers of people—the only time in my life that I have been important enough for this to happen to me' (Orwell 1970b: 265). He is the target of physical and verbal abuse for the native population. A pivotal opposition, between individual and group, is established immediately, one that will reverberate through the narrative. The narrator's position is complicated by the fact that he is antagonistic to the system he ostensibly represents: 'Theoretically—and secretly, of course—I was all for the Burmese and all against their oppressors, the British' (Orwell 1970b: 266). Further oppositions are established, between British and Burmese, colonizer and colonized, the powerful and the powerless. Yet while the narrator's relationship to the group, the large numbers who hate him, is clear, he stands in an ambiguous position as regards the other divisions; he is an anti-British Briton, an anti-Empire imperialist, and a figure of power put upon by those he has nominal power over.

The complexity of both situation and character is heightened by the fact that the narrator's condemnation of imperialism is equivocal. He states that he 'did not even know that the British Empire is dying, still less did I know that it is a great deal better than the younger empires that are going to supplant it' (Orwell 1970b: 266). The confused sense of time is important. The narrator confesses not to have known of something happening at the time of writing (that the British Empire *is* dying) or of something that will happen in the future (that the empires *that are going* to supplant it will be worse). In the latter case he has no logical way of knowing how the (unspecified) younger empires will operate. This confusion nevertheless strongly suggests that while all empires are evil, some are more evil than others.

The narrator's apparent inconsistencies threaten his role as a credible eye-witness. His 'character' is in doubt. This problem is overcome in paradoxical fashion by the self-revelation of racist and sadistic leanings. The narrator portrays the native population as laughing 'hideously', of possessing 'sneering little yellow faces', of being 'evil-spirited little beasts' (Orwell 1970b: 265-6). With one part of his mind he recognizes the British Raj as a tyranny, but with another part the narrator confesses 'that the greatest joy in the world would be to drive a bayonet into a Buddhist priest's guts. Feelings like these are the normal by-products of imperialism; ask any Anglo-Indian official, if you catch him off duty' (Orwell 1970b: 266). This shocking revelation functions in two ways. Acknowledgement of the brutalizing effect of imperialism on its own functionaries reinforces the attack on the system. More subtly, however, the narrator is shown to be acutely self-aware and disarmingly honest about his prejudices. The reader's trust in the 'character' of the narrator, with the consequent willingness to accept the perspective presented, is achieved by the revelation of alarming tendencies.

The construction of a self-revelatory narrator is a preamble to the central narrative, the shooting itself. Called upon as the local representative of imperial power, to put down what supposedly is a rampaging elephant, the narrator, on sighting the animal, recognizes that in the interim it has become harmless. Yet the hugh crowd of Burmese that have followed him force the narrator to a moment of crisis:

> I realized that I should have to shoot the elephant after all. The people expected it of me and I had to do it... I was only an absurd puppet pushed to and fro by the will of those yellow faces behind. I perceived in this moment that when the white man turns tyrant it is his own freedom that he destroys (Orwell 1970b: 269).

This illumination clearly approximates that described in 'A Hanging'. Similarly, it is normally taken to encapsulate the moral thrust of the piece. As in 'A Hanging', the narrator's insight does not alter the flow of the narrative; in the former, he observes an execution, in the latter he carries it out. Analysing his shooting of the animal, the narrator wonders 'whether any of the others grasped that I had done it solely to avoid looking a fool' (Orwell 1970b: 272). This opposition of individual and group is fundamentally important. What is striking is the strong sense of personal failure and inadequacy, the fear of looking a fool to the Burmese. In the moment he attempts to overcome these fears by shooting the elephant, in the moment he should triumph over the group, the narrator is the crowd's play thing, 'an absurd puppet'. Drained of any sense of self, the narrator's actions are determined not by personal or imperial forces, but by 'the will of those yellow faces behind'. The group triumphs over the individual, no matter that the narrator suspects, or hopes, that his true motivations remain hidden.

The dominance of the powerful mass over the impotent individual signals an apparent transfer of power from colonizer to colonized. The narrator's existential crisis, it would seem, turns the oppressor into the oppressed. The crisis, however, is that of an individual. Concentration on the self deflects attention from the larger material forces at work, from the mechanics of imperialism. The brutal realities of an imposed system are obscured by the foregrounding of individual impotence, the narrator's personal dilemma drawing attention away from the institution he represents. Furthermore, the narrator's human frailties, his apparent self-awareness and self-criticism, creates sympathies that function to validate his own perceptions of the incident. This in turn bolsters the narrators's more general assumptions: the differences between British and other imperial regimes, the disturbing 'otherness' of the Burmese, and the 'normality' of racism and brutality under imperialism.

The narrator's function as the personification of imperialism is seen clearly in the revelatory claim that 'when the white man turns tyrant it is his own freedom that he destroys'. This appears to indict imperialism, to provide an index of its dehumanizing impact. The stunningly myopic statement in fact blatantly ignores the effect of imperialism on the local population. Emphasis on, and a consequent empathy with, the white man's loss of freedom leaves that of the Burmese unconsidered. This one-sidedness is founded on the opposition of individual and group. The narrator, the solitary, vulnerable individual, is exposed as essentially powerless. In contrast, the Burmese are viewed as a largely undifferentiated, depersonalized, mass. Their very amorphousness suggests an ability to resist imposed pressures, to survive the impact of imperialism. The concentration on the narrator's individual crisis undermines a thorough-going critique of imperialism.

The eye-witness perspective would seem to imply an exploration of the self by the narrator, and to an extent this occurs in both 'A Hanging' and 'Shooting an Elephant'. In neither case, however, is self-definition or self-examination of prime importance. Instead, what analysis of both pieces foregrounds is the ideological and structural functions of the eye-witness, and the degree to which these two elements interact. The narrator, by defining and validating certain groups in 'A Hanging', and by remaining largely ill-defined, universalizes the attack upon capital punishment. Yet, consequently, this diverts attention from the realities of imperialism. In 'Shooting an Elephant', the juxtaposition of impotent individual and powerful, amorphous mass, functions to the same purpose.

Do these deflections from a full critique of imperialism constitute, in effect, a defence of that system? The question requires a separate answer in the case of each piece. In 'A Hanging', capital punishment is certainly dealt with in universal moral terms — the 'unspeakable wrongness' of extinguishing human life clearly is to be seen as relevant outside imperial Burma. But this does not reduce the setting to mere background, to exotic colouring, for clearly the imperial situation has unique elements that are deemed worthy of examination. If this is accepted, however, then 'A Hanging' can be seen to evade questions of dominance it appears to raise. In 'Shooting an Elephant', by contrast, the attack upon imperialism is explicit. The narrator acknowledges both the evil of the system and his antagonism to that system. Yet his stance is equivocal, and the narrative itself largely ignores an examination of imperialism in favour of an exploration of individual guilt and impotence. The strength of the proclamation of an anti-imperial position in 'Shooting an Elephant' is an index of the failure of that piece to fully prosecute that case.

Orwell's use of the persona of the eye-witness, then, has importance both in terms of the narrative and ideology. At the same time it seems clear that it is unnecessary to situate Orwell within either piece to validate interpretation. An understanding of the symbolic importance of the dog, and its role in the construction of the narrative of 'A Hanging', leads to the reconsideration of the narrator as himself a narrative component, rather than a narrative constructor. The invocation of Orwell as narrator is superfluous to an understanding of that tale. The same is true in 'Shooting an Elephant'. In terms of an eye-witness account it suffers from the fact that it was written at least eight years after Orwell had left Burma. His 'evidence' would hardly be credible in a court of law, nor can it be more so in a purported eye-witness prose work. Orwell considered writing the piece only after a request for contributions to John

Lehmann's periodical, *New Writing*. Without this prompt it might never have been written. Despite Orwell's avowed hatred of imperialism, it is an ideological position complicated by the fact that 'Orwell'—as a narrative construct—does not speak with the vehemence of the recent exposure to events that characterize and invigorate *The Road To Wigan Pier* (1981) or *Homage To Catalonia* (1979), which were to appear within two years of the publication of 'Shooting an Elephant'.

Mention of these later works invites a parting shot at the Orwell myth. Orwell is far too readily accepted in holistic terms, as a unified and consistent writer. His prose style is partly to blame, suggesting by its apparent simplicity a clear, coherent vision. And the various hagiographic characterizations of the man tend to draw attention away from his writings. These, in turn, are often read 'backwards', interpretations of Orwell's later and more famous works, *Animal Farm* (1978) and *Nineteen Eighty-Four* (1979), being taken as keys to all Orwell's work. The examination of texts like 'A Hanging' and 'Shooting an Elephant', however, suggests a more complex picture of a writer sometimes sure-footed, sometimes stumbling in his efforts to accommodate the demands of politics and literature. Moreover, by allowing the 'eye-witness' to recoil upon itself as a textual component, the boundaries between language and reference, fiction and auto-biography, become problematic. This is especially true of those early works like 'A Hanging' and 'Shooting an Elephant', written before Orwell (or even Blair) had become what we now accept as 'Orwell'.

Bibliography

Barthes, Roland (1977), *Image – Music – Text*, essays selected & translated by Stephen Heath, London, Fontana.
Crick, Bernard (1982), *George Orwell: A Life*, Harmondsworth, Penguin.
Orwell, George (1970a), 'A Hanging', *The Collected Essays, Journalism and Letters of George Orwell, Volume 1: An Age Like This, 1920–1940*, (eds Sonia Orwell and Ian Angus), Harmondsworth, Penguin, 66–71.
Orwell, George (1970b), 'Shooting an Elephant', ibid., 265–72.
Orwell, George (1978), *Animal Farm*, Harmondsworth, Penguin.
Orwell, George (1979a), *Homage to Catalonia*, Harmondsworth, Penguin.
Orwell, George (1979b), *Nineteen Eighty-Four*, Harmondsworth, Penguin.
Orwell, George (1981), *The Road to Wigan Pier*, Harmondsworth, Penguin.

8 'Pretending to be Me': Larkin *versus* 'Larkin'

Peter MacDonald Smith

If the title of this article seems at first ambitiously wide-angled that is because, to get a picture of the character Philip Larkin presents as his own in his poems, one needs a wide-angled lens. The poet himself is everywhere visible, to an extent unparalleled in the work of any other English poet of this century, and perhaps any other. To a unique degree, the subject of the poems is the poet and his life. The message, in the most modern manner, is the messenger.

This essay will make three observations about Larkin's so-called cult of personality. First, his poems present the actions of their author with the objectivity and detachment of a dramatist presenting a character. They erect a stage, and on this stage the poet himself performs. Second, the actions of this character ('Larkin' naturally enough) are precisely weighted and calculated to establish an attitude towards the subject of the poem in which they are described. In 'Church Going' (Larkin 1988: 97) for example, the poet donates an Irish sixpence not because he happens to find one in his pocket, but because he wants to strike an attitude towards the church. And third, that this stance, this attitude established by the poet's actions, will eventually be found wanting when the poem comes to reflect upon it.

Actions are described; actions are probed and reconsidered; actions are rejected. The result of this habitual about-face is that when the reader comes to look for the 'real' Larkin, (s)he must look—despite the poet's high profile in the poems—as through a glass darkly. For the irony remains that the more available Larkin seems to be—and at first he seems very available indeed—the more elusive he is. And the elusiveness is the chief result of the tension between how one behaves and what one believes: the kind of tension, in fact, that in other contexts—chiefly the context of prose fiction—has begun to be given the name postmodern.[1]

I am describing here an archetypal practice. Indeed, I am describing an archetypal poem. And one can certainly speak of the archetypal Larkin poem. Larkin speaks of it himself: 'I tend' he says,

> to lead the reader in by the hand very gently, saying this is the initial experience...and now you see that it makes me think of this, that and the other, and work up to a big finish—I mean, that's the sort of pattern...[Morrison 1980: 125].

Larkin's analysis of his own practice as a poet describes action (what stems from the 'initial experience'), then reflection (what culminates in the 'big finish'). What he omits from the analysis, however, is the relationship between the two, between action and reflection—a relationship that is inverse. For rather than illustrate the thinking of the poem, as one would expect them to do, the poet's actions illustrate the very reverse. His actions establish how not to behave, what not to do. And it is in the heart of this confusion, this antagonism between action and reflection, that Larkin's elusive 'self' takes cover. Larkin's unusual practice in this respect can be observed in a brief review of three poems in which the rules I have described are obeyed, and of a fourth in which they are bent, even broken.

The subject of the late poem 'Sad Steps' is that conventional romantic image, the moon [Larkin 1988:169]. Characteristically, the poet's actions are concentrated into the first half of the poem; they are detailed in a manner objective and detached; and they proceed to establish an attitude towards the moon without spelling that attitude out:

> Groping back to bed after a piss,
> I part thick curtains, and am startled by
> The rapid clouds, the moon's cleanliness.

The character the poet presents as himself is awkward, ungainly and down-to-earth. And this, in fact, is just the right adjective given his defensive reaction to the moon, his embarrassment:

> Lozenge of love! Medallion of art!
> O wolves of memory! Immensements!

The character's behaviour is calculated to convey the view that the moon is simply a tired prop of Romantic posturing, and this view, that the moon is irrelevant and absurd but good material for satire, is confirmed in the description he gives of it: 'High and preposterous and separate' he calls it—and indeed his descriptions have left no room for any other impression. But this is always the function of the poet's actions in these poems: to strike an attitude, one which his reflections—recorded in the 'big finish'—will question, then overturn.

For the poem as a whole is not satisfied with the character's performance. As action gives way to reflection, the mood changes, and the other side of the coin is held up to the light. 'No' the poet chides himself,

> One shivers slightly, looking up there.
> The hardness and the brightness and the plain
> Far-reaching singleness of that wide stare
>
> Is a reminder of the strength and pain
> Of being young; that it can't come again,
> But is for others undiminished somewhere.

Rather than preposterous, as it seemed at first, the moon is now revealed as moving: a dignified and serious symbol. And rather than separate, it hurts. The character's instinct, his impulse, is to deride and belittle. But the poem as a whole is sensitive and pained.

It is worth observing two points: that the initial attitude of the poet—scornful and defensive—is the polar opposite of his reflections, which are serious and plain-spoken. And that the poet's stance—ungainly, earthy and jovial—is the precise opposite of the poem he has written, which in the end is elegant and high-minded. To put the matter briefly, the poet presents as himself someone with whom, on the matter in hand, he disagrees. For not only is the character of 'the poet' different from the poem in which he appears, he is also different from the poet himself, from Larkin. Larkin presents as his own a performance with which, in the end, he cannot identify, one he must reject. And this is the kind of logical (or psychological) black hole into which one disappears when one goes in search of the elusive self in Larkin's poems.

The same patterns, and the same problems, arise with 'Church Going' [Larkin 1988: 97]. The poem presents the reader with a character who is occasional, awkward, sceptical and above all iconoclastic—altogether an identikit picture of that 1950s fiction, 'Movement man':

> ...Hatless, I take off
> My cycle-clips in awkward reverence,
>
> Move forward, run my hand around the font.
> From where I stand, the roof looks almost new—
> Cleaned, or restored? Someone would know: I don't...
> I sign the book, donate an Irish sixpence,
> Reflect the place was not worth stopping for.

Once again the actions of the character constitute the first stage of the poem. And once again, they are presented in a manner quite detached: with the exception of the fifth and last lines, we are told only what this character is doing, not what he is thinking.

But we can guess what he is thinking—indeed, we can only come to one conclusion: indifference to Christianity is something of an intellectual imperative; ridiculing the rituals of this anachronism is a thoroughly credible course of action. Donating foreign money is an eloquent rebuff to anyone old-fashioned, or superstitious, or merely cowed enough to want to keep the church going so to speak. On the face of it one must expect that when the poet turns his mind to reflect on the church, it will be written off as superfluous, irrelevant, even laughable. This expectation is confounded, of course, in the closing stanzas:

> It pleases me to stand in silence here;
>
> A serious house on serious earth it is,
> In whose blent air all our compulsions meet,
> Are recognized, and robed as destinies.
> And that much never can be obsolete,
> Since someone will forever be surprising
> A hunger in himself to be more serious...

It is a stirring peroration. But in fact the character of the poet has been neither silent nor serious, and his chief hunger was to be irreverent. The poem wonders what will happen when churches fall out of use, but donating foreign money will not help. More seriously, whereas the character is described specifically as 'awkward' 'bored' and 'uninformed', the poem as a whole (and by extension its author) is none of these things — elegant, wise and broad in his sympathies as he seems in the last lines quoted.

The result is that once again Larkin presents as himself a character with whom he disagrees, and presents as his own a pattern of behaviour of which he disapproves. 'I don't arse about in churches' Larkin told Ian Hamilton in an interview, but one feels that the poem as a whole tells us this already [Hamilton 1964: 74]. This character, as it happens, ridicules an institution that symbolizes 'marriage, and birth/And death, and thoughts of these' (Larkin 1988: 97) which are the proper province of Christianity of course, but which are also the material of art, and at least two of which are the prime material of Larkin's art. In delivering a rebuke to the character, as the closing stanzas seem to do, the poet appears to remind himself ('himself') what it is to take these things lightly.

The character of the poet is belittled, dwarfed, even humiliated by the sheer weight of the evidence against him. He defines himself by a show of scepticism in a place that demands faith, and behaves without dignity in an arena that commands respect. His behaviour is reproved by the findings of the poem as a whole. He is 'condemned' as R.S. Thomas says of the Welsh peasant, 'By man's potential stature' [Thomas 1955: 65]. The implications are much as they were in the matter of 'Sad Steps': the ordinary individual is small, and life defeats him; that he chooses wrong, and his behaviour fails to measure up; that his actions and attitudes are proved out of place by his reflections; that he is undone by his own second thoughts.

This thinking underwrites 'Mr Bleaney' [Larkin 1988: 102]. Here again the actions of the character are concentrated into the opening stanzas of the poem before performance gives way to reflection. And again there is the implication that action and reflection have opposite interests. Other than stubbing out cigarettes and 'stuffing' cotton-wool into his ears, the character of the poet acts once only, and then decisively, in the course of the poem: '"I'll take it"'. The character takes the room, but the poem as a whole rejects it, at once condemning the character for his want of ambition and sympathizing with him for his almost inhuman existence. Larkin 'agrees to tolerate the intolerable' comments Donald Davie, 'for the sake of those who don't find it intolerable at all'; but one might say of this poem that the character tolerates the room only for the poem as a whole — for the poet himself, indeed — to remind him how intolerable it is [Davie 1973: 69].

Larkin's poems at first seem empirically sound: from a particular event or experience a general conclusion is drawn. But actions and reflections, it seems, take opposite routes. They cannot be regarded as complementary. A man may introduce himself through the way he behaves, but it is through his words that he is to be defined. So, for all the prominence of the active poet on the stage the poems erect, words still speak louder than actions here: a man need not practise what he preaches. So one learns how to act by acting, and how to think by acting wrong. And it is this change of heart, at the interface between action and reflection, that lends Larkin's poems an unusually narrative (even dramatic) vigour.

In Larkin's poems in general, there is nothing unusual about this technique, this switch in direction; it is there too in those poems which aspire — in Robert Frost's phrase — to clarify life.[2] Such poems open in the classical manner, not with a performance but with a robust and provocative analysis of the way of things. But then, rather than explain or justify the analysis, Larkin proceeds to overturn it, or reject it. 'Oh, no one can deny,' runs the opening line of 'Self's the Man' [Larkin 1988: 117],

> 'That Arnold is less selfish than I'.

It is a proposal the poem proceeds, at first, to deny:

> But wait, not so fast:
> Is there such a contrast?
> He was out for his own ends
> Not just pleasing his friends

And then finally, to collapse:

> So he and I are the same,
>
> Only I'm a better hand
> At knowing where I can stand
> Without them sending a van —
> Or I *suppose* I can. [Larkin 1988: 117; my emphasis]

Alternatively, in 'Toad's Revisited' [Larkin 1988: 147]:

> Walking around in the park
> Should feel better than work

until it proves, on reflection, not to do so: 'it doesn't suit me'. Elsewhere:

> Talking in bed ought to be easiest.

But in practice, as the poem discovers, it is as hard as ever [Larkin 1988: 129]. The poet seeks in poems like these to set up, in his opening line, a 'stay upon confusion', but his attempts to accomplish this ideal are doomed, it seems, to failure; ending, at best, in 'Words at once true and kind,/or not untrue and not unkind' [Larkin 1988: 129]. It is the other side of the coin — and perhaps something in the inversion itself — that tells the 'real' truth.

There is one poem, however, where the various mechanics this essay describes can be found — the objectivized character, the emblematic performance, the voice-over analysis and the simmering tension between action and reflection — yet the poet steadfastly refuses to choose between the performance and the inverted interpretation. The subjects of 'Dockery and Son' are time, the passing of time, and death [Larkin 1988: 152]. The poet's journey by train, which this poem describes — between his old Oxford college, the scenes of his youth, and the northern industrial landscapes of his adult life — serves as a metaphor (and a rather conventional one) for his life as a whole.

The poem describes the train journey in some detail, indeed, the detail is part of the pleasure of the poem — the poet falling asleep and so on. The thinking of the poem in general is, again conventionally, that we cannot escape from the passing of time. And to the prospect of death there is no alternative:

> Life is first boredom, then fear.
> Whether or not we use it, it goes,
> And leaves what something hidden from us chose,
> And age, and then the only end of age

The journey from Oxford to Sheffield is the journey from youth to age, and then the only end of age: time, in short, is a vehicle from which it is not given to dismount.

In a conventional poem one might expect this thinking to be underwritten by the events of the poem. By his actions, this hypothetical poet would illustrate the ideas of the poem, and the general would be described in the particular. So the poet would be driven (we would expect) from the haunts of his childhood to the scenes of his maturer years, and on — one might almost say — to his final destination.

But the character the poet presents as his own in 'Dockery and Son' refuses to accept this. The poet's closing thoughts, which tell us that from the train through life there is no dismounting, are delivered when the character of the poet has in fact already dismounted; they are delivered when the poet has got down from the train, and '... walked along/The platform to its end'. It is from here, from a position of stasis, that the poet expounds on time's (and his own) inevitable motion. It is almost as if, in dismounting from the train, the poet refuses to accept the analysis he knows he will give: man cannot get off, he says, then off he gets. So once again, the poet's character defines his own stance by his actions. Once again action and reflection take opposite sides. Again the poet presents as his own a series of actions with which he fundamentally and explicitly disagrees. But where 'Dockery and Son' departs from the norm is in the tolerance with which the poet views his own rebellion against himself. The reader looking for the truth of Larkin's own view in the midst of this conflict will find the 'real Larkin' torn between the two poles of a dilemma that is not perhaps ever finally answerable.

Which dilemma is this? Principally, it is the gap between what a man wants to believe and what he must accept. As a general rule the poet's actions are shorthand for his desires; his reflections, by contrast, betoken what he knows he must accept. This is a dilemma with which Larkin's poems are intimately familiar. In 'Aubade', his last major poem [Larkin 1988: 208], it is death that the poet describes as something '... we can't escape,/Yet can't accept'. But the dilemma of what cannot be escaped yet cannot be accepted is typically (in Larkin's work) a matter of life, not death. The heroic achievement of Larkin's career as a poet lies in his struggle to come to terms with the here-and-now, and make his peace with present reality: to accept. Then again, the theme of much English poetry since Keats has been the struggle to come to terms with the here-and-now, given the impossibility — whether through memory or imagination — of escaping the 'real's' insistent clutches.

And in general it is probably best to think of the semantic gap revealed in these poems — a gap between action and reaction — as symbolizing a gap between impulse and conviction.³ It is the seriousness of what the church signifies that the character in 'Church Going' seeks to avoid and from which he attempts to hide his face—thoughts of matters serious, that demand respect: 'marriage and birth/And death, and thoughts of these'. And it is facing the meaning of the church squarely that reacquaints him with his own hunger 'to be more serious'. Or, to put the matter the other way, it is the character's impulse to deride but the 'surprising' of his hunger to be serious is a matter of conviction.

The same principles are at work in 'Sad Steps': again an impulse is attempted, then rebuked, and an opposing conviction put in its place. The facts have to be faced, the poet tells himself. And there is just the same understated severity about the poet's judgment on himself in 'Mr Bleaney'. When I speak of a rebellion in 'Dockery and Son', I mean that the impulse is tolerated, no doubt in part to dilute the hard facts of the conviction, and in part because of the sheer impotence of the impulse in this case, given that our convictions tell us — much against out will, no doubt—that there is no dismounting from time.

To put the matter into a literary context, the gap explored in these poems is the gap between the human individual and the planet on which (s)he finds himself: the gap between the world as it is and that other world of which (it seems) man can but dream. Larkin's mentor, Thomas Hardy, was much possessed with 'the radical imperfection of the universe'—a familiar feeling in the present context—and its 'inability to accommodate the human emotions' [Millgate 1982: 120]. Larkin inherits something of this tradition in the poems I have been describing: the difference between what Man wants and what he must take. Against these truths the poet rebels and from them he seeks to escape. Such attempts at insurrection and escape from the ways of the world are written into the poems through the mechanism this essay has outlined.

Or there may be a simpler explanation. In 'An Interview with *The Observer*' Larkin muses on the possibility of a sinecure position as a poet-in-residence [Larkin 1983: 51]: [But] 'I couldn't bear that' he confesses, 'It would embarrass me very much. I don't want to go round pretending to be me'. Superficially, at least, it is difficult not to conclude that in poems like 'Church Going' 'Sad Steps' 'Mr Bleaney' and 'Dockery and Son' and in many others besides ('Lines on a Young Lady's Photograph Album' for example, 'The Whitsun Weddings', 'I Remember, I Remember', 'Reasons for Attendance', 'Aubade' on so on'), the character the poet presents as himself is wandering around, pretending to be Larkin.

Notes

1. See my essay, 'The Postmodernist Larkin' in *English*, Vol XXXVIII, No. 161 (Summer 1989), pp. 153–161, one aspect of which this essay amplifies and refines.
2. Cited in William Pritchard (1987: 62).
3. See F.W. Bateson (1966: 60), for an analysis of the 'semantic gap' which Bateson sees as a principle of major poetry.

Bibliography

Bateson, F.W. (1966), *English Poetry* (revised edn), London, Longman.
Davie, Donald (1973), *Thomas Hardy and British Poetry*, London, Routledge and Kegan Paul.
Hamilton, Ian (1964), 'Four Conversations: Philip Larkin', in *London Magazine*, IV, 71-77.
Larkin, Philip (1983), *Required Writing*, London, Faber and Faber.
Larkin, Philip (1988), *Collected Poems*, London, Faber and Faber.
MacDonald Smith, Peter (1989), 'The Postmodernist Larkin', in *English*, XXXVIII, No. 161, 153-161.
Millgate, Michael (1982), *Thomas Hardy*, Oxford, Oxford University Press.
Morrison, Blake (1980), *The Movement*, Oxford, Oxford University Press.
Pritchard, William (1987), 'Philip Larkin', in *Raritan*, 6, No. 4, 62-80.
Thomas, R.S. (1955), *Song at the Year's Turning*, London, Hart-Davis.

9 Language, Knowledge, and the Stylistics of Science Fiction
Peter Stockwell

This paper will be concerned with language in relation to the genre of Science Fiction (SF), and will deal with the practice of stylistics and the reading of texts. In the spirit of SF itself, the discussion will draw on work from a variety of disciplines which will be brought to bear on a short story 'The Night', by the American SF writer, Ray Bradbury.[1] Firstly, however, to facilitate this discussion I would remind the reader of the story of the roadrunner. In those cartoons, first shown in the 1960s but regularly re-run, the basic plot centred around the efforts of a wily coyote to chase and catch a small, fast bird—the roadrunner. The animators of that cartoon imposed rules on themselves in its production: there was to be no dialogue; the roadrunner was to remain on the road; the bird never directly harmed the coyote; and so on. The coyote employed a variety of tools and techniques to catch the roadrunner, but the roadrunner always escaped, and the coyote was always destroyed by his own plan. Each episode that made up the programme was completely independent of the others, so the coyote could miraculously be brought back to life and start again. But the point to emphasize is that the coyote always began again from scratch. Even if only a small part of a particular plan didn't work, instead of learning from the mistake and improving the plan, the coyote always abandoned it completely in favour of something different. He never learned from his mistakes, and his method of proceeding was to suppose that if a plan of attack did not work perfectly the first time, then it was totally useless. The principle that underlies this procedure is that the failure of part of a theory in action leads to the complete abandonment of the whole theory. I will call the tendency in people to do this the 'coyote complex'.

This rather frivolous example is used here to make two serious points. One is concerned with *pragmatics*, about which more later. The other is to suggest that what I've jokingly called the 'coyote complex' is a pervasive practice in the methods of most disciplines of inquiry into knowledge, but especially in literary studies. In almost any book on literary theory, the author will spend a substantial part of the book orientating him or herself in relation to other theories or ways of reading a text. Previous theories will be demolished on the basis of a contradiction that is characterized as a 'fatal flaw' in the theory, leaving the way open for the author's own views to be presented. This practice of theory-abandonment, on the basis of theoretical discussion without any regard for the practical circumstances of application, is so widespread in literary theory as to have attained the status of a consensus methodology. A good, concentrated example can be seen in surveys of literary theory such as Eagleton (1983). The 'coyote complex' is the product of a sort of academic purism and a failure to understand the nature of theory.

One of the best discussions of this for the present purposes is an article by the neo-classical economist Milton Friedman (1971), originally written in 1935. Friedman begins by asking whether a theory, hypothesis, or model can be tested by a judgement of the realism of its assumptions. He decides that the assumptions are irrelevant to whether a theory works or not — in other words, whether it has predictive or usable power. Assumptions allow a theory to be abstract and complete — E doesn't equal mc^2 more or less, or only on Wednesdays, but always and exactly, in theory. But when the theory is applied in practice, it changes its nature. It is up to the observer — economist, scientist, linguist or critic — to assess whether the affecting circumstances in practice have any material relevance or significance in altering the results. A theory can be abstract and ideal because it does not have to take account of circumstances in the real world. Friedman uses an example from Euclidian geometry: a line in theory connects two points in the shortest distance. It is a measure only of length, in one dimension. Of course, an actualized Euclidian line is not possible. The theory assumes a line with no width and no depth. But no matter how fine the pencil or how faint the line, a real line drawn on a surface will have volume, will be three-dimensional. This reality does not invalidate the theory. The idea of a Euclidian line is still useful in physics and mathematics, but actual lines must be thought of differently. This is because the theory is a metaphorical representation of an idea from reality. A theory cannot therefore be right or wrong, only applicable or inapplicable in different specific circumstances. A metaphor such as 'Juliet is the sun' (to use the favourite example of the academic literature) cannot be said to be true or false; it is, of course, literally false, but this would be an inappropriate response to the metaphor. Theories are useful, says Friedman, only if the economist (or anyone) remembers the significance of circumstances in the actualization of the theory.

There are three points to emerge out of this. Firstly, that theory is only useful when actualized and the circumstances taken into account. Secondly, that theory is abstract and complete, but the actualization does not have to be, and can still be valid. Thirdly, that some circumstances will vary so far from the assumptions of the theory as to render the theory invalid in those circumstances. For example, the significance of 'error' is small when a Euclidian line for a building design is actualized with a fine pencil, but the 'error' is significant if actualized by a thick marker.

The inherent assumptions of a model often implicitly specify the circumstances under which it will work — in other words, a model only works within its own frame of reference. For example, in physics Newtonian mechanics was the prevailing theory of motion for almost two centuries. Around the turn of this century, it was discovered that Newtonian mechanics only applies in the circumstances of low velocities and short distances, and that strange things happen in the actual circumstances of velocities approaching the velocity of light, which can only be accounted for by relativity theory. Of course it would be silly to abandon Newtonian mechanics completely on these grounds, since it is still applicable in the frame of reference of our every-day world in which we drop objects and drive cars around and so on. If the 'coyote complex' held in physics, then perhaps cars would be designed using relativity theory, which could probably be done but which would be extremely circumlocutionary and redundant. No single frame can be applied to all frames of reference. In literary terms, no reading theory has a monopoly on truth. The critic who does not adapt theory to the practice of analysis will end up with an unrepresentative analysis. Chuck Jones, creator of the roadrunner, said: 'People who look through keyholes are apt to get the idea that most things are keyhole shaped' (quoted in Hall 1968: 28).

The method of the following discussion will proceed in accordance with the implications of Friedman's guidelines. The assumptions (or, at least, some of them) underlying this paper will be presented as articles of faith that the reader is asked to accept simply so that the discussion can move beyond them. I hope to justify them, not by theoretical argument, but by showing how they apply to the practice of reading; not proof, therefore, but demonstration of the frame theory in its appropriate frame of reference and circumstances. The first article of faith partly underlies what has been said so far.

Actualization of a model demands context consideration

It is this principle that forms the basis of the descriptive model of language functions in De Beaugrande (1980). De Beaugrande sees the virtual (abstract) system of grammar in language as a default system which texts can override in utilization. In other words, a text can construct its own grammar in reading, and can be found meaningful. Text is an actual system which is derived from the virtual system of language. Any discussion of a text in terms of the virtual system is therefore meaningless. De Beaugrande's orientating frame, also followed in this paper, is based on *functionalism* and *pragmatics*. Pragmatics here holds both the everyday meaning of being concerned with the circumstances of specific application, as well as being that branch of linguistics which is concerned with utterances (language in a social context, eg Levinson (1983)). Pragmatics avoids the 'coyote complex'.

De Beaugrande differentiates between features of *textuality* (which make a text processable by the human brain), and *design* which is where he locates qualitative judgement of the text. Design criteria include efficiency (greatest returns for least effort) which gives effectiveness (relevance) and appropriateness (of the text in a particular situation). Qualitatively 'bad' texts are thus those which are inefficient, ineffective, or inappropriate. All of these are evidently inherently concerned with a specified reader in a specified circumstance. Evidence from the textual aspect can therefore provide a basis for a judgement of value (ie validate) but it cannot on its own assign value (ie evaluate). Value is a contextual feature of texts that is culture- and subject-based.

De Beaugrande also dismisses discussion of texts that look at potential ambiguities as products of the abstract system of *langue* rather than the actualized system of *parole*. Although ambiguities occur in the context of real utterances, these are seldom misunderstood because the brain matches and predicts the probable specific meaning in the context of utterance. However, De Beaugrande does not elaborate the importance of probability, and in later articles he even seems to view it as being less significant. The importance of an understanding of probability can be seen when the process of actualization is applied to the theory. The basic traditional model of probability says that in tossing a coin there are two possible outcomes, so each side has a 50 per cent chance of selection — in theory. But in actualization, this theory must change its nature and a sort of 'bookmaker' probability will take over (formalized as that branch of mathematics known as Bayesian statistics). In a race with five horses, simple probability would say that in theory each has a 20 per cent (1 in 5) chance of winning. But no bookie would ever give that as a starting price. This is because bookmaker probability — or, more properly, Bayesian statistics — takes account of circumstances, of previous performance, of expectations; it is cumulative and context-dependent. A coin that comes down 90 times heads and 10 times tails still, in theory, has 50 per cent probability either way. But, in practice, the observant gambler would choose heads. The same is true of the reading process, what De Beaugrande calls 'utilization'. Readings are thus disambiguated not absolutely, but to an acceptable level of probability in order to be processed under a principle of efficiency — maximum processing returns for least processing effort. A sentence 'means' not only in isolation, but based on everything that has gone before it in the text, itself interpreted probabilistically. This is how a text generates its own grammar, rules for its own reading. How else could the reader make sense of a sequence like 'The king was pregnant'? Ungrammatical in the default system, but perfectly grammatical in Le Guin's *The Left Hand Of Darkness* (1981: 89) since the context has been established of the alien winter-world of Gethen, with its single-sex humans capable of becoming male or female for a few days once a month for the purposes of reproduction. So, a second article of faith.

A text-reading is acceptably determinate because of cumulative probability

The appropriateness of this framing theory for the frame of reading interpretation can be demonstrated by looking at the alternative. If cumulative determination did not hold, then the brain, in the primary stage of reading perception, would have to run through every possible entry of a lexical item in its neural network. For such an apparently simple sentence as the opening of 'The Night' — 'You are a child in a small town' — I calculate 432 possibilities (without metaphorical connections). Longer, more complex sequences would produce hundreds of thousands of potential alternatives. Clearly the brain has neither the size nor the speed to run through this many possibilities. The brain reads pre-selectively, basing its selection on its accumulated rules in the text.

Cumulative interpretation is qualitative not merely quantitative, depending not only on the frequency of occurrence of previous items but also on a judgement of their significance (foregrounding or weighting). And it holds at every level of interpretation, from word-interpretation as shown above, to the history of genres. Hans Robert Jauss (1982) seems to imply this in seeing the reader as a cultural consensus, in the second thesis in *Toward An Aesthetic Of Reception*:

> The analysis of the literary experience of the reader avoids the threatening pitfalls of psychology if it describes the reception and the influence of a work within the

objectifiable system of expectations that arises for each work in the historical moment of its appearance, from a pre-understanding of the genre, [and]... from the form and themes of already familiar works. (Jauss 1982: 22)

The consequence of the two circumstances of cumulative interpretation process and the specificity of context is that every reading is a new and different one, even a second reading of one book by one reader. Doris Lessing articulates this in *Briefing For A Descent Into Hell*:

Sometimes when you read a book or story, the words are dead, you struggle to end it or put it down, your attention is distracted. Another time, with exactly the same book or story, it is full of meaning, every sentence or phrase or even word seems to vibrate with messages and ideas, reading is like being pumped full of adrenalin. (Lessing 1972: 155)

Cumulative probability must work right down to the most basic level of decision-making in the brain: the *bit* (binary digit), which is defined as the operation needed to make a decision between two equally probable events. This leads to the third article of faith.

Function and identity are co-definable

The idea that language *is* what it does underlies functional and descriptive linguistics. In terms of inquiry into processes, it is the function that is primary, and deeper levels — whether they are called *deep structure, langue, competence, universal grammar* or whatever — are inferred from the surface utterance. Michael Johnson, in *Mind, Language, Machine* (1988), has pointed to the co-incidence of function and identity at every stage of interpretation — from the primary code of syntactic and semantic processing in the language centres in the brain, to the micro-code of conceptual-semantic networks in the neural networks, down to the neurochemical code in basic neuroanatomy. It would seem that this regression of codes has no ending, going down to the DNA code and beyond, with the actual uncoded, untransformed real meaning (S) in the deep structure never attained, ever receding infinitely. Johnson 'explains' this by a mystical invocation of Derrida, saying the meaning is continually deferred. This seems to me inadequate as an explanation, and evidence for a more appropriate model can be found in the brain and in evolution, and embodied in a fourth article of faith.

Environmental and textual interpretation are co-terminous

That is, they have common boundaries. The language centres in the brain are predominantly Broca's area and Wernicke's area in the left hemisphere, dealing with syntagmatic structure and paradigmatic structure respectively. These areas are adjacent to the visual areas around Exner's centre and the auditory cortex, which analyses sound. Fossil remains show Broca's area (and thus the origin of language capacity), as enlarged about two million years ago, which, in evolutionary terms, is not long enough for these areas to become totally discontinuously specialized. Writing and reading use existing brain structures wholly, beginning only eleven thousand years ago. So the parts of the brain that deal with environmental orientation are the parts that we use to interpret texts. There is a biological analogy here as well: the area in the brain that reconstructs two-dimensional visual data into three-dimensional space-concepts occupies the same position in the right hemisphere as the language area in the left, suggesting that environmental orientation and textual orientation work in the same way.

This analogy indicates that the grammar of neural connections lies in spatial relations. Different qualities of perception, cognition and emotion activate different nerve cells and fibres, all operating at once (in parallel). So, brain activity must be measured as a dynamic map, as spatial relations in progress. Meaning depends on a configuration of the map; a meaning, in other words, is a frozen mapping — an experience at a point in time. This culminates in, and metaphorically supports, the final article of faith.

Style is meaning

Information is form, materially true in the brain. Grammar is topological.

This is how the transformation of encoded meaning proceeds — not forever deferred in infinite and abstract regression, but into a configuration which can be imaged — in much the same way as a computer can image complex fractal repetition structure from relatively simple equations (cf. Peitgen and Saupe (1988) and Gleick (1988: 90-103)). Perhaps one day there will be the technology to map the status of every brain cell and synapse in this complex process. Simmons (1973), in an article on semantic networks, suggested that:

> The meaning of any node is an ordering of the rest of the nodes of network with which it is related. Assuming a richly interconnected network, the complete meaning of any particular node may involve every other node in the system. (Simmons 1973: 78)

But complexity is even less of a reason for abandoning a theory than the 'coyote complex'.

The roadrunner cartoon was used at the beginning of this paper, not only to make a serious point, but also to provide a link into a discussion of SF. In the April 1968 edition of *Psychology Today*, Mary Harrington Hall interviews Chuck Jones, the creator of the roadrunner, and Ray Bradbury, the American SF and fantasy author. In the interview, among other things, they discuss what makes a narrative science fiction. Chuck Jones says:

> People think there is one set of rules for every form of literature and another set for fantasy, and that's where most mistakes in analyzation are made. The rules are exactly the same. (Hall 1968: 29)

It is the difference in emphasis of the discourse rules that makes SF. SF is a form of fantasy, but one of the things that differentiates it from pure fantasy is the degree to which it literalizes metaphors — actualizes them, to use consistent terminology. If you can imagine a story in which Juliet really *is* the sun, and the sun was a sentient being capable of generating solar and magnetic storms to influence the climate in Verona, that story would be a SF story; indeed, the idea of stars having consciousness appears in Olaf Stapledon's *Star Maker* (1972). Many of Isaac Asimov's stories take metaphysical problems and actualize them in technological form to work them out. Chuck Jones says:

> You must build an entire world that is believable. Everything about this world must ring true, and the facts of the imagination must become as acceptable as the facts of reality. (Hall 1968: 29)

He talks about imaginative facts being actualized as text-facts. Ray Bradbury adds: 'What you must do is take one simple, fantastic idea and implement it on every sensual level' (Hall 1968: 29). On every sensual level in a text, means at every linguistic and cognitive level. In creating belief-worlds of this sort, SF has been variously characterized as 'possibility fiction', or 'context manipulation fiction', or 'speculative fiction'. I would suggest 'epistemic fiction' as a good descriptive label, conveying the idea of a fiction to do with knowledge, the impact of knowledge on humans and how we deal with it. (I mean here something different from Dolezel's (1976) modal categories, under which SF would be part of an *alethic* system.) A stylistic analysis of an SF text must therefore take account of the knowledge structures that the reader brings to the text. This can be demonstrated by what Chuck Jones calls an 'analyzation' of a text — 'The Night' by Ray Bradbury.

An exhaustive analysis is precluded here because of considerations of space and because only two interrelated aspects of the text are relevant to the previous discussion. The construction of the text-world and the orientation of the reader towards that world are matters of the epistemic features of the text. I have already said — it is the fourth article of faith — that environmental and textual orientation are almost the same process. This assumption underlies the theory of *scripts* or *frames* developed in artificial intelligence. In that field it is mainly text-*production* that is of interest, but Erving Goffman (1974) has given frame theory a textually descriptive and analytic slant. When people frame an event or text in order to make sense of it, Goffman says, they assign the frame a particular operational status. Two of these are *keying* and *fabrication*. Keying is the process by which play is derived from 'real' activity; reality and game are distinguishable more as a consequence of their assigned status than by inherent properties. A fabrication is an attempt to transform the frame-belief of someone else — it is intentional deception. These seem to me to correspond to the difference between realism and fantasy. Realism in fiction is marked by a process of keying: minimal fictiveness. Fantasy such as SF is based on fabrication: a marked fictiveness that is significantly different from the reader's knowledge of the real world. Fabrication is achieved by building up a new belief-world, and strategies used to do this in SF generally can be seen at work in 'The Night'.

The construction of the belief-world of 'The Night' involves orientating the reader into a new identity, that of the eight-year-old boy, Doug. The narrator does this by orientational sequences that are outside the narrative progression of events in the story, ie the plot. The first paragraph of the story is the most obvious example of these sequences:

> You are a child in a small town. You are, to be exact, eight years old, and it is growing late at night. Late, for you, accustomed to bedding in at nine or nine-thirty; once in a while perhaps begging Mom or Dad to let you stay up later to hear Sam and Henry on that strange radio that is popular in this year of 1927. But most of the time you are in bed and snug at this time of night. (Bradbury 1976: 154)

This establishes the age and location of Doug, the year, and a particular social environment. Throughout the story, these orientational sequences form the knowledge-base accumulated by the reader. Textually, they are characterized by several features. Firstly, there is much direct propositional content such as 'You are a child in a small town', or 'Skipper is your brother' (p.155), or 'There are a million small towns like this all over the world' (p.160). Secondly, there is a high degree of additional informativity, elaborating on details such as 'Skipper is your brother. He is your older brother. He's twelve and healthy, red-faced, hawk-nosed, tawny-haired, broad-shouldered for his years, and always running' (p.155). Thirdly, there is a high occurrence of generic propositions. These are propositions with a proverbial flavour which are presented as timeless truths; the classic example, though ironic, is the opening of Jane Austen's *Pride And Prejudice* (1813): 'It is a truth universally acknowledged that a single man in possession of a good fortune, must be in want of a wife'. In 'The Night', a sentence like 'The reedy playing of minor-key violins is the small-towns' music' is a generic sentence. Finally, these orientational epistemic sequences are characterized by high certainty modality, which is the attitude expressed by the narrator to the subject. This can be seen in many of the modal auxiliaries: 'You *should* feel encouraged' (p.158), 'You *must* accept being alone' (p.159–60)—my emphasis; and also in modal and evaluative adverbs, adjectives and phrases: 'to be exact' (p.154), 'which is natural' (p.155), 'certainly' (p.159).

The certainty of the belief-world thus constructed is then undermined as the story progresses. Uncertainty is expressed by questions in the narration: by low value modality 'Blackness *could* come swiftly' (p. 159), my emphasis; by confusion in collocational clashes such as 'thick green odour' (p.157); by the animation of the unknown and inanimate 'the whole ravine is tensing' (p.160) and 'Doubts flush you' (p. 159); and especially by underlexicalization 'the dark dark dark' (p.155) and 'All of the nameless things are there' (p.158). The certainty of the frame is restored at the end, with the high value modality and directness of the last paragraph (p.162), and the last sentence: 'It is'. The victory over the unknown, and the reassertion of the timeless certainty of the family united at the end, is what the story is about. It is, then, an epistemic story, a story about knowledge and certainty.

Intertwined with all this is the textual aspect by which the point of view of the narrator is realized. A precise way of examining textual point of view has been developed by Roger Fowler (1986) from work by Boris Uspensky (1973). On the psychological or perceptual plane of point of view,[2] Fowler delineates four categories: A, B, C and D. Type A is narrative from within the text, as if from within a character's consciousness. Type B is narrative as if the narrator has knowledge of the character's thoughts and feelings and can move around them at will. Type C is external to the characters, as if an objective reportage of events, with minimal interference (typical of Hemingway). Type D is narrative in which the persona of the narrator is highlighted, trying to reconstruct an event from outside (as in Fielding or Kafka). I have summarized these categories A to D as *mimetic, omniscient, objective* and *interpretative* narratives respectively.

The problem with 'The Night' is that the narration does not seem to fit any of these categories very well. Starting from the beginning, the first two paragraphs would seem to indicate a type C narrative point of view. It is very factual and apparently objective — it seems to evaluate as little as possible; in fact it seems similar to the 'invisible' narration of an instruction manual. However, it is not precisely that. The sense of a narrative presence is strong, realized by evaluative modalities ('to be exact' and 'perhaps'), as if there is a narrator constructing a character, building him up by presenting propositions of his external behaviour; so this is type D. But perhaps it is not an external narration at all, neither C nor D. After all, this narrator seems to *know* the character, internally. The reader has to be informed of his/her fictive role in the narration, providing the narrator knows more about the character than the character/reader himself ('him' because it is Doug). Later, for example, the narration runs: 'He'll be here, you say, knowing very well that he will be' (p.156). The narrator here has knowledge of Doug's consciousness, and presents Doug's feelings and evaluations throughout the story as he thinks them; so is it a type A narrative? At times — most notably in the orientation sequences already mentioned — the narration seems more like type B: 'Is there, then, no strength in growing up? no solace in being an adult? no sanctuary in life? no flesh citadel strong enough to withstand the scrabbling assault of midnights?' (p. 159). The lexical range here is not that of an eight-year-old boy. The narrative is not even wholly felicitous to the point of view of Doug. Occasionally it moves into the mind of his mother: 'she cannot look anywhere, in this very instant, save into her heart, and there she'll find nothing but uncontrollable repugnance and a will to fear' (p. 159). In the third person, this is like the omniscient narrator of a type B narrative point of view.

It would seem, then, that if a story as short as 'The Night' can contain all of these narrative points of view, then Fowler's categories are not much use. When this first occurred to me, I tried to save the model by rewriting the categories along the lines of the grammatical person in which the narrative was realized. So, between Fowler's type A (first person) mimetic narrative and his type B (third person) omniscient narrative I inserted a third type of narrative point of view in the second person, which I called the *instructive* or *ghost* narrative. It is this ghost narrator that appears in 'The Night'. A ghost or instructive narrative seems to alternate between being internal and external, present and disengaged: present in the deixis such as 'that strange radio' and 'this year of 1927' (p. 154); present in the internal knowledge of the character; present in assimilating reported speech into the narrative 'full with "chocolate on top, yes!" ' (p. 154). Yet at the same time it is disengaged in external comments such as 'to be exact' (p. 154) and 'which is natural' (p. 155); disengaged in shifting to the future tense 'Later, when you have grown you'll be given names to label them with' (p. 158). The shift between the two occurs from sentence to sentence and even within sentences (a phenomenon known as *slipping*): 'It is a wide ravine that cuts and twists across the town, a jungle by day, a place to let alone at night, Mother has often declared' (p. 157) — here a narrative description slips into free direct speech. My point is that the level of narrative presence corresponds with the level of uncertainty at various points in the text. The linguistic and orientational cognitive levels of the text all work together in the thematic progression of the narrative.

My reformulation of Fowler's categories seems, therefore, to work in this instance. However, from a general overview, there are not many narratives that would fall into the category of instructive point of view. It can therefore be borne in mind more as an exception to the rule. What I hope I've done is to demonstrate how a theoretical model has to undergo alteration when it is actualized by application to a text. Fowler's categories remain useful, since my necessary modification of them was derived from components of the theory and selected according to the circumstances of the text. In being aware of this, I avoid the 'coyote complex' and retain a useful theory of narrative point of view.

To draw to an accumulated conclusion, I will make some outrageously generalized comments about SF, derived from the previous discussion, in the hope that they will provoke interest and further research. I claim 'The Night' as archetypal SF, though it might not seem to be. There are no bug-eyed monsters, no flying saucers, no aliens, no technological hardware. It is not set in the future, there is no time travel besides tense shifting. There are not even any impressive field equations. And yet 'The Night' *can* be read as SF, for the following reasons. Firstly, it is SF by association (metonymically SF?) since it is found in a collection of fantastical stories that are more recognizable as SF, written by a famous writer of SF. The reader will probably therefore come to the story with the expectation of reading in the convention of SF. Secondly, SF deals not with the impact of technology on humans, but with the impact of *science* on humans (where science is 'knowledge', from the Latin *scientia*). Doug's story is about the impact of knowledge. Thirdly, and very generally, many critics have noted the twentieth-century tendency in literature towards internalization. In mainstream fiction, this tendency has often taken the form of psychological exploration where a character usually corresponds with an individual. In the SF genre, the idea of character often corresponds with humanity itself, and so the cultural tendency towards internalization here takes the form of philosophical and epistemological exploration, since philosophy can be said to be the thought of the mind of humanity. 'The Night' is therefore typical of SF in that it is an epistemic story; it is about the state of knowledge of typical eight-year-old boys — in 'a million small towns like this all over the world' (p. 160) — when faced with the unknown. Even more modern SF, that problematizes the concept and status of knowledge — in the work, for example, of Philip K. Dick or Brian Aldiss — still concerns itself with epistemological exploration.

Finally, the critic Mark Rose (1981) has identified the area that SF explores as being the relationship of the human to the non-human — reinstating concerns of Romantic literature in the dialogue between humanity and nature, and of previous literatures including medieval romance. The human and the non-human is also the subject and the other, the known and the unknown, the finite and the infinite, which is what confronts Doug at the edge of the ravine. SF, as in 'The Night', is an attempt to name the infinite; to bring, through language, as much knowledge as possible within human understanding. In other words, the aim of SF is to transform *scientia* (knowledge) into *sapientia* (wisdom — which is knowledge in use, applied knowledge). It is this therapeutic, cathartic, broadly political, non-escapist, practical aspect of art that Bradbury refers to when, in the *Psychology Today* article, he grandly declares:

> The so-called realists are trying to drive us insane, and I refuse to be driven insane. I go with Nietzsche who said: 'We have art that we do not perish in the truth'. (Hall 1968: 29)

It is with this kind of overblown statement, which is also typical of SF, that this paper should end.

Notes

1. The short story is 'The Night', which is stylistically interesting in that it is written in the second person. It is most easily found in the collection *The Small Assassin* (Bradbury 1976: 154-162). SF has been, from its 'pulp' magazine origins, a genre of the popular paperback, and so page references to this story and to the other SF works mentioned in this paper are from the paperback editions of the books.
2. For ease of reference I have here summarized the categories of perceptual point of view in narrative, adapted from Fowler (1986: 127-146). For a new approach to point of view in terms of modality, see Simpson (1990).

Internal

Type A: The *mimetic* narrative, inside a character's mind. Usually in the first person, with high evaluative modality.

Type B: The *omniscient* narrative, with knowledge of character's thoughts. Often in the third person.

External

Type C: The *objective* narrative, outside characters' thoughts. Usually in the third person, with no evaluative modality.

Type D: The *interpretative* narrative, with persona of narrator highlighted. Typically in the first person.

Bibliography

De Beaugrande, R. (1980), *Text, Discourse, and Process: Toward a Multidisciplinary Science of Texts*, Norwood (N.J.), Ablex Publishing Corp.
Blakemore, C. (1977), *Mechanics of the Mind*, Cambridge, Cambridge University Press.
Bradbury, R. (1976), *The Small Assassin*, St. Albans, Granada.
Dolezel, L. (1976), 'Narrative Modalities', *Journal of Literary Semantics*, 5: 5-14.
Eagleton, T. (1983), *Literary Theory: An Introduction*, Oxford, Basil Blackwell.
Fowler, R. (1986), *Linguistic Criticism*, Oxford, Oxford University Press.
Friedman, M. (1971), 'The Methodology of Positive Economics', in Breit, W. and Hochman, H.N. (eds) (1971), *Readings in Microeconomics* (second edition), Hinsdale (Illinois), Dryden Press, 23-47.
Gleick, J. (1988), *Chaos: Making a New Science*, London, Cardinal.
Goffman, E. (1974), *Frame Analysis*, New York, Harper & Row.
Le Guin, U.K. (1981), *The Left Hand of Darkness*, London, Futura.
Hall, M.H. (1968), 'A Conversation with Ray Bradbury and Chuck Jones: The Fantasy Makers', *Psychology Today*, 1(11): 28-37 & 70.

Jauss, H.R. (1982), *Toward an Aesthetic of Reception*, Brighton, Harvester Press.
Johnson, M.L. (1988), *Mind, Language, Machine: Artificial Intelligence in the Post-Structuralist Age*, Basingstoke, MacMillan.
Lessing, D. (1972), *Briefing for a Descent into Hell*, London, Grafton.
Levinson, S.C. (1983), *Pragmatics*, Cambridge, Cambridge University Press.
Peitgen, H-O and Saupe, D. (eds) (1988), *The Science of Fractal Images*, New York, Springer-Verlag.
Rose, M. (1981), *Alien Encounters: Anatomy of Science Fiction*, Cambridge (Mass.), Harvard University Press.
Simmons, R.F. (1973), 'Semantic Networks: Their Computation and Use for Understanding English Sentences', in Schank, R.C. and Colby, K.M. (eds) (1973), *Computer Models Of Thought And Language*, San Francisco, Freeman, 63–113.
Simpson, P.W. (1990), 'Towards a Modal Grammar of Point of View', *Liverpool Papers in Language and Discourse*, 3: 40–80.
Stapledon, O. (1972), *Star Maker*, Harmondsworth, Penguin.
Uspensky, B. (1973), *A Poetics of Composition*, (trn. Valentina Zavarin and Susan Wittig) Berkeley, University of California Press.

10 Narrative Voice and Focalization: The Presentation of the Different Selves in John Fowles' *The Collector*

Dominique Costa

In 1963 the publication of *The Collector* initiated John Fowles' career as a full-time writer.[1] In the first novel the story of Frederick Clegg, an emotionally disturbed young man from an unhappy lower middle-class family, and of Miranda Grey, an attractive art student from an upper-class family, is recounted to us in a most distinctive manner.

The aim of this paper is to examine Fowles' use of two specific narrative devices — voice and focalization — in order to present in a realistic way two fundamentally different selves, Clegg's and Miranda's; one static and destructive, the other striving for self-knowledge and improvement, each representative of two distinct social groups: 'the Few' and 'the Many'. For this analysis I shall use the concepts and terminology introduced by the French theorist Gérard Genette in his major work *Narrative Discourse: An Essay in Method* (1980).

The main plot of the novel may be conveyed in a few words. Having unexpectedly won a football pool, Clegg prepares to fulfil his secret aspiration of possessing Miranda with whom he is deeply obsessed. Letting his fantasies dominate his life, he kidnaps the young girl using chloroform as he does for his butterflies. Being a collector he keeps her for a long period in the cellar, especially prepared for her imprisonment in the old cottage he has recently bought, until she dies. Throughout the novel it is the strange relationship that develops between these characters — Clegg, the imprisoner and Miranda, the imprisoned — which unfolds dramatically in front of the reader's eyes.

The Collector opens with Clegg's account of the events which precede Miranda's kidnapping, followed by those during her captivity in the cellar, halting abruptly at a crucial moment during her illness, within a few days of the girl's death. In fact, having arrived almost at the middle of the novel, Part Two suddenly starts not with Clegg's continuation of the events but, instead, with Miranda's account of the events her captor has already described. The main difference is that events are now seen by her and recounted from her own perspective, and I quite agree with Perry Nodelman (1987: 333) who considers that 'it is this surprising switch of perspective *in medias res* that forms readers' attitudes to both Clegg and Miranda'. Fowles' selection of two distinct, traditionally called, 'first-person' voices and sharply contrastive focalizations on the same events — a selection that allows Clegg and Miranda to narrate the story of their relationship in their own manner with their own words — is, as will be seen, crucial to the presentation of these characters. By inserting in Part Two Miranda's narrative voice within, rather than before or after, Clegg's narrative sections, together with the juxtaposition of their contrastive voices, the author shows the narrators' differing, clashing viewpoints on the situation enhancing their different selves, and simultaneously causes the form of the novel to mirror the content. Miranda's story becomes entrapped in Clegg's, paralleling in this way her personal entrapment by him. These two sections of *The Collector*, in which Clegg's and Miranda's voices show their personal views on the situation, form the bulk of the novel and are followed by two shorter ones in which Clegg, taking up the narrative once more, unfolds in Part Three a chilling account of Miranda's last moments, finally ending in Part Four with the disclosure of his plans for his next victim.

By permitting direct access to his protagonists' narratives, Fowles removes himself from his novel leaving the reader to pass judgement alone. With the absence of the authorial voice the illusion that the characters themselves shape their own text is effective. While authenticity and credibility are thus achieved by having two 'surrogate authors' — Clegg and Miranda — provide their own narratives, their different selves become apparent to the reader.

I now want to look in more detail at the narrative voice which provides the frame of the novel, Clegg's. In the opening sentence of the novel we are at once confronted with the occurrence of two personal pronouns lacking any antecedent:

> When *she* was home from her boarding-school *I* used to see her almost every day sometimes, because their house was right opposite the Town Hall Annexe (my emphasis). (C: 9)

The 'I' of this 'etic opening' — ie one characterized by the absence of narrative preliminaries with predominance of personal pronouns without references — can here only indicate the narrator, a narrator whom the traditional theoretical studies on perspective generally and confusingly name a 'first-person narrator' failing, as Genette points out, (1980: 186–9) to distinguish between *mode* (Who sees?) and *voice* (Who speaks?). As the opening sentence shows, this narrator is present as a character within the world of fictional events. He is what Genette calls a 'homodiegetic narrator' and, because he functions as the protagonist in the story he is narrating, he is also 'autodiegetic' — ie what is traditionally called a 'protagonist-narrator'.

Genette's crucial separation of mode and voice — distinguishing between the question 'Who sees?' (focalization) and the question 'Who talks? (narration) — is of great value here since a differentiation between Clegg the protagonist, whose perception orients the narrative perspective (the focus), and Clegg the narrator, who presents the events (the voice), is essential for the way in which Clegg's narrative is recounted and for the way the reader perceives his self. Basing their argument on Genette's concept of focalization, two later theorists, Mieke Bal (1985) and Shlomith Rimmon-Kenan (1983), call such an agent the 'focalizer'; he is the vehicle of focalization 'through whose spatial, temporal and/or psychological position the textual events are perceived' (Lanser 1987: 141). What the focalizer perceives—all that is related to himself, Miranda and her captivity—is named the 'focalized object'. The relationship between focalizer (Clegg) and focalized object (Miranda) is offered from an 'internal focalization' since it is, as the following example reveals, through Clegg's thoughts, feelings and perceptions that the story is presented:

> *Seeing* her always made me *feel* like I was catching a rarity, going up to it very careful, heart-in-mouth as they say. A Pale Clouded Yellow, for instance. I always *thought* of her like that (my emphasis). (C: 9)

In his narrative then, Clegg plays a double role. He is at the same time a character within the story he is telling—the protagonist who underwent the experience in the past, the focus through which all is seen—and also the one who narrates it in the present, the narrating voice. Genette posits that these two identities—the narrating focus and the narrating voice—though found within the same character, are quite different in function as well as in the degree of their knowledge. He considers the following:

> The narrator almost always 'knows' more than the hero, even if he himself is the hero, and therefore for the narrator focalization through the hero is a restriction of field just as artificial in the first person as in the third. (Genette 1980: 194)

Because of the 'restriction of field' and especially because of the duality of focus-narration, the reader rapidly senses Clegg's unreliability as a narrator. Knowing, in fact, before the beginning of his narration what the end of Miranda's captivity will be, Clegg colours his treatment of the events from the very beginning and distorts reality to his advantage.

The reader also rapidly becomes aware that in Clegg's presentation of Miranda's captivity, certain terms and expressions are used to conceal his faults and to make him feel less guilty about her condition. For instance, he never directly refers to her as his prisoner but calls her his 'guest'. Furthermore, a similar process, a process of self-deceit by which Clegg distorts reality in his own favour in order to justify his actions and eliminate any responsibility, is frequently used, as the following example illustrates:

> About what I did, undressing her, when I thought after, I *saw it wasn't so bad; not many would have kept control of themselves*... it *was almost a point in my favour* (my emphasis). (C: 87)

Other negative aspects of Clegg's self, such as his obsession with collecting, quickly become noticeable in the novel. First, Miranda's name is revealingly marked in his entomological observations diary and throughout his narrative she is frequently compared to butterflies, as in 'It was like catching the Mazarine Blue again or a Queen of Spain Fritillary' (C: 31). On one occasion Fowles explicitly draws our attention to his protagonist's obsession by making him refer to Miranda as 'it' instead of 'she': 'For a moment I thought her, *it* looked so different (my emphasis). (C: 80) This obsession is characterized in him by a need of possession. 'Having her', declares Clegg, 'was

Nothing needed doing: I just wanted to have her' (C: 95). As with his butterflies, he is interested on in her image not in her self, as Miranda rightly observes:

> The sheer joy of having me under his power, of being able to spend all and every day staring at me. He doesn't care what I say or how I feel — my feelings are meaningless to him — it's the fact that he's got me ... It's me he wants, my look, my outside; not my emotions or my mind or my soul or even my body. Not anything *human*. He's a collector. That's the great dead thing in him. (C: 161)

The writer's choice of the girl's name — Miranda, the Latin gerundive of *miror*, referring to 'she who ought to be wondered at' — clearly enhances this.

From the beginning of his narrative Clegg's language shows certain distinctive features. His personal way of narrating the events in a matter-of-fact, colloquial style, using banal expressions, emphasizes his low social background and poor level of education. The type of language and tone used by the narrator is frequently inappropriate to, and clashes with, the events that are being narrated. In his analysis of one of the most dramatic passages of the novel, when Clegg coldly describes Miranda lying dead in her bed (C: 274), Ronberg (1985: 107) notes that 'the language does not accord with the field of discourse', a conflict arising from 'form not matching function'. This observation can be applied to other passages of the novel and it is also through such a device that Clegg's emotional, psychological, sexual and social inadequacies are revealed. Language is thus primarily used by the author as a means of revealing the deficiencies of his narrator's intellect and education, and exposing his emotional stuntedness and moral blindness. At the end of his narrative, Fowles shows how little Clegg has learned by letting us witness how, without any sense of guilt, he is prepared to repeat what he has done. The only difference is that this time he will catch an 'ordinary common shop-girl' — his previous mistake, he tells us, having been that of 'aiming too high' (C: 282).

By means of such narrative Fowles lets his reader see how Clegg's disturbed mind works, how his obsession rules his and Miranda's lives. According to Clegg, his failure with Miranda has been caused by class difference: 'There was always class between us' he says (C: 41). His resentment and sense of inferiority are quite evident when, in an outburst, he tells his prisoner:

> If you ask me, London's all arranged for the people who can act like public schoolboys, and you don't get anywhere if you don't have the manner born and the right la-di-da voice — I mean rich people's London, the West End, of course. (C: 14)

Miranda's views of her captor indicate that she sees him as, to some extent, a victim himself, as when, for example, she writes: 'I know he's a victim of a miserable nonconformist suburban world and a miserable social class, the horrid timid copycatting genteel in-between class' (C: 161). Clegg is what he is as a result of social conditions, unequal opportunities, childhood deprivation and poor education, and Fowles asserts that in the this novel he has tried 'to establish the virtual *innocence* of the Many' (Fowles 1989: 10). The recurrence of expressions like 'I don't know why' or 'I don't know how' indicate that most of the time Clegg is at a loss, unable to understand what is happening. He has, as

Fowles stresses in his preface to *The Aristos*, no control over what he is. Miranda clearly sees this when she tells him 'You're the one imprisoned in a cellar' (C: 58).

Considering now Miranda's narrative voice, the beginning of her narration in Part Two of *The Collector*, with the date 'October 14th?', indicates at once that she is writing a diary in which her thoughts, feelings, perceptions and experiences about her present situation are going to be confided. In her diary she records all the events concerning her imprisonment and the painful experiences which accompany it, and at the same time she is able to recall memories of the past in which she can take refuge.

Miranda is, thus, in this part of the novel, as Clegg was in the others, an autodiegetic narrator since she is a narrator who tells a story in which she simultaneously plays a part as one of the fictional characters. It is she who acts as the focalizer—the agent of the narrative who concentrates her attention on the focalized object; ie all which concerns her present and Clegg, and also her past and G.P., George Paston, her artistic mentor. Her presentation of the fictional world, like Clegg's, is self-centred in that it is offered through her thoughts, memories and feelings—from an internal focalization. With such a process the reader is able to follow Miranda closely, observing her struggle and the transformations which her captivity effects in her inner self.

Fowles claims that Miranda 'is an existentialist heroine groping for her own authenticity', but he adds that 'her tragedy is that she will never live to achieve it. Her triumph is that one day she would have done so' (Newquist 1964: 255). Elsewhere he comments:

> I'm interested in the side of existentialism which deals with freedom: the business of whether we do have freedom, whether we do have free will, to what extent you can change your life, choose yourself, and all the rest of it. Most of my major characters have been involved in this 'Sartrian concept of authenticity and inauthenticity'. (McSweeney 1983: 105)

While Clegg makes use of his memoir primarily as a means of self-justification, Miranda on the other hand uses her diary in order to discover her self. Writing is for her a creative activity. Through introspection and self-criticism she is able to expose her old self and her narrative allows us to follow the transformations she is undergoing:

> I want to use my feelings about life. I think and think down here. I understand things I haven't really thought about before. (C: 142)
> I am beginning to understand life much better than most people of my age. (C: 145)
> I'm growing up so quickly down here. Like a mushroom. (C: 156)

For Fowles (1989: 42), 'we must evolve to exist'. Contrasting with Clegg's spiritual inertia, deadness—subtly pointed out by his last name 'Clegg' which can be phonetically associated to the French 'clef', indicating his role as gaoler, but mainly in its meaning in dialect: a vampirish horsefly, and in its consonance with 'clog', suggesting heaviness and woodenness—Miranda is on the other hand to be seen as a symbol of moral growth, struggling to understand and become better. In *The Aristos* (1989: 157) Fowles considers the following distinction: 'Adam is hatred of change', he 'is stasis or conservatism... Eve is the assumption of human responsibility, of the need for progress and the need to control progress... She is kinesis or progress'. Such distinction is clearly embodied in these two protagonists: Clegg (stasis or conservatism); Miranda (kinesis or progress).

Since she lives in the present of her captive world and she most desperately wants to escape from it, one sees Miranda making use of her memories, of her recollections of her past outside world, in order to escape, at least mentally if not physically, from her confined situation. She discloses this when she writes:

> I felt I was going mad last night; so I wrote and wrote and wrote myself into the other world. To escape in spirit, if not in fact. To prove it still exists. (C: 157)

Remembering the past, and especially her relationship with G.P., helps her in her present confinement. It is through the introduction of a certain type of 'analepsis' or 'flashback'—designated by Genette as 'external', whose 'only function is to fill out the first narrative by enlightening the reader on one or another "antecedent"' (Genette 1980: 50)—that Fowles permits his reader to know his protagonist better. Through such analepses one is in fact able to follow Miranda's progress from her 'old Ladymont self' into a new and better self, her growth through suffering and her striving for self-knowledge. On one occasion she even goes so far as to admit:

> A strange thought: I would not want this not to have happened. Because if I escape I shall be a completely different and I think better person. Because if I don't escape; if something dreadful happened, I shall still know that the person I was and would have stayed if this hadn't happened was not the person I now want to be. (C: 251)

Being an artist with a creative temperament, Miranda's narrative voice is presented in her diary in various ways. She decides to use a variety of forms in her fiction including dialogue with stage directions, lists of thoughts and feelings and fictive letters. Her creativity can also be noticed in her use of language, offering a sharp contrast with her captor's. About her style Peter Wolfe (1979: 79) rightly states that 'Miranda's literary style gauges her personality, her values, and her ability to adapt to change'.

Throughout her diary Clegg has been referred to as one of 'the Many' or, as she derisively names him, one of the 'New People'—'the new-class people with their cars and their money and their tellies and their stupid vulgarities and their stupid crawling imitation of the bourgeoisie' (C: 207)—while she sees herself as one of 'the Few': 'a sort of band of people who have to stand against all the rest' (C: 208). 'In this situation', Miranda claims, 'I'm a representative' (C: 206), but being a representative of 'the Few' does not mean that she is to be regarded as perfect and that the author's viewpoint is to be identified with his heroine's. Fowles himself draws our attention to this when he clearly asserts: 'That does not mean that she was perfect. Far from it she was arrogant in her ideas, a prig, a liberal-humanist snob, like so many university students' (Fowles 1989: 10).

Miranda's flaws are apparent in her narrative. Like Clegg she makes use of clichés 'I love life so passionately, I never knew how much I wanted to live before' (C: 118), prefers avoiding verbal 'impropriety', and refers, for instance, to people by initials. What Fowles wants us to understand is that contrary to Clegg, who learns nothing, who cannot change or mature, 'if she had not died', he says about his heroine, 'she might have become something better, the kind of being humanity so desperately needs' (Fowles 1989: 10). The author further explains his views on *The Collector* when he remarks:

> The actual evil in Clegg overcame the potential good in Miranda. I did not mean by this that I view the future with a black pessimism, nor that a precious *élite* is threatened by the barbarian hordes. I meant simply that unless we face up to this unnecessary brutal conflict (based largely on an unnecessary envy on the one hand and an unnecessary contempt on the other) between the biological Few and the biological Many; unless we admit that we are not, and never will be, born equal, though we are all born with equal human rights; unless the Many can be educated out of their false assumption of inferiority and the Few out of their equally false assumption that biological superiority is a state of existence instead of what it really is, *a state of responsibility* — then we shall never arrive at a more just and happier world. (Fowles 1989: 10)

With Miranda's second 'autodiegetic narration' Fowles enhances the unbridgeable gap that exists between her and her captor. Through her narrative, Clegg's version of the events is complemented and often corrected, striking contrasts and ironies becoming thus apparent. Events which have been previously narrated by Clegg are treated differently in Miranda's narrative, disclosing to us his distorted self. Throughout the novel Clegg and Miranda appear to misread each other constantly. When he expects some understanding from her, none is shown, and when she sympathizes with him, he is not able to see it. Their mutual incomprehension is illustrated by Miranda when she writes 'We'll never understand each other. We don't have the same sort of heart' (C: 84), and also by Clegg when at a certain point he declares: 'We could never come together, she could never understand me, I suppose she would say I never could have understood her, or would have anyhow' (C: 87). Apart from the different treatment of the events, the intersection of the autodiegetic narrations primarily reveals the fundamental differences between these two antagonistic selves.

This narrative process through which the writer presents his two autodiegetic narrators is fundamental for an effective treatment of the subject and points primarily to the two different selves of the protagonists. In *The Collector* Fowles appears thus as an author in full control of his material offering, through an effective handling of two specific narrative devices — voice and focalization — an existential parable which delineates Clegg's destructive *being* and Miranda's creative *becoming*.

Notes

1. *The Collector* (1986, Pan Books). All quotations from the text are from this paperback edition (hereafter referred to as C), and page references will be in parentheses within the text.

Bibliography

Bal, M. (1985), *Narratology: Introduction to the Theory of Narrative*, London, University of Toronto Press.
Fowles, J. (1986), *The Collector*, London, Pan Books.
Fowles, J. (1989), *The Aristos*, London, Triad Grafton Books.
Genette, G. (1980), *Narrative Discourse: An Essay in Method*, (tr. Lewin, A.E) New York, Cornell University Press.
Lanser, S.S. (1987), *The Narrative Act: Point of View in Prose Fiction*, Princeton, Princeton University Press.
McSweeney, K. (1983), *Four Contemporary Novelists*, Montreal, McGill Queens's University Press.
Newquist, R. (1964), 'John Fowles', in *Counterpoint*, Chicago, Newquist, 217-25.
Nodelman, P. (1987), 'John Fowles' Variations in *The Collector*', *Contemporary Literature*, 28, 3: 332-46.
Rimmon-Kenan, S. (1983), *Narrative Fiction: Contemporary Poetics*, London, Methuen.
Ronberg, G. (1985), 'Literature and the Teaching of English as a Foreign Language at University Level', *Triangle*, 4: 103-12.
Wolfe, P. (1979), *John Fowles, Magus and Moralist*, Lewisburg, Bucknell University Press.

11 Feminism, Language or Existentialism: The Search for the Self in the Works of Clarice Lispector

Barbara Mathie

The title of this paper might seem to propose three alternative and mutually exclusive readings of the works of the Brazilian writer Clarice Lispector: that is to say, a feminist, a poststructuralist and an existentialist reading. However, I have no wish to propose one 'correct' reading; rather, I intend to show how all three readings can—I hesitate to say should—be simultaneously accepted.

Whereas existentialist and narratological readings of Clarice's work have already been widely discussed,[1] as has her poststructuralist stance regarding language and the construction of reality—a stance shared by many other Latin-American writers of the same period, for example Borges and Cortázar[2]—as Marta Peixoto points out in her article '*Family Ties*: Female Development in Clarice Lispector', the feminocentric nature of her writing is only now being recognized (1983: 287ff).

Obviously in this short paper I cannot hope to examine in detail the whole body that comprises the fiction of Clarice Lispector.[3] I shall, therefore, limit my analysis to two collections of short stories: *Laços de família* (*Family Ties*) (1970) first published in 1960, about halfway through Clarice's writing life, and a later collection, *A via crucis do corpo* (*The Via Crucis of the Flesh*) published in 1974.

My intention in choosing these two collections is to show that, despite her reluctance to be labelled as a *female* writer (a position echoed by her later champion Hélène Cixous, and by the theorist Julia Kristeva), and leaving aside the feminocentric surface structure—for example, a predominance of female characters—at the level of deep structure there lie firmly embedded in her work elements of recent (French) feminist theory, such as that introduced by both Cixous and Kristeva. Hélène Cixous herself considers the fiction of Clarice Lispector as a superlative example of *écriture féminine*.[4] Although Julia Kristeva does not, however, allow for the existence of an '*écriture féminine* or a *parler femme* that would be inherently feminine or female' she does allow for the concept of a marginal writing, bisexual rather than specifically feminine in nature; she does not allow for biological determinism however (in Moi 1985: 164).

Yet, between the two collections of stories cited here there is a fundamental difference. Fitz has already pointed out how *A via crucis do corpo* differs stylistically from Clarice's previous writing, and signals it as the text of 'a writer in transition' (Fitz 1988: 47). He sees the stories as considerably less lyrical in tone and as marking a change in the author's concerns; prior to *A via crucis do corpo* the concern is with the internal, isolated human, whereas those books that follow it are concerned with the external, and with the possibility of human communication.

However, it is my suggestion that while one can validly interpret the theme of *Laços de família* as being the (universal) isolation of the human condition, that is to stop short. What is common to almost all of the stories in this collection is the lack of space for discourses other than the patriarchal, a discourse which because of its adherence to a belief in an ultimate transcendental signifier, the phallus, necessarily renders the subject *être-en-soi* (being-in-itself).[5] This causes the protagonists to live inauthentic existences, as we shall see in the first part of this paper.

In the second collection of stories, however, Clarice adopts a new stance, positing a solution to this problem of lack of space. In the second part of this paper, I should like to examine how Clarice attempts to open up this new space and construct a discourse that is neither phallo- nor logocentric.

Laços de família (hereafter *LF*) is a collection of short stories of which three have male protagonists, although they are no less insignificant for being male.[6] All the other progatonists are female, although one of these females, in the story 'A galinha' ('The Chicken'), is a chicken.

Each story centres around an epiphany, or *Gestalt*; that is to say a moment of supreme consciousness and self-awareness instigated by the protagonist's changed perception of an everyday object.[7] In 'Amor' ('Love') for example, the protagonist, Ana, is precipitated into a state of crisis and self-awareness by the sight of a blind man chewing gum. I find it significant that the man is blind since it prevents Ana from being, in her relationship to him, an *être-pour-autrui*, an object in the eyes of others, which according to existentialist theory is an act of extreme *mauvaise foi* and one of the reasons underlying Sartre's proscription of love (Cranston 1962: 55-57).

Another element common to many of these stories is that the moment of awareness, the epiphany, although actually caused by the perception of an everyday object, occurs when the protagonist's social role remains temporarily undefined. For example, Ana's epiphany takes place when she is not limited and defined by her role of an urban, middle-class wife and mother. Ana herself speaks of 'na hora perigosa da tarde, quando a casa estave vazia sem precisar mais dela, o sol alto, cada membro da família distribuído nas suas funções' (during that dangerous hour in the afternoon when the house was empty, no longer needing her, the sun high in the sky, each member of the family elsewhere, busy with his own things) (*LF*: 19).[8]

The idea that women within patriarchal society are merely playing a role was first posited by Simone de Beauvoir, and explains her famous statement 'one is not born a woman, one becomes one'; in *Le Deuxième Sexe* (1956), de Beauvoir discusses the issue that within the confines of patriarchal society, the (biological) female *qua* female is always *other*, alienated without an individual identity and allocated the sole function of confirming male identity. This echoes Freud's concept of the gaze, 'a phallic activity linked to anal desire for sadistic mastery of the object', for the female of patriarchy is rarely considered as more than (an) object; that is to say, as a male possession (Moi 1985: 134).

A theory of the gaze, Sartrean rather than Freudian, is the pivot around which the story 'Preciosidade' ('Preciousness') functions. In this story the young, female protagonist adopts a stance of *indifférence*. This is 'a kind of "blindness" towards others, or, more exactly, a deliberate refusal to accept that others are looking at me' (Cranston 1962: 57). And so she, the protagonist, intentionally avoids any interaction with those who surround her, except for in the classroom where, as we are told, she can be like a boy: 'Até que, enfim, a classe de aula... onde ela era tratada como um rapaz' (Until, at last, the classroom... where she was treated as if she were a boy) (*LF*: 98). For the girl to adopt this stance of *indifférence* is, as Naomi Lindstrom points out, an act of *mauvaise foi*, and also, in view of the protagonist's conscious efforts to be unkempt and unfeminine, indicative of her shirking her role as an adult woman within the confines of patriarchal society (Lindstrom 1982: 190).

The crisis in her (non-)existence occurs when she becomes aware that she is being followed by two young men (*LF*: 101). The sexual aspect of the fear of a young girl on her own is, of course, obvious but for her what is overriding is her fear that they might look at her; 'Êles vão olhar para mim, eu sei não, há mais niguém para êles olharem e êles vão olhar muito!' (They are going to look at me, I know it, there is no one else for them to look at, and they're going to look at me a lot!) (*LF*: 102). The climax of this episode occurs when they touch her and she is finally forced to recognize her existence *pour autrui*, as the alienated other, as the female sex object (*LF*: 102–3). The story ends, after her deliberating with herself, with her acceptance of her role as *être-pour-autrui*: ' "Preciso cuidar mais de mim", pensou' ('I need to pay more attention to my appearance', she thought) (*LF*: 107). Thus she abandons her stance of *indifférence*: 'Até que, assim como uma pessoa engorda, ela deixou, sem saber por que processo, de ser preciosa' (Until, in the same way as someone puts on weight, without realizing how, she stopped being 'affected') (*LF*: 108).

Yet, as the above quotation makes clear, this transformation was not so much a decisive action on her part, as ineluctable destiny.

What almost all the stories is this collection have in common, over and above their being structured around an epiphany, is the failure of the female protagonists to act upon what their 'experience' reveals to them. They do not initiate the quest for that eluding, indefinable grail which is an authentic existence as a semiotic *être-pour-soi*, as opposed to the inauthentic and symbolic state of *être-en-soi/pour-autrui*.

In these stories, as in Iberian Golden Age dramas, the modern detective story or the fairy story, any subversive action or event that threatens the monolithic order of the symbolic is *always* overcome, and harmony is restored.

In 'Amor' ('Love') Ana, while still in a state of crisis, finds herself drawn to the Botanic Gardens. The lyrical description of the gardens mentions their tropical lushness and abundance, but also present are death and putrification (*LF*: 23–25). This is a retreat to a pre-Lapsarian imaginary, or to Kristeva's semiotic *chora*.

Kristeva's theory of language acquisition substitutes the Lacanian terms of the 'imaginary' and the 'symbolic order' with the terms the 'semiotic' and the 'symbolic'. As with Lacan's concept of the imaginary (1977), the semiotic precedes the entry into language, and therefore, also the Oedipal crisis (the resolution of which results in the rupture of dyadic unity). This is reflected in the polysemy of the semiotic *chora*, 'which receives all things and in some mysterious way partakes of the intelligible and is most incomprehensible' (Moi 1985: 165): as there is no transcendental (phallic) signifier, there can be no fixed meaning. This means that love and hate, life and death and other such pairings—mutually exclusive within the confines of patriarchal binary thought—may co-exist; for, as Toril Moi points out, the pre-Oedipal mother is both masculine and feminine (1985: 165).

Yet, the semiotic cannot replace the symbolic (Moi 1985: 170). At the same time, however, 'there is no space for resistance within the terms of the symbolic order, and women who do not wish to repress their true femaleness can have no access to it' (Weedon 1987: 65). The use of the term 'femaleness' in the previous sentence does, however, require modification: for Kristeva, there is no such thing as a woman except in the most negative of senses. It is the phallocentric discourse of patriarchy which defines woman, and any such definition is in negative, marginalizing terms; as Kristeva says: 'I therefore understand by "woman" that which cannot be represented, that which is not spoken, that which remains outside naming and ideologies' (in Moi 1988: 163). What Kristeva advocates in place of 'femininity' is a theory of marginalization and subversion, not restricted in its application to the biological woman.

In this respect, Marta Peixoto points out the significance of the title of the collection of stories under discussion. The *family ties* of the title are what define and limit the female protagonists' existences (Peixoto 1983: 289). As we saw above, with reference to the story 'Amor' ('Love'), Ana's crises (or epiphanies) occur *only* when she is not fully participating in the role of middle-class wife and mother. Patriarchal society is, of course, structured around the family, at the head of which is the father and his law, a law founded on the possession of the phallus: in Cixous' terms, it is the 'realm of the proper'.

Yet these defining bonds are not permanent as is illustrated in the story 'Feliz aniverário' ('Happy Birthday'). As Peixoto points out in her article, the party in honour of the protagonist's eighty-ninth birthday is reduced to the level of empty ritual (1983: 287). The protagonist, the birthday girl, is described in passive terms, impotent now she holds only a puppet role:

> E, para adiantar o expediente, vestira a aniversariante logo depois do almoço. Pusera-lhe desde então a presilha em tôrno do pescoço e o broche, borrifara-lhe um pouco de água-de-colônia para disfarçar aquêle seu cheiro de guardado— sentara-a- à mesa. E desde duas horas a aniversariante estava sentada à cabeceira de longa mesa vazia, têsa na sala silenciosa. (*LF*: 61).
> (And, to speed things up, she had dressed the birthday girl immediately after lunch. She had, at that point put the necklace around her neck and fastened it; she had sprinkled her with a little toilet water to hide that musty smell she had, and she had sat her at the table. And for last two hours the birthday girl had been sitting up straight at the head of the long, empty table in that silent room.)

The rest of the family are more concerned with themselves and with doing what is expected of them: her son José, the eldest of six sons, is especially worried about saying the correct thing (*LF*: 63ff).

The grandmother's moment of awareness occurs with the ritual cutting of the cake, symbolizing, for her, the final severing of the family ties. With a sudden show of rebellion, the grandmother spits vehemently, thereby upsetting everyone. Order is almost immediately re-established. However, the final words of the story reflect the pessimism of existentialism: of the grandmother we are told, 'A morte era o seu mistério' (Death was her mystery) (*LF*: 75), introducing the Sartrean belief that after death there is nothing, and that, consequently, a man or woman is the sum total of his or her acts. (Death is a favourite concern of Clarice, and in one of the stories of *A via crucis do corpo* — 'Antes da ponte Rio-Niterói' ('Before the Bridge at River-Niterói')—she, as the intradiegetic narrator, considers the possible nature of death.)

In the title story of 'Laços de família' maternal love is, again, the theme. By an act of chance (*le hasard*) the protagonist Catarina is thrown together with her mother in a taxi, and this results in Catarina's consciousness of her overwhelming love for her mother: 'Ninguém mais te pode amar senão eu ... Não, não se podia dizer que amava sua mãe. Sue mãe lhe doía' (No one else can love you apart from me ... No, she couldn't say that she loved her mother. Her mother made her ache) (*LF*: 112). This awareness of a primeval, semiotic love is all the more important as we have already been informed that Catarina's post-Oedipal tie was, as is the normal case, with her father (*LF*: 111-12). This awareness of love also occasions in Catarina a new awareness of the world surrounding her (*LF*: 114ff). It is also reflected in her relationship with her son who, since he has not yet fully mastered use of language nor acquired a sense of his own identity, is therefore pre-Oedipal:

> Em que momento é que a mão, apertando uma criança, dava-lhe esta prisão de amor que se abateria para ser sempre sôbre o futuro homen... Quem saberia jamais em que momento a mãe transferia ao filho a herança. E com que sombrio prazer. Agora mãe e filho comprendo-se dentro do mistério partilhado. (*LF*: 117-118).
> (At what moment is it that a mother, hugging her child, gave him this prison of love that would descend forever upon the future man... Who could know at what moment a mother transferred to her son that inheritance. And with what sombre pleasure. Now mother and son understanding each other, together in the mystery they share.)

As Peixoto (1983: 293) points out, the father resents his exclusion from the dyadic unity between mother and infant, and uses his power to install the *feminine*: 'Mas tinha-se habituado a torná-la feminina dêste modo' (He had become used to making her feminine in this way) (*LF*: 118-19). It is, perhaps, superfluous to point out that the above quotation justifies the belief shared by de Beauvoir and Kristeva, amongst many, that a woman is created by patriarchy.

The third element that links these stories is the ineffable nature of the epiphanies. In 'Laços de família', despite Catarina's burgeoning feelings for her mother, 'não tinham o que falar' (they had nothing to say) (*LF*: 112). Likewise Ana, the protagonist of 'Amor' ('Love'), attempts to communicate with her son, but cannot; she ends up frightening him instead with her momentary intensity (*LF*: 26).

This inability of the protagonists to vocalize, and therefore to lend reality to their new found consciousness, is, of course, because a return to the semiotic is a return to a state preceding language where the heterogeneous subject is, as yet, unsplit. Within the discourse of the symbolic, based on one transcendental signifier, the *logos* is fixed in meaning and the polysemic nature of the semiotic is, therefore, ineffable.

In her novel *A paixão segundo G.H.* (*The Passion according to G.H.*) (in Lucas 1976), Lispector examines fully the quest for authenticity and reality through language, and the ensuing muteness:

> Ah, mas para chegar à mudez, que grande esforço da voz. Minha voz é o modo como vou buscar a realidade; a realidade antes da minha linguagem, existia como um pensamento que não se pensa, mas por fatalidade fui e sou impelida a precisar saber o que o pensamento pensa... A realidade é a matéria prima, a linguagem é o modo como vou buscá-la... Mas — volto com o indizível. (Lucas 1976: 16–17)
> (Oh, but in order to become mute, what great efforts of the voice are required. My voice is the means by which I shall seek reality; reality even before my language existed as a thought, which is never thought, but by destiny I was and I am impelled to find out that which the thought thinks... Reality is the raw material, language is the means through which I can reach it... But — I always return with that which cannot be spoken.)

From an existentialist–poststructuralist point of view, if one accepts the fact that it is through language that any given reality is made manifest or created, if the *indizível* (that which cannot be spoken) were articulated in the (phal)logocentric discourse of patriarchal society, it would be fixed; that is to say, rendered *être-en-soi*.

The story entitled 'A menor mulher do mundo' ('The Smallest Woman in the World') is, perhaps, the only story in this collection that is in any way optimistic. Although, as Peixoto points out, this pygmy woman is representative of every possible minority — she is small, black, pregnant and female, in other words completely defenceless and marginalized — she has, nevertheless, succeeded in preserving her identity (1983: 301–02); she survives against all odds, including cannibalistic neighbours. Towards the end of the story she is described as being in possession of her own authentic identity:

> E então ela estava rindo. Era um riso como sòmente quem não fala ri. Êsse riso, o explorador constrangido não conseguiu classificar. E ela continuou fruindo o próprio riso macio, ela que não estava sendo devorada. Não ser devorado é o sentimento mais perfeito. Não ser devorado é o objectivo secreto de tôda uma vida. (*LF*: 84)
> (And then she was laughing. It could only be the laugh of someone who does not speak. This laugh the troubled explorer could not classify. She, who was not being devoured, continued enjoying her own smooth laugh. Not to be devoured is the most perfect sentiment. Not to be devoured is the secret objective of one's whole life.)

We are also told that in this community, a child is given his liberty 'quase que imediatamente' (almost immediately), thus freeing the mother from a subjugated existence as *autrui* (*LF*: 78). It is further related that this woman has a tree of her own, in which she lives; automatically, one thinks of the tree of life, although, it is also possible to interpret the tree as phallic, especially as it is spoken of as a *possession* (*LF*: 86). Yet it is my opinion that, although in possession of a tree and her own identity, Pequena Flor (Little Flower) who is named by (and perhaps therefore appropriated by) the explorer, is not situated within patriarchal discourse. This is because we are also told, more than once, that Pequena Flor cannot speak. Furthermore, her concept of love is of a love which does not devour the individuality of either party (*LF*: 84–85); that is to say a love in keeping with the tenets of existentialism (Cranston 1962: 57).

However, there are also three stories in the collection which have male protagonists. In the story 'Começos de uma fortuna' ('Beginnings of a Fortune') the adolescent Arturo is learning about life in the adult world. What is apparent throughout the story is Arturo's unease and tentativeness faced with the exploitative nature of capitalist (and patriarchal) society. Like the protagonist of 'Preciosidade' ('Preciousness') he is adolescent, but unlike her, for she attempts to resist entry into the adult world, he is both curiously tempted and repelled. Having recognized his parents as individuals (*LF*: 123), and acknowledging his growing separateness from them, he reflects upon the establishment of his own dynasty: 'Quando eu tiver minha mulher e meus filhos... tudo será diferente' (When I have my own wife and children... everything will be different). In this respect he obviously sees his own future as within the structures of patriarchy, with himself in the role of subject (*LF*: 124).

At the same time, he is unsure as to whether or not he wishes to take on this adult role, represented in the story by his indecision over whether or not to borrow money from his friend in order to take a girl to the cinema (*LF*: 125ff). In the end, after having been teased, he capitulates and borrows the money without being sure if the girl whom he took to the cinema was exploiting *him*, or if perhaps he should have taken advantage of *her* (*LF*: 128).

'O crime do professor de matemática' ('The Crime of the Mathematics Professor') features a protagonist whose career would point to him being the very embodiment of logic and rationality, as Di Antonio remarks (1985: 28); however, even he is unable to avoid certain feelings of Sartrean 'nausea'. His crisis is caused when he comes across a dead, unburied dog, which he determines to buy in an attempt to expiate his guilt over having earlier abandoned his own pet dog. This, however, he never manages to do. Di Antonio identifies the dog with the (instinctive) Jungian unconscious, which the professor is unable to buy under the tree of knowledge (1985: 29). It is not implausible to extend this interpretation, seeing the dog, an animal and therefore without language, as representing the semiotic and the act of burial as an attempt on the part of the symbolic, rational man to isolate himself from the subversive within himself. While Julia Kristeva maintains that it is impossible for the semiotic to take over the symbolic, she nevertheless posits a theory of the *sujet en procès*, or the disrupted subject. In the same way that Freud's repressed is never fully repressed, so too there are semiotic pulsions which can be released into the symbolic through expulsion or rejection. This allows for a subversive or revolutionary discourse, based on semiotic motility and the *sujet en procès* (a semiotic *être-pour-soi*). This is the theory in the philosophy of Julia Kristeva which is correlative and substitutive of Cixous' concept of *écriture féminine* (Moi 1985: 170).

It is, of course, entirely possible to interpret 'O crime do professor de matemática' ('The Crime of the Mathematics Professor') on a purely existentialist level. In Sartrean philosophy freedom is absolute: there is no absolute or transcendental moral code by which one can live one's life. Consequently, one has to make choices by which one can either be saved or be damned; one is responsible for these choices, and for one's acts. The concept of salvation and damnation might seem paradoxical when one is dealing with what, in the case of Sartre, is an atheist philosophy. This problem is examined in Sartre's *Huis clos*, where the three protagonists are in hell, but a hell of their own making: they are each other's hell ('L'enfer, ce sont les autres'). They are damned precisely because they are dead, and therefore can perform no new acts to wipe out their past deeds. Garcin asks: 'Can you judge a whole life by one act?', to which Inès responds 'It is deeds alone which show what a man has willed' (Cranston 1962: 35).

In Lispector's story there is no Sartrean hell; there are no other people; the crime is known only to the mathematics professor. His crime was not so much the abandoning of his pet as, rather, his attitude towards the dog: he tried to objectivize both himself and the dog in their mutual relationship, as in the Sartrean proscription of love. Love is seen as a process of 'infinite regress', since in wanting to be loved, or in being loved, one's own transcendence is curtailed and one is objectivized, at least in relation to the person by whom one is loved. Correspondingly, in loving someone, one curtails the beloved's liberty (Cranston 1962: 56). This is complicated by the paradox that in desiring love, one merely seeks to be loved oneself; in desiring love/to be loved, one is an *être-pour-soi* seeking to be *en-soi*, and as such, one seeks to avoid ethical responsibility.

The professor's crime is, therefore, the former relationship with his dog, whom he even gave a human name: 'dei-te o nome de José para te dar um nome que te servisse ao mesmo tempo de alma' (I gave you the name José to give you a name that would, at the same time, serve as a soul) (*LF*: 143). Obviously, since the professor mis-recognizes his crime, he cannot expiate his crime.

The final story in *Laços de família* I want to consider is 'A imitação da rosa' ('The Imitation of the Rose'). In this story, the protagonist, the childless Laura, has recently suffered a nervous breakdown. Although recognizing society's need to rationalize and to name everything, she attributes her illness to an 'insuficiência ovariana' (hormonal imbalance) (*LF*: 43). In an effort to compensate for her reduced social role—she has no children to furnish her with an identity as *autrui*—she takes an excessive interest in her home: 'em fazer da sua casa uma coisa impessoal; de certo modo perfeito por ser impessoal' (In making her house something impersonal; in a certain way perfect in its impersonal appearance) (*LF*: 39). It is the contemplation of some wild roses that causes Laura's delicate mental balancing act to fall apart. These roses represent the freedom and the integrity—they merely *are*—that are missing in Laura's life. Although she gives away the roses, it is too late, and when her husband returns home she was 'de nôvo alerta e tranqüila como num tren. Que já partira' (once more alert and serene, as if in a train. That had already left) (*LF*: 58).

In her attempts to exist *pour-soi*, she is considered as mad since society cannot accept her. In her outlining of the impossibility of an outright rejection of the symbolic, Toril Moi points out that a failure to engage in human relationships, that is to say discourse, would result in Lacanian psychosis (Moi 1985: 176).

Before discussing how in *A via crucis do corpo*, Clarice manages to resolve the problem of the lack of space for authentic existence as *être-pour-soi* within the discourse of patriarchy, I should like briefly to consider two novels which are situated chronologically between the two collections of short stories. These are *Uma aprendizagem ou o livro dos prazeres* (*An apprenticeship or the book of pleasures*) (1969) and *Água viva* (White Water) (1973).

Uma aprendizagem ou o livro dos prazeres, published in Brazil in 1969, is the novel that, in my opinion, marks Clarice's passage to a new phase of maturity, in which her characters are no longer quite so isolated in their human angst, managing instead to establish communication with their fellow humans. It is a text that differs considerably from those that precede it. First there are two central characters, and secondly, there is a much greater use of dialogue than previously common in Clarice's work. Like Clarice's other novels, the two characters embark upon a metaphysical journey. Here, however, Lóri and Ulisses are successful in attaining the grail, which is the fulfilment of love. In contrast to the constraining and limiting love of *Laços de família*, the love between the two protagonists of *Uma aprendizagem* is not based upon the infinite regressing of mutual objectivizing; it allows for individual freedom and self-fulfilment as an ever-growing *être-pour-soi*. As Fitz (1987: 431) points out, this psychological achievement is represented in the novel by the physical consummation of their love.

Água viva, published three years later in 1973, once again deals with the themes of love and freedom. Unlike *Uma aprendizagem* it is, however, more concerned with internal, psychological reality than with external relationships. As Fitz indicates, the novel is an unbroken stream of consciousness, centring around the female narrator's quest for rebirth as an individual. This will come about through the successful termination of a previous objectivizing relationship: ' "Fui ao encontro de mim ... Simplesmente eu sou eu. E você é você ... Olha para mim e me ama, Não: tu olhas para ti e te amas" ' (I went to an encounter with myself ... I am simply me. And you are you ... Look at me and love me, No: you look at yourself and love yourself) (Fitz 1985: 85).

Like *Laços de família*, *Água Viva* is once again highly lyrical in its language: it is, perhaps, a return to what preceded *Uma aprendizagem*. The novel ends with the female protagonist still in a state of flux, that is to say as *être-pour-soi*, yet, as Fitz points out, it is not quite a conclusion: we do not know whether the former lover will achieve that same degree of liberation — Fitz suggests that he will not (1985: 91). However, following on from the argument expressed in this analysis, for there to be any one, concrete 'conflict resolving conclusion' would involve a breach of existentialist and poststructuralist philosophy.

It is with the publication of *A via crucis do corpo* (hereafter VC) that the trend established in *Uma aprendizagem* continues to be expanded and developed. Like its forerunner, this collection of short stories affirms the possibility of successful human interaction, with non-hierarchical, non-exploitative relationships, although not in every story. Another similarity between *Via crucis* and *Uma aprendizagem* is the sexual element featured in both — often, though not always, as the means of communication, as in the story entitled 'Melhor do que arder' ('Better than to burn'). As Fitz remarks, there is a link between sexuality and a sense of identity, for example in the story 'Miss Algrave' (1988: 43).

The sexual element included in these stories is, of course, announced by the title of the collection: *A via crucis do corpo* (*The Via Crucis of the Flesh*). The translation of the title into English, however, ignores the dual meaning of the word in Portuguese, where *corpo* can also mean body. Although a valid interpretation of the title could be 'salvation through the flesh' — for the pain of the Way of the Cross (the Via Crucis) is superceded by the Resurrection — it is, perhaps better, to see this work as an example of the much heralded 'return of the body'. This return (or perhaps resurrection) of the body in literature is the replacing of the fixed, and allegedly transcendental, *logos*/phallus with the polysemic signifier that is the body; man's/woman's primal impulses (*triebe*) are corporal. Furthermore, for both Freud and Kristeva, 'the body forms the basis for the constitution of the subject' (Moi 1988: 166). For Kristeva, the disruption of the symbolic by the semiotic is through oral and anal expulsion or rejection; and since these impulses and desires, those of the pre-Oedipal child, are, contrary to patriarchal thinking never mastered, the subject is endlessly *en procès* (Moi 1988: 170). (Any total satisfaction of desire would, as Freud pointed out in 'Beyond the Pleasure Principle', result in death, although this mastery of desire (death drive) is what the phallocentric subject strives for.)

The return of the body is apparent in the story entitled 'Melhor do que arder' ('Better than to Burn'), the protagonist of which is a nun troubled by irrepressible sexual desire: 'Mas na hora em que o padre lhe tocava a boca para dar a hóstia tinha que se controlar para não morder a mão do padre' (But at the moment when the priest touched her mouth to give her the Sacrament she had to stop herself from biting his hand); 'Não podia mais ver o corpo quase nu do Cristo' (She could no longer look at the half-naked body of Christ) (VC: 92).

Although she attempts to annul and repress her desires by mortifying herself, she does so in vain, for as we have seen the primal impulses of the semiotic can never be fully repressed by the symbolic. In this story, however, the symbolic, as represented by the Church, is overthrown when the protagonist leaves the religious life and marries. Yet the use of the term 'overthrow' is misleading, for we have already seen how one cannot retreat into the semiotic; rather we should see this victory as a positing of the possibility of new parameters within which the subject is not redefined, but can be repositioned.

In one of the two title stories, 'O corpo' ('The Body'), it is through female solidarity, however, that communication between the two protagonists is established, enabling once again an overthrow of the dominant phallogocentric symbolic. As well as meaning flesh and body the *corpo* also means corpse. The corpse in the story is that of Xavier, who is described as a *superhomem* (superman) and compared to that symbol of male sexuality, the bull (VC: 30–31). Not content with living bigamously with two women, he also frequents a prostitute, and it is this which leads the two women to rebel. First of all they go on strike in the kitchen and eventually go on to plan and carry through his murder (VC: 31–34). The solidarity between the two women in Xavier's life is built up gradually: we are told that Carmen would let Beatriz read her diary, and then that 'apesar de não serem homossexuais, se excitavam uma à outra e faziam amor. Amor triste' (although they were not homosexuals, they would caress each other and make love. Sad love) (VC: 30).

They murder Xavier, using one knife each, but yet they are not censured: in order to avoid excessive paper work, the police suggest that the two women flee to Montevideo and no more will be said of the matter. The phallus, Xavier, the *superhomem* who, as he admits, cannot be satisfied by the two women he lives with, is displaced. It is interesting that what replaces exclusive heterosexuality is not exclusive homosexuality, but bisexuality. Unlike some radical feminists who posit lesbianism as the only solution to the problem of patriarchy, Cixous, a passionate champion of Lispector, adheres to a solution of *other bisexuality*, which as Moi points out is 'multiple, variable and everchanging' (Moi 1985: 109). This postulation does not contradict Kristeva's aim of deconstructing the false and metaphysical gender identities defined by patriarchal discourse with its (would-be) transcendental signifier of the phallus.

The creation of (apparently) false gender identities is also the subject of the story 'Praça Mauá'. The protagonists of the story are Luísa-Carla, a cabaret dancer, and the homosexual drag queen Celsinho-Moleirão. In their work at a nightclub they both assume false identities on a physical level: Luísa-Carla's make-up transforms her into 'uma boneca de louça' (a china doll) and Celsinho-Moleirão is, as mentioned, a transvestite who uses false eyelashes, and who, through taking hormones, has acquired a 'fac-simile de seios' (something akin to breasts) (VC: 79&81). The two protagonists fall out over a man whom they both desire, and Luísa-Carla accuses Celsinho-Moleirão of not being 'um homem de verdade' (a real man); he retorts that, since she does not even know how to crack an egg, she is not a real woman.

In this story, therefore, we see not only how the concept of 'womanhood' is defined, created and imposed by patriarchal discourse, but also an undoing of the traditional boundaries of 'masculine' and 'feminine'. In the first instance, Luísa-Carla is seen as not being a woman by Celsinho-Moleirão since she does not know how to cook, and, unlike him, she is also childless; yet at the same time, made-up and performing her erotic dances, she is the epitomy of male fantasy, though still not a real woman. Celsinho-Moleirão, like the character Molina in Manuel Puig's film *El beso de la mujer araña* (*The Kiss of the Spider Woman*), does not conform to patriarchal society's concept of the masculine, nor is he really a woman (he can have no idea of what it is like to be a (biological) woman from childhood in a patriarchal society) despite Luísa-Carla's admission at the end that Celsinho, who towards his adopted daughter was a 'verdedeira mãe' (a true mother) was 'mais mulher do que ela' (more of a woman than she) (VC: 80–81&84). In this story we are made to realize the arbitrariness of traditional gender divisions, and, as in the whole collection, there is not only a return of the body, but also a return of the marginalized subject; that is to say a repositioned subject who is *not* defined and written around the phallic signifier.

This repositioning of the subject is a theme explored again in 'Miss Algrave'. Fitz maintains that 'the sexually-orientated scenes of *The Via Crucis of the Flesh* link a character's sexuality with the same character's sense of identity' (1988: 43). Yet, it must be pointed out that the sexuality expressed in these stories is, on the whole, a sexuality that within the context of patriarchal discourse is always marginalized. The non-phallocentric sexuality in this collection is the nucleus around which the stories are structured, and demonstrates the repositioning of the subject. It is a discovery of her sexual identity that liberates Miss Algrave, as Fitz remarks:

> the essential personality is established in terms of her being sexually repressed, isolated in her solitude, and painfully discontent with a superficial and inauthentic existence. Suddenly the unanticipated event happens and her sense of being is irrevocably altered. (1988: 47)

This 'unanticipated event' is the appearance of an extra-terrestrial being who initiates Miss Algrave sexually, giving her her sexual, and therefore, psychological freedom (VC: 20). When she asks who he is, she is given the answer 'Eu sou um eu' (I am an I): that is to say he is a being defined solely in relation to himself (VC: 20).

This process of liberation and self-discovery will and does continue, for we are told that Ixtlan will return (VC: 21). Yet this does not mean that Miss Algrave, now 'uma mulher realizada' (a whole woman) forms her life entirely around the extra-terrestrial; she has and will continue to have sexual relations with other men (VC: 22ff). Her social liberation is represented by her freeing herself from patriarchal domination in the form of the Church and her previous exploitative employer.

Although in this collection of short stories Clarice succeeds in establishing a non-phallogocentric discourse, there are nevertheless cases of exploitation. In 'Mas vai chover' ('But it's going to rain') the widow's sexual satisfaction in her relationship with the gigolo is short lived; it is not long before he begins to exploit her (VC: 98). He eventually demands a million *cruzeiros* as an inducement to continue his relationship with her, and leaves her when she cannot pay, despite her pitiful pleas. Although it may seem that in this story the evils of patriarchy are winning through, this is not entirely so. Once again, in this story, the primacy of the phallus is undermined for we are told that at the age of twenty-seven the gigolo, Alex, will become impotent.

Another distinctive feature of this collection that separates it from Clarice's previous fiction is that, unlike A *paixão segundo* G.H. and *Laços de família*, language plays a role, not as a lyrical mediator in the quest for authenticity, but as a means of communication. Fitz is correct in his assertion that these pieces are extremely unlyrical in tone, and there is little expressive dialogue between the characters; it is in the re-writing of a (his-)story that language becomes central, as well as the importance given to non-verbal language, in the form of sex (Fitz 1988: 41). It is this communication of the author to the reader that is essential.

Unlike *Laços de famíla*, some of these stories have an intradiegetic narrator. In 'Ruído de passos' ('The Sound of Footsteps') it is a third person narrator who directly addresses the protagonist: 'É a vida, senhora Raposo, é a vida. Até a benção da morte' (That's life, senhora Raposo, that's life. Until the blessing of death) (VC: 71). In this story the elderly female protagonist has to achieve sexual satisfaction on her own: once again Clarice posits an alternative, non-phallic form of sexual activity as valid.

In 'Antes da ponte Rio-Niterói' ('Before the Bridge over the River Niterói') the intradiegetic narrator is not only first person, but also admits to being unreliable. The narrator tells us:

> Mas estou me confundindo toda... As realidades dele são inventada. Peço desculpa porque além de contar os fatos também adivinho e o que adivinho aqui escrevo, escrivã que sou por fatalidade. Eu adivinho a realidade. (VC: 73)
> (But I'm getting all confused... All its realities are invented. Forgive me, for in addition to recounting the facts I also guess and what I guess I write down here, as the predestined writer that I am. I guess at reality.)

The story being told us is about a young girl whose leg is amputated, causing the girl's boyfriend to abandon her, even though she does not have long to live. In his relationship with her, the boyfriend has been cheating on the woman with whom he lives (VC: 74). This woman, however, decides to retaliate and pours boiling water into his ear leaving him 'surdo para sempre, logo ele que não perdoara defeito físico' (deaf for the rest of his life, he who would not forgive a physical imperfection) (VC: 75).

This obviously poststructuralist stance regarding the creation of fiction and reality, and the explicit blending of the boundaries between the two, is not unique to this story, occurring also in other stories such as 'A via crucis'. However in 'Rio-Niterói' it is constantly pointed out that the narrator (not necessarily the author) is inventing and imagining an event which took place in the distant past, if ever at all, and this could, in the light of the betrayed woman's revenge and the tone of the other stories in the collection, be seen as another example of subversive discourse in which the marginalized (woman) is able to depose the patriarchal.

Whereas in the stories of *Laços de família* Clarice's prose is highly lyrical and the stories themselves more drawn out, the style of *A via crucis* is more prosaic and the stories pared to the point of being almost schematic. This contrast in style between the two collections is a reflection of a shifting of what one might term the 'campo da batalha' (the battlefield). Prior to *A via crucis* the characters of her fiction tend to attempt to realize authenticity within the confines of patriarchal discourse and, naturally, fail. In *A via crucis* however, the struggle for realization of the self/subject is centred around the return of the pre-Oedipal body. It is only by substituting the polysemy of the pre-Oedipal body for the phallic signifier of the symbolic (with its concommitant desire for possession and mastery), that authenticity as *être-pour-soi* or *sujet en procès* can hope to be achieved by anyone (biologically) male or female, since the fixed phallogocentrism of patriarchal discourse must needs demand rigid, intransigent boundaries and definitions.

Notes

1. See, for example, Nunes (1973), de Sá (1979), and Fitz (1985).
2. See, for example, Fitz (1987).
3. For a detailed bibliography and biography, see Fitz (1985: 1-19).
4. See Cixous (1989).
5. In this study I am employing the Lacanian concept of the phallus, as defined by Weedon (1987: 53).
   > meaning and the symbolic order as a whole, is fixed in relation to a primary transcendental signifier which Lacan calls the phallus, the signifier of sexual difference, which guarantees the patriarchal structure of the symbolic order. The phallus signifies power and control in the symbolic order through control of the satisfaction of desire, the primary source of power within psychoanalytic theory.
6. These are: 'O Crime do Professor de Matemática', 'O Jantar', and 'Começos de uma Fortuna'.
7. For a more detailed discussion of the role of epiphany in Clarice Lispector, see Palls (1984).
8. All translations are my own.

Bibliography

Anderson, R. (1985), 'Myth and Existentialism in Clarice Lispector's O crime do professor de matemática', Luso-Brazilian Review, Vol. XXII(1): 1-7.
de Beauvoir, S. (1956), Le Deuxième Sexe, Paris, Gallimard.
Cixous, H. (1987), 'Reaching the Point of Wheat, or a Portrait of the Artist as a Maturing Woman', New Literary History, Vol. 19(1): 1-21.
Cixous, H. (1989), L'Heure de Clarice Lispector, Paris, des Femmes.
Cranston, M. (1962), Sartre, Edinburgh and London, Oliver and Boyd.
Di Antonio, R. (1985), 'Myth as a Unifying Force in O crime do professor de matemática', Luso-Brazilian Review, Vol. XXII(1): 27-35.
Fitz, E.E. (1980), 'Freedom and Self-realization: Feminist Characterization in the Fiction of Clarice Lispector', Modern Language Studies, Vol. 10(3): 51-61.
Fitz, E.E. (1985), Clarice Lispector, Boston, Twayne.
Fitz, E.E. (1987), 'A Discourse of Silence: The Post-Modernism of Clarice Lispector', Contemporary Literature, Vol. 28(4): 420-436.
Fitz, E.E. (1988), 'A writer in Transition: Clarice Lispector and A via crucis do corpo', Latin American Literary Review, Vol. XVI(32) (July/August): 41-52.
Lacan, J. (1977), Ecrits: A Selection, London, Tavistock Publications.
Lindstrom, N. (1981), 'A Feminist Discourse Analysis of Clarice Lispector's "Daydreams of a Drunken Housewife" ', Latin American Literary Review, Vol. 9 (Fall/Winter): 7-16.
Lindstrom, N. (1982), 'A Discourse Analysis of "Preciosidade" by Clarice Lispector', Luso-Brazilian Review, Vol. IX(2): 187-195.
Lispector, C. (1969), Uma aprendizagem ou o livro dos prazeres, Rio de Janeiro, Editôra Sabiá.
Lispector, C. (1970), Laços de família (5th edition), Rio de Janeiro, Editôra Sabiá.
Lispector, C. (1973), Agua Viva, Rio de Janeiro, Editôra Sabiá.
Lispector, C. (1974), A via crucis do corpo (1st edition), Rio de Janeiro, Editôra Artenova.
Lucas, F. (1976), Poesia e Prosa no Brasil, Belo Horizonte, Interlivros de Minas Gerais.
Moi, T. (1985), Sexual/Textual Politics: Feminist Literary Theory, London and New York, Routledge.
Nunes, B. (1973), Clarice Lispector, Bela Vista, São Paulo, Edições Quiron.
Palls, T.L. (1984), 'The Miracle of the Ordinary: Literary Epiphany in Virginia Woolf and Clarice Lispector', Luso-Brazilian Review, Vol. XXI(1): 63-78.
Piexoto, M. (1983), 'Family Ties: Female Development in Clarice Lispector', in Abel, E., Hirsch, M. and Langland, E. (1983), The Voyage In: Fictions of Female Development, Hanover (N.H.) and London, University Press of New England for Dartmouth College, 287-303.
de Sá, O. (1979), A Escritura de Clarice Lispector, Rio de Janeiro, Editôra Vozez Ltda.
Senna, M. de (1986), 'A Imitação da Rosa by Clarice Lispector: An Interpretation', Portuguese Studies, Vol. 2: 159-165.
Weedon, C. (1987), Feminist Practice and Poststructuralist Theory, Oxford, Basil Blackwell.
Wheeler, A.M. (1987), 'Animal Imagery as Reflection of Gender Role in Clarice Lispector's Family Ties', Critique, Vol. 23(3): 125-134.

12 Portrait of the Subject as a Young Man: The Construction of Masculinity Ironized in 'Male' Fiction
Lynda Broughton

> Women [in Freud's introduction to his 1932 lecture on 'Femininity'] are considered merely as the *objects* of desire, and as the *objects* of the question. To the extent that women 'are the question' [of what is femininity], they cannot *enunciate* the question; they cannot be the speaking *subjects* of the knowledge or the science which the question seeks.
>
> [Freud's] question: 'what is femininity? in reality asks: what is femininity—*for men?* (Felman 1981: 20; author's emphasis)

In her extraordinary 1981 article 'Rereading Femininity', in which she presents a reading of Balzac's story 'The Girl with Golden Eyes' through Freud's 'Femininity' (1932), Shoshana Felman places herself, and by implication the reader of all three texts involved—that is, Freud's, Balzac's and her own—in the position of the woman reader (re)reading femininity in a 'male' text. In so doing she anticipates Jonathan Culler's question in *On Deconstruction* (1983) of what happens to a text when one reads it *as a woman*; that is, from the position of a woman experiencing a text from a female perspective, so far as that can ever be identified. In other words, Felman is asking, as I should like to ask, what happens to a (male) text if we come to it with other than male assumptions, which are so often presented as in some way neutral or universal?

Culler's question, while useful as a starting point in feminist literary study, is of course flawed in that it assumes that to 'read as a woman' is to perform an undifferentiated, singular act of reading—the same as reading 'as a man'—only from the opposite side, as it were. The question itself represents an important division in feminist literary studies; a division which, it seems, has to be addressed whenever the problem of feminist interpretation of the 'male' text is discussed. Culler's question—which we might, with some justification, refer to as seminal—requires that we cut loose from the constraints imposed by patriarchal critical practice and read from a position which does not even attempt to pass itself off as anything but partisan. To 'read as a woman' is not only to read from a position defined by one's experience of being female, particularly of being female in a patriarchal culture; it is to place oneself as reader within a specific, identifiable, feminist critical practice. Notwithstanding the variations in feminist literary theory, 'reading as a woman' is an act of interpretation of the literary text which takes account of a concept which, for feminism, is as formative as it is double-edged: the idea of the otherness of the feminine, and the interpretation and analysis of the uses to which, historically, the idea of the otherness of femininity has been put. It must be stressed, however, that to concentrate feminist energies on this work of rereading 'male' texts is not to deny the importance to feminist scholarship of the study of women writers; neither is it to undermine the need for radical reassessment, within educational institutions at all levels, of the texts which are offered to pupils and students as being of value. On the contrary, the rereading of the 'male' text is an essential part of this work. Indeed, I would argue strongly for the need to encourage those we teach to become rereaders, rather than just readers, of the texts we offer them; to encourage them to become aware that their position as readers in relation to the text is not, cannot be, 'objective' or neutral; to politicise the act of reading. To 'read as a woman', therefore, to reiterate Culler's phrase, is to read as the other, from the stated position of the other; it is also to locate otherness in the text, to problematize the position of the subject. This kind of rereading of 'male' texts — that is, as far as it can be defined, texts written from a perspective which privileges what are traditionally understood to be patriarchal values — allows us to apply a form of effective cultural critique; we ask awkward questions of the text and see what happens.

What happens in the case of reading Balzac's story, Felman argues, is that a new level of reading, particularly of reading sexual difference, is opened up so that the story becomes, through Felman's reading of it, 'a provocative erotic riddle' in the course of the solution of which the structure of sexual difference is revealed. This comes about by means of an examination of the analogy between the structures of wealth (the acquisition and possession of gold) and the structures of gender and power. The hero's quest for possession of the (idealized and initially un-known) love-object, whom he knows only as 'the girl with the golden eyes' transforms her, according to Felman's analysis, into a metaphor for *male* sexuality; signifying not herself, but him. The girl, Paquita, represents a 'package' of knowledges which he must unwrap; a 'problem' he must solve and so possess a solution to the riddle of femininity. Felman defines this process as follows:

> Defined by man, the conventional polarity of masculine and feminine names woman as a *metaphor of man*. Sexuality, in other words, functions here as the sign of a rhetorical convention, of which woman is the *signifier* and man the *signified*. Man alone thus has the privilege of proper meaning, of *literal* identity: femininity, as signifier, cannot signify *itself*; it is but a metaphor, a figurative substitute; it can but refer to man, to the phallus, as its proper meaning, as its signified. (Felman 1981: 25; author's emphasis)

The resulting hierarchy of sexualities, Felman argues, has as its consequence the suppression of woman's difference from man, shown in the absence, within male discourse, of her subjectivity; within her silence as speaking subject. The function of femininity within patriarchal discourse, therefore, as revealed within the Lacanian psychoanalytic discourse which informs Felman's playful reading, is both to define and to justify male sexuality.[1]

It is this relation, which places femininity at the service of masculinity, which informs both the characteristics of 'male' fiction (and thereby fictionalizes both masculinity and femininity) and the rhetoric of pornography. Clearly, to make such an assertion is to equate 'male' writing with pornography, a generalization which is obviously false and one which, were I to make it, would invite the charge of feminist extremism. To examine the rhetoric of the 'male' text, from the position of the woman reader, however, is to be able to identify those textual strategies which such writing uses to reinforce patriarchal interests, principal among which is the subordination of women. However, rereading 'male' fictions also enables the feminist reader to apply the same playful analysis to the subject of masculinity, since this is frequently the 'hidden' subject of 'male' writing. Masculinity's sense of itself, recent commentary on the question has suggested,[2] is a construct so frail that it must be constantly reinforced, constantly rewritten; the woman reader of the 'male' text frequently finds herself, to use Simone de Beauvoir's phrase (1953), in the position of one listening to a little boy telling himself stories, rebuilding himself as subject through the hierarchical structures of sexual difference.

The purpose of this paper was originally to produce a reading of Ian McEwan's (1975) short story 'Homemade', to be presented to a meeting of a feminist theory group at the University of Strathclyde in the context of the general question of whether it is ever possible to identify such a thing as a 'male' text—that is, a text not only (or not even) written by a male author, but one which could be said to be recognizable as belonging within 'male' discourse. The enterprise itself begs several questions, as the group's subsequent discussion of the story came to reveal. How, we wondered, do we as readers recognize a 'male' text? What criteria are we to apply? Are we to concern ourselves solely with the sex of the author? Obviously not. With the content? Possibly. With the position of the narrator, or the tone of the narrative voice? Perhaps. With the representation of received knowledges about sexual difference? Easier. With the language? Or the story's sexual politics? Or the length and syntactical structure of the sentences? Or any combination of these or other possible markers of 'male' writing? Whose categories are these anyway? Is a 'male' text one which privileges patriarchal values, or one which is written from an obviously male perspective so that the viewpoint we, as readers of the text, are given and invited to share is inevitably a male viewpoint, a discursive power strategy which effectively marginalizes the dissenting woman reader? Most unsettling of all, given unmarked extracts from texts we do not know, how do we decide whether these are 'male' or 'female' texts?; the question, of course, which brings the argument back full-circle—how do we recognize the gendered text?

The answer, which can only lend ammunition to those for whom feminist critical practice is flawed by a lack of 'rigour', is that there is no 'scientific' method of doing this. This is not to say that there are not recognizable markers of 'male' texts. In the 'male' text, whatever the sex of the writer, the subject of discourse is male and the narrative celebrates the characteristics of the hero: singular, sublime, mediating the world through the special consciousness of the transcendental subject, privileged, central, essential; characteristics which, it will become apparent, the subject-narrator of McEwan's story ascribes to himself. This is a view of the heroic which encompasses both Romantic texts in which the writer is the hero of his own narrative, and the Bradleyan view of Shakespeare's tragic heroes: masculinity as glorious, noble fantasy.[3] In 'male' fiction the unitary (and usually male) consciousness is elevated to the status of an icon, and the male writer's version of individual experience, which enjoys privileged status and canonical recognition, has continued to occupy the literary high ground. Moreover, texts can be 'male' (in that they privilege a more or less mythologized masculinity and incorporate patriarchal values) even if they have been written by women; an important distinction which complicates the question still further. As an article in *The Guardian* accusing feminists of forcing the exclusion of Martin Amis' novel *London Fields* from the shortlist for the 1989 Booker Prize suggested, violence and pornography cannot be said to be markers of 'male' writing if women write pornographic and violent fiction, can they?[4] The question (at least as I am posing it) is not rhetorical, of course, but ironic.

If a 'male' text is not, however, necessarily one written by a male author, can we argue that it is one written from within a set of patriarchal discursive strategies — 'male' texts being texts which are conservative in the assumptions about sexual difference which inform them? Accordingly, in a 'male' text we are likely to find that received ideas about masculinity and femininity are reproduced, and that the uses to which these stereotyped ideas are put reinforce the naturalization of sexual difference. 'Male' texts reproduce patriarchal myths about women, particularly about women's sexuality, and reinforce the ideology of fear and control which informs male attitudes to woman as a sexual being. 'Male' texts, then, however authored, categorize and stereotype women: angel, whore, wife, mother, witch, bitch, pricktease, jailbait, her indoors, she who must be obeyed; the demonology of fear and loathing with which we are all tediously familiar. These stereotypes, we know, limit and define women in relation to men, and to what received male wisdom 'knows' femininity to be in terms of the metaphorical relation identified by Felman; women is (or should be) the signifier, man the signified.

Feminist critique of the sexual politics of the text in the second half of this century has shown that in a 'male' text, woman functions in precisely this metaphorical way. She is presented and defined, as in Balzac's story, as in McEwan's, in relation to man, constructing him out of her own otherness. He is subject, she is object; her image is refracted through a masculine lens so that the version of femininity which is available to the reader is mediated through male fantasies. Female sexuality, in 'Homemade' as elsewhere, is construed in terms of appearances and mythologies, of an object-status which is not limited to the quasi-pornographic arena of 'pulp' fiction; Charlotte Brontë's *Jane Eyre* does it too. This paradox, in which the active object constructs the passive subject, is one of the many irrationalities which is revealed when we begin to consider the means by which what we recognize as sexual difference comes to have meaning. The privileging of male subjectivity is so entrenched that, in a 'male' text, a hierarchy of meanings is assumed so that what a man is, knows, desires, sees, thinks, does, is privileged over what a woman is, knows, desires, etc. Thus 'male' writing recreates a fictionalized discourse in which man is the subject and woman is the object, even if a woman writes it; even if the speaking subject — the 'I' of the discourse in a first-person narrative — is female, as it often purports to be in pornographic writing. If 'male' fiction tells the story of woman, it is woman as seen, 'known' within the parameters of a discourse which has been appropriated by patriarchy.

In *Psychoanalysis and Feminism* (1974) which is subtitled 'a radical reassessment of Freudian psychoanalysis', Juliet Mitchell argues that 'however it may have been used, psychoanalysis is not a recommendation *for* a patriarchal society, but an analysis *of* one' (Mitchell 1974: xv). However much this may read like wishful thinking given the central preoccupations of Freudian psychoanalysis which appear irredeemably patriarchal,[5] Mitchell's argument, which suggests that psychoanalysis can be read against itself, is helpful in the sense that it offers a feminist position from which to read an apparently patriarchal body of texts. Moreover, Shoshana Felman's playful rereading of Balzac, using the word-play which proceeds indirectly from Freud's recognition of the function of metaphor and pun in the unconscious and in dreaming, gives scope for an even more subversive feminist reinterpretation of the 'male' text. As hostile feminist critics of psychoanalysis have argued, Freud's analysis of the origins of sexual difference and the processes by which gender identity is acquired, places a scientific gloss on ancient theological theories of gender, which themselves were rationalizations of primitive, and, it would appear, pancultural fears and fantasies about the female body and its functions. The institutionalized inferiority of women is justified by Freud, as we know, in terms which privilege the phallus without distinguishing clearly enough between the literal (the flesh and blood penis) and the metaphorical (the phallus, symbol of power and privilege). In the resulting confusion the phallus, literal or otherwise, thus becomes a metaphor for the self: it is the letter 'I', the number 1, the singular, unique subject of its own discourse and the story of 'I' displaces all other stories in a single, privileged act of writing—the construction of the subject.

The problem with this, for feminism, is that the position of woman within the set of values which inform 'male' writing is, as in McEwan's story, ambiguous. The feminine is both known—defined, stereotyped, all wrapped up—and unknown—alien, chaotic, terrifyingly 'other'. In 'Homemade', the subject of the story presents himself, within the context of a series of literary allusions, as the Romantic hero whose quest is the search for the 'fleshly grail' of adult knowledges, the last and most desirable of which is the female body, the 'last fur-lined chamber of that vast, gloomy and delectable mansion, adulthood' (McEwan 1976: 12). The 'freshly grail' he seeks, it is revealed, is cunt—the hero does not yet know what it is, but he knows that, like Everest, it is there. It is the unknowability of the dark gothic mystery, woman, which makes it desirable; once incestuously known, the female body is no longer desired and is left, ten years old and weeping, on the edge of the bath while the 14-year-old hero celebrates the success of his quest in glorious self-absorption, alone.

Thus the story appears to reproduce the familiar textual strategy of glorifying the notion of the hero as a man alone—singular, complete, unified; the integrated, inviolable 'I' elevated to mythic status—while at the same time ironizing it. The hero's introspection, his celebration of his separateness from the society in which he finds himself—the world of petty domestic routine, of meaningless competition and ill-paid, repetitive and ultimately futile work—belongs to the tradition of high romance which the literary allusions in the story reinforce. The story is told from a self-consciously literary perspective, and is peppered with allusions to other texts which similarly celebrate male quests, the acquisition of knowledges and specifically male journeys from innocence to experience. This is the boy as hero of his own narrative, the male self celebrated as conqueror. And yet there are ironizing devices in the text which turn it back on itself; or rather, they produce an internal distancing effect. There is, admittedly, in this text, a narrative voice which represents itself as the locus of meaning, but it is a voice which is consistently aware of the ironic spaces in its discourse; a double irony which opens up the making of the text as it opens up the making of the subject.

The story traces the hero's progress from innocence to experience under the tutelage of his friend Raymond, who is a year or so older and confers on the hero a series of knowledges which, ironically, he himself cannot use. Raymond introduces the hero to the pleasures of an adolescent version of the adult world—alcohol, dope, crime, dirty stories, horror movies, masturbation—all of which the hero takes to with considerable pleasure and success while poor Raymond finds only discomfort and boredom. The hero despises and rejects the realities of adult life in the repressed, 'respectable' social class from which he comes: dull and unrewarding work, loyalty to exploitative employers, petty family responsibilities. His father's gifts of pocket money and homespun wisdom are pathetic in the face of the hero's growing knowledge and economic power, since by selling stolen books—stolen knowledges—to a second-hand dealer in the Mile End Road he can earn more than his father and uncles can after a week's backbreaking work. Most of all, he despises the stupefying dreariness of domestic life, represented in the story not so much by his parents' lives (as in many children's stories the parents are conveniently absent or ignored throughout, except when a point is to be made), as by his little sister's fantasy games of 'Mummies and Daddies'.

As he gains experience of the 'adult' pleasures provided by Raymond, the hero acquires, through his own detachment from it, a knowledge of human futility. There is a sequence in the story when, as the detached and superior spectator at a school cross-country race, he takes pleasure in waiting until the final stragglers—one of whom, of course, is Raymond—are painfully finishing the race, long after the winners have gone home:

> ...and then suddenly...discern[ing] on the far side of the field a limp white blob slowly making its way to the tunnel, slowly measuring out with numb feet on the wet grass its micro-destiny of utter futility. And there beneath the brooding metropolitan sky, as if to unify the complex totality of organic evolution and human purpose and place it within my grasp, the tiny amoebic blob across the field took on human shape...just life, just faceless, self-renewing life to which, as the figure jack-knifed to the ground by the finishing line, my heart warmed, my spirit rose in the fulsome abandonment of morbid and fatal identification with the cosmic life process—the Logos. (McEwan 1976: 17)

This futile struggle, analogous at once to conception, birth and death, becomes, within the story, a metaphor for life itself as most people he knows will live it—painful, without reward, noble and at the same time profoundly comic: ' "Long before I knew it" ', the narrator says, ' "I was a student, a promising student, of irony" ' (McEwan 1976: 15). The narrative constantly operates on this double level, recounting the events which constitute the hero's progress from innocence to experience with the detached, adult literariness of the narrator.

The last of the knowledges the hero is to acquire is, of course, sexual knowledge, knowledge of woman; for him and for Raymond the most terrifying knowledge of all, and yet from the point of view of the narrator the most comic, absurd and ultimately squalid. The boy already knows the theory, from sitting in cafés listening to men talking about their sexual encounters. These stories of male sexuality, overheard without understanding by the boy but recalled with relish by the skilled adult narrator, are told in terms of 'an unreal complex of timeworn puns and innuendo, formulas, slogans, folklore and bravado' which the hero stores away for future reference and out of which he constructs, 'augmented by a quick reading of the more interesting parts of Havelock Ellis and Henry Miller' a reputation as a juvenile 'connoisseur of coitus ... [and] all this after only one fuck — the subject of this story' (McEwan 1976: 14). Promised an encounter with a girl called Lulu Smith, whose reputation for sex is of legendary proportions:

> [a] heaving, steaming leg-load of schoolgirl flesh who had, so reputation insisted, had it with a giraffe, a humming-bird, a man with a iron lung (who had subsequently died), a yak, Cassius Clay, a marmoset, a Mars Bar and the gear stick of her grandfather's Morris Minor (and subsequently a traffic warden) (McEwan 1976: 13)

in the course of which he will be allowed to 'see it for a shilling', the hero decides to make preliminary reconnaissance, to increase his prior knowledge, by seducing his ten-year-old sister. He lures her into his parents' bedroom as part of her favourite game of 'Mummies and Daddies' and attempts, without success, to have sex with her with the only humiliating result that she laughs both at the idea and at him — or rather at his signifier, his ineffectual penis, ' *"So silly, it looks so silly"* ' — until, as he is about to give up, she touches him on the elbow: ' "I know where it goes" ', she says (McEwan 1976: 23; author's emphasis). In this shocking moment the child Connie acquires a different kind of significance; from being a petulant, unattractive little-sister figure, she assumes in that moment the mythic, symbolic status of woman — the idea of woman as the terrifying, knowing, unknowable other which informs 'male' fictions. Connie both has knowledge and is herself the embodiment of knowledge — *con/naissance*.

Thus in the text sexual difference becomes word-play, a matter of conning. To 'con' is both to learn and to trick someone by supplying them with false meanings, as in 'con-man'. The translinguistic pun on *connaissance* reminds us that *con* is French for cunt; used in France as an insulting epithet, as well as a pejorative term for the vulva and vagina, as it is in English. 'Knowledge' has well-known sexual connotations in English, in which 'to know' has a double meaning. Thus, among its other literary allusions, the story includes an echo of the mythology of the Fall of Man, in which both knowledge and sex are placed in the province of Woman, whose misuse of them caused Man to be thrown out of paradise and thereby brought suffering and death into the world, and the punishment of eternal subordination upon herself. *Con/naissance* is both knowledge, and birth (*naissance*) through knowledge: birth through the *con* and birth of a *con*. The story of the Fall shows that this birth is also death: the death of the body, the 'death' of orgasm, the cosmic beginning and end of everything. It is the universal rite of passage of all humanity, all (with superhuman, mythic exceptions) experiencing birth through that fleshly access route to life. This final, carnal *connaissance*, this 'dawning of his sexual day', this birth of the hero triumphant, literalizing his phallic subjectivity into his erect penis, joining 'that superior half of humanity who had known coitus and fertilized the world with it', is thus a kind of *con/naissance* of the subject — the birth of the hero-as-a-man takes place through the con/quest of Con/nie; at once the knowing little girl and the innocent 'inter-galactic-earth-goddess-housewife' (McEwan 1976: 20), who is both desired knowledge and abstract, feared, unknown cunt; both desire itself and its object.

The irony of Connie's knowledge — '"I know where it goes"' — problematizes her in relation to the hero. Connie 'knows' instinctively, just knows, is in charge of the game for a second; her knowledge, which seems to come from nowhere is what the hero has been searching for all along and has been unable to find. In his knowledge, knowledge which he steals from her, is born her suffering and his disaffection. We seem to be firmly back in the province of male meanings, in the area of discourse which privileges the male order of things and celebrates the hero's search for knowledge; there are references in the story to *The Divine Comedy*, to *Faustus*, to *The Prelude*. However if, as I am suggesting, the story can be read against itself so that, in Shoshana Felman's words, we can 'interfere' with the relationship between the signifier and the signified in this story, what is there to disrupt the hierarchical division between author and reader who, however much she may wish to dissent, is placed by the narrator's celebratory tone in the position of admiring voyeur whether she wishes to collude with the story or not?

The narrative is constructed so that the narrator controls the pace of the encounter, teasing the reader — 'you must be patient' — so that the effect is of a hierarchy of knowledges in which the narrator, who 'knows' the story, is in a superior position to that of the reader who does not. The events of the story are recounted out of chronological sequence so that the narrator is able to privilege his sexual initiation over the other knowledges he acquires: important though it is that the reader should know how, and by what means, his entry into the adult world is achieved, it is the 'terrifyingly obscure' territory of female sexuality which he most desires to conquer and colonize — recognizably 'male' strategies which the reader is invited to endorse and celebrate. Woman — the feminine — is present in the story as a set of grotesque, depersonalized, bestial and territorial images. The hero's mother is 'vast' — continental in proportions — and monstrously hideous, her skin 'hanging from her like flayed toad-hides' (McEwan 1976: 14), in the manner of Spenser's female monsters in *The Faerie Queene*. His sister is 'an ugly bat'. The initial object of his sexual curiosity, Lulu Smith — the name suggests both sexual availability and the anonymity of the most common English surname, a kind of sexual Everywoman — is also described in terms of monstrosity and physical grossness: huge, her 'physical enormity was matched only by the enormity of her reputed sexual appetite' (McEwan 1976: 12). Woman in this adolescent male discourse is an unknowable space, a dark continent, ('Zulu Lulu'), known only in fantasies, innuendo and male mythologies constructed in word-games over mugs of tea. Woman is a fictional device; her 'otherness' is both the cause and the effect of the hero's fantasies. Her body, the 'last room in the mansion', is simultaneously a challenge and the object of unspeakable terror. The hero's imagination constructs female sexuality in Mediaeval terms; the grotesqueness of the imagery represents female sexuality as bestial and alien, a chaotic darkness into which the hero must plunge. All of these are familiar literary devices, constructing a fictionalized masculinity out of its difference from fictionalized versions of the feminine.

I want to suggest, however, that by playing games with what might be called the 'writerliness' of the text, the story offers ironic fissures through which a rereading of it is not only made possible but seems positively to be invited. Not only the unpleasantness of the story, but the manner in which it is told, function as ironizing devices in that the reader is being asked to collude within the 'literary' genre of the short story, with a tale of 'innocent' subjectivity which reveals itself as monstrous, being constructed out of cruelty, perversion and an unrepentent criminality which suggests a pornographic psychosis. On the surface the story appears to be the unproblematized recounting of a particularly unpleasant domestic crime (incest, child-abuse), from a subject position within a disordered version of patriarchal authority: the events of the story are described with shocking detachment and chillingly good-humoured affection from an adult perspective which appears to invite the reader to share both its misogyny and its celebratory tone, both of which are presented unproblematically. The shock of this 'adult' detachment—the coolness with which the narrator remembers the torture of birds in the park, for example; the roasting alive of a budgerigar, feeding glass splinters to pigeons— combines with his celebration of adolescent male competitiveness (competitions in getting drunk, shoplifting, masturbating, which the hero always wins) to present what is, according to the criteria already given, a text which is 'male' to excess. And yet it is this very detachment which signals the literariness of the text. The reader is invited to read the story within a certain literary context, at least one example of which tells the story of the quest for knowledge as ultimately futile; having used up his life in the meaningless and rewardless quest for the 'grail' of delight Faustus, damned, descends to hell for ever. The very notion of the grail is a metaphor for futile searching: the reward is nothing, because there is nothing there[6].

This literariness in turn signals the construction of the story of acquired masculine knowledge—or masculinity *through* knowledge—as a textual strategy, the writing of a story about the writing of a story; masculinity itself as a work of creative fiction; *homme*/made. The possibilities for word-play and punning make this text-within-a-text a series of secrets to which the reader is admitted, replicating the strategy of the text itself so that the story becomes entirely self-referencing, signposting its own construction. In a replication of the sexual relation between the boy and his sister it allows the reader to participate in its knowledges, its areas of *connaissance*, with the result that, through the devices of language, we are able to gain access to an ironizing layer of meanings. Which is not to say that it ceases to function as a rather nasty piece of pornography.

Which must alert us, as feminist readers encountering this story, to a further problem—how far *can* a text like this be ironized? How far is it self-ironizing? (One is reminded of the recent television series *Blackeyes* which was supposed to ironize male fantasies of women and failed.) How do we recognize the markers of irony if a woman-hating story is offered, apparently unproblematically, within a context of woman-hating discourses[7] in a woman-hating society? The hero calls himself 'a promising student of irony'—*what* is he ironizing? His own acquired masculinity? To what extent can we read this story against the grain of its own declared assumptions? Are there openings in the text through which an ironic reading is made possible, or does the text impose a (masculine) closure on itself and forbid such acts of feminist contradiction?

How far is the writer teasing us? Is the narrator telling the truth? Could it be that the author is playing a double game, offering both a feminist and an anti-feminist text at the same time, attempting, as it were, to subvert sexual difference entirely by having it both ways? These are questions which the story itself appears to taunt us with, questions which are inextricably linked with the problematic relation between feminism and pornography, and with reading (and representing) femininity in a patriarchal culture.

Postscript

When we discussed these questions at the original session at Strathclyde, some members of the group wanted to have nothing to do with the debate, feeling that to credit the story with being self-ironizing was to collude with its sexual politics and that a more radical definition of 'male' discourse than mine should be applied. It is, after all, depressingly easy to imagine 'Homemade', or something very like it, appearing in the pages of some sleazy 'men's magazine', where pleasures very different from mine might be elicited from the text. The pleasure of 'Homemade' for me is an entirely subversive one, a matter of rereading and revision of what I am calling a 'male' text; and here the scare-quotes are appropriate, I feel, since it is never entirely clear whether in fact this is a 'male' text at all.

Notes

1. In *Reading Woman: Essays in Feminist Criticism* (1986), Mary Jacobus suggests that Balzac's hero 'can be viewed as a man in search of his own phallus' in his pursuit of the girl with the golden eyes. Woman in the text thus functions as a metaphor for man as the phallus is in metonymic relation to him; it is himself he seeks. Jacobus' (double-edged) argument derives from Lacan's analysis of the relation of the signifier to the signified in language in 'Agency in the Letter of the Unconscious, Or Reason Since Freud', in Lacan (1977), p 146-178.
2. See, for example, Tolson (1977), Metcalf and Humphries (1985), Chapman and Rutherford (1988).
3. Jane Ellison, 'Battle Fields', *The Guardian*, October 12 1989: 21 and subsequent correspondence.
4. See Bradley (1971), 'lecture 1', for an outline of this still influential view.
5. Lacan (1977: 281-92) has extended Freud's castration complex into a total metaphor for female deprivation.
6. In the Renaissance period the word 'nothing' could be used to stand for the female genitals; hence the pun in the title of Shakespeare's play *Much Ado About Nothing* or Hamlet's response to Ophelia's 'I think nothing, my Lord' — 'That's a fair thought to lie between maids' legs' (*Hamlet* 3.2. 113-4). See David Willbern (1980) for a psychoanalytic reading of the use to which the notion of 'nothing' is put in Shakespeare. 'Nothing' also denotes absence, lack: in Freud's description of sexual difference the girl's 'castration' (lack of the penis/phallus which distinguishes masculinity by its presence) is the mark (stigma?) of femininity, as well as an object of horror and anxiety for the boy. McEwan's hero is rewarded with many aspects of 'nothing': his triumph is both literally and metaphorically hollow. Feminist objections to Freud's apparent literalizing of the metaphorical phallus however would include the observation that this is a con/tradiction, since an absence is being

defined in terms of a presence. What 'lies between maids' legs' is not nothing, but something.
7. The other stories in *First Love Last Rites* are equally problematic in content. In one, 'Solid Geometry', a woman is made to disappear through a fold (a vulval implication?) in time and space. In another, 'Butterflies', a small girl is murdered by a young male psychopath.

Bibliography

de Beavoir, S. (1953), *The Second Sex* (tr. H.M. Parshley), Harmondsworth, Penguin.
Bradley, A.C. (1971), *Shakespearean Tragedy*, London, MacMillan.
Chapman, R. and Rutherford, J. (eds) (1988), *Male Order: Unwrapping Masculinity*, London, Lawrence and Wishart.
Culler, J. (1983), *On Deconstruction*, London and Henley, Routledge & Kegan Paul.
Felman, S. (1981), 'Rereading Femininity', *Yale French Studies*, 62: 19-44.
Freud, S. (1932), 'Femininity', in Freud, S. (1964), *The Complete Psychological Works of Sigmund Freud*, Vol. XXII (1932-36) (tr. James Strachey), London, The Hogarth Press and The Institute of Psycho-analysis, 112-135.
Jacobus, M. (1986), *Reading Woman: Essays In Feminist Criticism*, London, Methuen.
Lacan, J. (1977), *Ecrits: A Selection* (tr. Alan Sheridan), London, Tavistock Publications.
McEwan, I. (1975), 'Homemade', *First Love Last Rites*, London, Pan Books, 9-24.
Metcalf, A. and Humphries, M. (eds) (1985), *The Sexuality of Men*, London, Pluto Press.
Mitchell, J. (1974), *Psychoanalysis and Feminism*, Harmondsworth, Penguin.
Tolson, A. (1977), *The Limits of Masculinity*, London, Tavistock Publications.
Willbern, D. (1980), 'Shakespeare's Nothing', in Schwartz, M. and Kahn, C. (eds) (1980), *Representing Shakespeare*, Baltimore, Johns Hopkins University Press, 224-263.

13 The Spaced-out Subject: Bachelard and Perec
Jamie Brassett

> A certificate tells me that I was born. I repudiate this certificate: I am not a poet but a poem. A poem that is being written, even if it looks like a subject. (Lacan, 1979: viii)

Introduction

Contemporary continental philosophy has destroyed the subject. It has produced a rigorous critique of the notion of subjectivity, as it has been stated at least since Kant, arguing against the accepted belief in a homogeneous, internalized, located-just-behind-the-eyes, individual subject. Contemporary philosophy forces us to look at what was called the subject, not as the spring of consciousness but as something which is structured from without. The importance of external forces in the development of subjectivity has been accentuated by thinkers such as Marx and Freud, whereas the rejection of the idea of a simple subject has been undertaken by Nietzsche and his contemporary followers.

The critique of the subject by contemporary philosophy is not what I'm going to argue against. Indeed, I take its premisses and agree with its project. Nevertheless, I think that it is important to provide a new way of looking at what we still call/think of as the subject. For even though we can do away with the Western metaphysical idea of the unified, interior *Ursprung* of consciousness, we cannot get away from the fact that the spatial situation of our bodies (with respect to others, or to society as a whole) acts as a particular locus for experience (if we want to be existentialists); a surface upon which intensities flow (if we want to follow Deleuze and Guattari); or, a site of the interpenetration of texts (if we want to be Derridians).

In the following essay, I want to argue that the ordering principle behind the construction of our notion of subjectivity is space. We move in space, through spaces. We think and remember ourselves in spaces; to have a childhood memory, or to remember an event from one's childhood (and I will return to this theme later with respect to Perec), is to re-enact an event according to the space in which it happened. This is what I call constructing. Furthermore, this (self-)constructing happens by means of stories — memories are told (to oneself or an other) and are themselves structured to make a story; sometimes textualized, often fragmentary, but structured nevertheless. Stories in space.

As such, the notion of subjectivity with which I am going to work—maybe I should say, put to work—is one which is always heterogenous, fluid and collective: heterogenous because the story one tells to oneself of one's own life is one that is made up of disparate elements—perceptions, memories, fantasies, etc[1]—this fictionalization only marking a temporary solidification; and collective because what can be more 'interindividual territory' than space? The space that I will examine is, specifically, lived-in space—ie the house—and will begin with an examination of the same theme in Gaston Bachelard's (1958) *La Poétique de l'espace*,[2] followed by a further examination of the subject/space motif in some of Perec's works, notably (1970) *La Vie mode d'emploi*.[3]

In the first section using Bachelard, I outline his theory of topo-analysis. Briefly—because I will return to it in more detail—this consists in moving through literary texts (usually, in Bachelard's case, poetic ones) remarking upon various psychological, psychoanalytical, philosophical themes, motifs, or repressions, which appear to be at work within them. Topo-analysis, then, is a method which in being primarily eclectic, cannot help but view the text as a disunity. For how could the psycho-philosophical contours of a text be charted if it were seen as a homogeneous whole, living and residing, finding its meaning within itself? Topo-analysis, as a philosophical method, already admits of heterogeneity of/between texts; and its product realizes itself as a fictionalizing, itself a story-telling. The motive force of my analysis of the texts of Bachelard and Perec will be topo-analytical, although of a different brand to Bachelard's. This essay will move through the different stages of the texts I've chosen to study, with the aim of producing a map, or draughting the structure, of the spatial construction of the subject.

The Subject of the House in Bachelard

> ...the house images move in both directions: they are in us as much as we are in them, and the play is so varied that two long chapters are needed to outline the implications of house images. (Bachelard 1969: 19)

Bachelard devotes the two opening chapters of *The Poetics of Space* to the house: chapter one—'The House. From Cellar to Garret. The Significance of the Hut'; chapter two—'House and Universe'. In the first chapter, as in the 'Introduction', Bachelard outlines his method for analysing the house/subject image. He calls this strategy topo-analysis:

> Descriptive psychology, depth psychology, psychoanalysis and phenomenology could constitute, with the house, the corpus of doctrines that I have designated by the name of topo-analysis. On whatever theoretical horizon we examine it, the house image would appear to have become the topography of our intimate being. (Bachelard 1969: xxxii)

A topo-analysis, then, involves a multidisciplinary reading of our intimate space; by looking at those spaces which constitute our 'intimate being'—the best places, for Bachelard, are in the imaginative reveries of poetry—Bachelard will accomplish a multitude of ends. He will examine the dialectical movement that inscribes the house within us simultaneously as we situate ourselves in a place; explore a new way of looking at poetry; and—as he describes it—perform a phenomenology of the imagination. The limits that I have imposed upon myself in approaching this text, however, mean that I will only deal with the dialectic of subject and house.

It is through/with topo-analysis that we find the subject of the house: the subject as it is constructed in the house, and the importance of the house for the subject. The examination of the 'quite simple images of *felicitous space*' seeks

> to determine the human value of the sorts of space that may be grasped, that may be defended against adverse forces, the space we love. For diverse reasons, and with difference entailed by poetic shadings, this is eulogized space. (Bachelard 1969: xxxi)

This quotation emphasizes the human valorization of space(s): the one I quoted above emphasizes the spatial, topographical nature of the subject; topo-analysis serves to articulate the field upon which these two notions will come into contact (combat/play).

As has already been mentioned, Bachelard's topo-analysis will map the (textual) area traced by the image of the house in various literary/poetic texts. Furthermore, because topo-analysis is an 'auxiliary of psychoanalysis' (Bachelard 1969: 8), it will focus upon those images that come in/as a reverie, or day-dream. Day-dreaming is an important process for Bachelard—one that he favours more than the normal or psychoanalytic night-dream. Yet day-dreaming—as it is articulated within a literary text—bears an important resemblance to the psychoanalyst's appraisal of dreams; that is, it has been textually structured. It seems to me that the Freudian idea of secondary revision—with reference to the manifest dream—has often been overlooked. Freud (1976), in describing the processes that structured a dream, identified four such processes. Secondary revision was the last—after condensation, displacement and symbolization—and refers to the transformation that the analysand makes to structure and dream into a textual whole—a story—in order to relate it to the analyst. Thus secondary revision denotes an unconscious process that privileges a particular way of telling the dream.

Day-dreams as they occur in poetry, for example, are already textually spaced; and the day-dreamer is already spaced: '... if I were asked to name the chief benefit of the house, I should say: the house shelters day-dreaming, the house protects the dreamer, the house allows one to dream in peace' (Bachelard 1969: 6). And it is because day-dreams can be regarded as the textual articulation of memories, the structured thoughts of things past, that they become ideal for topo-analysis. Bachelard situates the day-dreamer in the space I have described above—the double dialectic of subject and house; dreamers simultaneously structure themselves spatially and valorize the space in which they dream. Sometimes, in the first chapter of *The Poetics of Space*, Bachelard seems only to emphasize the latter; for example at one point he writes:

> the house is not experienced from day to day only, on the thread of a narrative, or in the telling of our own story. Through dreams, the various dwelling-places in our lives co-penetrate and retain the treasures of former days. (Bachelard 1969: 5)

THE SPACED-OUT SUBJECT: BACHELARD AND PEREC 149

This quotation shows that, in his effort to distance himself from the singularity of psychoanalysis, Bachelard has forgotten that the dreamer is always already a storyteller. For it is via the dreaming, the remembering that happens in a house, that 'one's own story' is told. The dreamer, in the house (*because* of the house), becomes the subject of the dream; the dreamer is made into a subject by the dream-house:

> At times we think we know ourselves in time, when all we know is a sequence of fixations in the spaces of the being's stability—a being who does not want to melt away, and who, even in the past, when he sets out in search of things past [*quand il s'en va à la recherche du temps perdu*], wants time to 'suspend' its flight. In its countless alveoli space contains compressed time. This is what space is for. (Bachelard 1969: 8)

This reinstatement of the importance of the spatially-constructed subject is not worded as directly as the previous privileging of the subject's valorization of (a) space. If we move down a storey, into the subtext of this quotation, we find that Bachelard is emphasizing the construction of a subject position: space—in its suspension/compression of time—provides the place in which the subject (a day-dreamer, no doubt) seeks to fix itself. For the subject-dreamer it is easier to build itself as existing continually through space(s), than it is to do so in time. Bachelard shows that temporalization is a mere twist in the body of space; this is the importance of the topo-analytic method. Topo-analysis charts the 'countless alveoli' of the subject-dreamer's space and it is with this method that I will confront the works of Georges Perec.

Perec's Stories and Memory

> [T]hat which seems to make the difficulty is this, that this consciousness being interrupted always by forgetfulness, there being no moment of our lives wherein we have the whole train of all our past actions before our eyes in one view, but even the best memories losing sight of one part whilst they are viewing another; and we sometimes, and that the greatest part of our lives, not reflecting upon our past selves, being intent upon our present thoughts, and in sound sleep having no thoughts at all... I say, in all these cases, our consciousness being interrupted, and we losing sight of our past selves, doubts are raised whether we are the same thinking thing.... (Locke 1977: 212)

My essay so far has been emphasizing what I have been calling the dialectic of house and subject. I should like now to turn to the works of Georges Perec. Although I will focus mainly upon *Life: A User's Manual* (1987), I shall make references to other of his texts—*Espèces d'espaces* (1974), *W, ou, le souvenir d'enfance* (1975b)[4] translated as *W, or, The Memory of Childhood* (1988), and *Tentative d'épuisement d'un lieu parisien* (1975a).

I shall begin with an anecdote. On Perec's death in 1982, there was found among his notebooks an outline for an autobiography. Unlike other autobiographies, Perec planned to write his to a spatial schema; that is, rather than organize the narrative of the events of his life temporally, Perec proposed to structure such a text according to places and spaces he'd occupied.[5] Yet, even without recourse to the invocation of a projected spatial-story, we can see that the theme, idea, motif, intuition and image of space has played an important part in the work of Perec. In this section of my paper, then, I would like to chart the spaces in the ('other') texts I mentioned above and then relate them to memory and remembering in *W, or, The Memory of Childhood* before turning to *Life: A User's Manual*.

Espèces d'espaces expands upon the brief, textual, situating game that most children play, which Perec articulates as follows:

> Georges Perec
> 18, rue de l'Assomption
> Escalier A
> 3ᵉ étage
> Porte droite
> Paris 6ᵉ
> Seine
> France
> Europe
> Monde
> Univers. (Perec, 1974: 113)

Each of the chapters in this book deals with an element of this form of address. But, as if to explain the line which leads into this address '*j'ai écrit ainsi mon adresse*', the first chapter of the book describes textual space and is called 'La Page'. Before any spaces can be discussed, described, even valorized, the co-ordinates of the space upon which this is done must be given (I shall deal with the importance of writing to memory with reference to *W, or, The Memory of Childhood* later). The rest of the book, in keeping with the map of the mode of address quoted above, moves through space — lived-in space — beginning with the room and finishing with space. In *Tentative d'épuisement d'un lieu parisien* Perec describes what he sees happen over a period of a few days in a particular place in Paris; things moving through a space in which he is (more or less) stationary. In *Life: A User's Manual*, however, both of the above strategies are employed; for at the same time as various characters are situated within various parts of the apartment-block in which the novel is set, Perec also expands each of these spaces by describing past (and possible) stories and events that have taken/take/will take place within those spaces. At the same time as he builds the apartment-block upwards he also builds outwards. This way of writing is allegorized in *Espèces d'espaces* in chapter four, 'L'appartement', a section on walls. Herein, Perec describes what happens when a picture is placed on a wall. Walls define the space that is the apartment, yet, in placing a picture on a wall, a double effacement takes place:

> the wall is no longer that which delimits and defines the place where I live, no longer that which separates it from other places where others live; it is no more than a support for a picture. But I also forget the picture, I no longer look at it, I no longer know how to look at it. I have put the picture on the wall in order to forget that there was a wall; but in forgetting the wall, I also forget the picture... Pictures efface walls. But walls kill pictures. (Perec 1974: 55; my translation)

If we remember the section above on Bachelard, we find there a similar dialectical movement between house and subject. Here, in *Espèces d'espaces*, we are shown the blurring of the boundaries between picture and wall in the very act which emphasizes their stability. With respect to *Life*, this movement describes that which I sketched briefly above: for as the apartment-block is fixed in space, as it is built storey by storey, it is simultaneously destroyed, insofar as the stories it generates move us outside its walled boundaries — literally (literarily) all over the world. As the picture is placed on the wall, as the story is told in/of/about the house, as the subject constructs in space, then that wall/house/space is strengthened and demolished. The subject, in making itself in a space, valorizes that space, but negates it insofar as it becomes a subject. Similarly with the space — it aids the constructing of a subject, it valorizes and destroys that subject. Here would be a good place to move into the house of *Life*, but before I textualize my plan for a topo-analysis of that novel, I will turn to *W, or, The Memory of Childhood* in order to further situate such an analysis.

I mentioned memory very briefly above in discussing Bachelard's notion of day-dreaming. Day-dreaming, I stated, was the always already textualizing process that structured memories; daydreaming provides the map *as* it opens the way in our 'search of things past'. The dreamer, I said, is a storyteller. Perec's *W, or, The Memory of Childhood* charts such a story. 'W' is the name of a story that Perec wrote when he was thirteen. It tells of an island off the coast of Tierra del Fuego, called W, whose inhabitants live according to the ideals of sport; W is like an enormous Olympic village. These bare bones of a story were all Perec could remember of his childhood tale; yet he has reconstructed it and interwoven it with some of his childhood memories. Perec's story — the autobiography, part I, chapter 2 — begins 'I have no childhood memories' (Perec 1988: 6). That is, the narratable events of Perec's life (he asserts) come to only two lines; he explains that History, 'with a capital "H" ' (avec sa grande hache)[6] (Perec, 1988: 6) intervened in his own story. 'W', then — the childhood story, the story in words and pictures that Perec constructed when he was thirteen — rather than depicting the events of his childhood can come to stand in for them; that is, insofar as the composing of it and the memory of it play a certain role, have a particular importance, in Perec's own story. Another manifestation of this type of idea in this text comes in chapter 4 — here Perec relates his 'two earliest memories' (Perec 1988: 13).

Although these memories are not implausible, Perec explains that, 'the many variations and imaginary details I have added in the telling of them — in speech or in writing — have altered them greatly, if not completely distorted them' (Perec 1988: 13). This observation gains importance in the relating of another of Perec's memories. this involves a particular injury, sustained when he'd been knocked over by a sledge whilst ice-skating at the bottom of a piste. He writes:

> I fell backwards and broke my scapula; it is a bone that cannot be set in a plaster; to allow it to mend, my right arm has been strapped tight behind my back in a whole contraption of bandages that makes any movement impossible, and the right sleeve of my jacket flaps emptily as if I really had lost my arm. (Perec 1988: 79)

Many years later Perec met a man who was living in the same village as he was during the war, and who was of the same age. This Louis Argoud-Puix could not remember Perec, even when Perec reminded him of the strange injury and its manner of being set, but he could remember another boy called Philippe, and, indeed, could remember the details of the skating accident and the broken scapula as having happened to Philippe. Perec's memory of Philippe's accident was imagined, varied and distorted so that *he* became the brave owner of a strangely-strapped broken scapula. But this does not annul the value of the story as a *memory*. Although it is an imagined, or fantastical event, it still bears an important relationship not only to the thoughts, feelings, and actions of the child (and here, maybe, we could begin our psychoanalysis...) but also of the importance of the childhood to the adult. All in all, the 'memory' still makes-up Perec's own story. It, for example, articulates a preoccupation with *suspension*, remoulding and its related motifs and emotions. In this way 'W' does relate to Perec's story. The ideal Olympic community soon becomes the image of the concentration camps: History — that *grand récit* — has intervened on little Perec's story. His father is killed fighting in the early stages of the war (in fact, on the day of the armistice between France and Germany, marking France's surrender) and his mother is soon transported to one of the death camps; the 'they' in the following quotation refers to Perec's parents:

> I am not writing in order to say that I shall say nothing, I am not writing to say that I have nothing to say. I write: I write because we lived together, because I was one amongst them, a shadow amongst their shadows, a body close to their bodies. I write because they left in me their indelible mark, whose trace is writing. Their memory is dead in writing; writing is the memory of their death and the assertion of my life. (Perec 1988: 42)

Memory and writing become like the wall and the picture. To write the story is to structure the memory; such a structuration is one that organizes not only Perec's story, but also positions him as a subject within the story of his family. Furthermore — and this is a point I will return to in the next section of this essay — writing is here linked with mourning: the erection of a *memorial* to his parents. Writing becomes the vault wherein Perec not only projects/situates his memory, but also the data from which he reads his own life.

Life: A User's manual is *about* (in both senses of the word) the apartment-block situated at 11 rue Simon-Crubellier. Each of the chapters is named after a space in the house: for example, we have chapter one, 'The Stairs, 1'; chapter two, 'Beaumont, 1'; chapter three, 'Third Floor Right, 1'. We are presented with the 'neutral' space of the stairs or the lift, or the lived-in space designated by the name of the person who occupies a particular flat. The room-chapters (as I will call the latter of these) begin with a description of the space:

> Madame de Beaumont's drawing room is almost entirely filled by a concert grand... In the left-hand corner of the room there is a large modern armchair made of a huge hemisphere of steel-ringed Plexiglass on a chromed metal base. (Perec 1987: 6, the opening of chapter 2)

These descriptions are extremely meticulous; each possible detail is given — such spaces are clearly valorized. Yet what usually begins as the description of these humanly valorized/valorizing spaces — depicting the present-day story of its inhabitant — often takes a turn to writing the story of the room, of its previous inhabitant(s) and their stories. Indeed, what always begins as firmly entrenched between the walls of a particular flat or room soon becomes a story which transgresses these boundaries. In order to write a character into a room, the story of that room is told — like the Homeric epics the present-day character is *subjectified* within a historical space which, as it is so constructed, constructs. Each character in Perec's novel must be situated; the story of their lives is told by examining the stories of the space in which these lives are delimited. It is important to remember — the following will be expanded upon in the next section of this paper — that the stories (and the story) of the apartment-block are being remembered by one of the book's characters, one of the inhabitants of the house, Valène. As we will see, Valène is remembering, dreaming, constructing stories and storeys of the house and its inhabitants, of himself.

Stor(e)y by Stor(e)y with Valène[7]

> To go upstairs in the word house, is to withdraw, step by step; while to go down into the cellar is to dream, it is losing oneself in the distant corridors of an obscure etymology, looking for treasures that cannot be found in words. To mount and descend in the words themselves — this is the poet's life. To mount too high or descend too low, is allowed of poets, who bring earth and sky together. Must the philosopher alone be condemned by his peers always to live on the ground floor? (Bachelard 1969: 147)

As the prefatory quotation suggests, in this section I shall be looking at the chapters of *Life: A User's Manual* entitled 'On the Stairs', the fifty-first chapter (my favourite) and chapter seventy-four called, 'Lift Machinery, 2'. But, first, why the stairs?

For Bachelard, the stairs facilitate dreams. It is via the stairs that we transgress the boundaries of our personal space; the stairs are not our *own*, no one *owns* the stairs. It is, therefore, important that those *escaliers* chapters that are not descriptive of a particular scene seen from a particular place, deal with the thoughts and feelings of — I would argue — the novel's central character, Valène. Furthermore, the book opens on the stairs, 'in this neutral place that belongs to no one, where people pass by almost without seeing each other, where the life of the building regularly and distantly resounds' (Perec 1987: 3). This first chapter describes a woman going to inspect the rooms of the recently deceased puzzle-maker Gaspard Winkler. Indeed, all traces of the craftsman are soon to be removed:

> Not much is left of these three small rooms in which Gaspard Winkler lived and worked for nearly forty years. His few pieces of furniture, his small workbench, his jigsaw, his miniature files have gone... The woman is going up the stairs. Soon, the old flat will become a charming pied-à-terre, two recept. + bedr., all mod. cons., open outlook, quiet. (Perec 1987: 5-6)

Already we are presented with an inextricable link between a character and a room; it is not yet clear whether the dwelling-space constructs the subject, or whether the personality of the occupant imbues the room. Nevertheless, when Winkler dies, so must his room.

The next 'On the Stairs' chapter is number seventeen. It begins 'On the stairs the furtive shadows pass of all those who were there one day' (Perec 1987: 59). There follows an impersonal ('He remembered') descriptive catalogue of past and present tenants. Over the page, after a space, a new paragraph begins, again impersonally: 'He was...'; it is established that 'he' has lived in the block longer than anyone else. It is not until the next-but-one paragraph that 'he' is named—he is the painter, Valène. Valène is on the stairs, musing, remembering... waiting?

> He tried to resuscitate those imperceptible details which over the course of fifty-five years had woven the life of this house and which the years had unpicked one by one... The stairs, for him, were, on each floor, a memory, an emotion, something ancient and unpalpable, something palpitating somewhere in the flickering flame of his memory. (Perec 1987: 61–62; translation modified)

It is for Valène only that the stairs lose their 'neutrality'. It is as he climbs the stairs—an activity that spans the whole book, except the epilogue—that he constructs the stories of the block of flats, re-constructs the memories that call to him from the spaces. Valène's life/being is one that has been ordered by the block—a point I shall return to in connection with 'The Fifty-First Chapter'—'when the opportunity arose of finding a larger flat or even a real studio, he realized he was too attached to his room, to his house, to his street, to leave' (Perec 1987: 60–61). The next time we encounter the stairs—in chapter twenty-eight—the scenario is the same: Valène is remembering. He is remembering the last time he saw Bartlebooth, at this point on the stairs. The most striking paragraph of this chapter—and one which I will quote in full below—is constructed from Valène's musing; it is one which is separated from the rest of the text on the same page by blank spaces:

> Sometimes Valène had the feeling *that time had stopped, suspended*, frozen around he didn't know what expectation. The very idea of the picture he planned to do and whose laid-out, broken-up images had begun to haunt every second of his life, furnishing his dreams, squeezing his memories, the very idea of this shattered building laying bare the cracks of its past, the crumbling of its present, this unordered amassing of stories grandiose and trivial, frivolous and pathetic, gave him the impression of a grotesque mausoleum raised in the memory of companions petrified in terminal postures as insignificant in their solemnity as they were in their ordinariness, as if he had wanted both to warn of and to delay these slow or quick deaths which seemed to be engulfing the entire building storey by storey: Monsieur Marcia, Madame Moreau, Madame de Beaumont, Bartlebooth, Rorschach, Madamoiselle Crespi, Madame Albin, Smautf. And himself, of course, Valène himself, the longest inhabitant of the house. (Perec 1987: 127; my emphasis)

For Valène, the house represents a *memorial* not only to others, but also to himself. It gives the rule to the construction of his life—the stories of his friends and co-habitants—and to the compilation of a painting: story by story, as well as storey by storey. This paragraph stands apart, within its spatial surround of blankness, tracing and traced by the events of the house. In this brief space we are witness to the freezing of time and the construction of subjects; the apartment block is the spatial alveoli *par excellence*. Yet there is a part of the book where this idea is shown even more forcefully, the fifty-first chapter.

This chapter is not a stairs-chapter. It is, at least nominally, a room-chapter and is called 'Valène (Servants' Quarters, 9)'. As with the two chapters I dealt with above, it begins impersonally; unlike the previous chapters, this one never identifies who its 'he' is—I assume it is Valène because of the title, and the fact that this 'he' is a painter. This chapter stands out for many reasons: first, textually, it is the centre of the book and is called the fifty-first chapter as opposed to chapter fifty-one, which would follow the pattern of the others; secondly, schematically, unlike the other chapters of its kind—the other room-chapters—it never once meticulously describes Valène's room, or Valène's past for that matter; but perhaps the most striking feature of this chapter is a combination of these. It opens describing four ways that the artist can paint himself into his picture; each way is enclosed in its own piece of text, surrounded by its own bit of blank space. The first three depict ways in which 'he' can insert himself into his painting: in a crowd (the way Renaissance painters did); in a corner; or, at the edge, in the process of painting, as Dali did, say. The fourth example is different insofar as the painter painting has become the subject of the picture. He will paint himself painting the picture, and to include his surrounding space will be to depict the original subject of the picture—the house. This fourth chunk of text ends 'and all around the long procession of his characters with their stories, their pasts, their legends' (Perec 1987: 228). There follows a long, numbered (from 1 to 179) list of events, scenes and stories that have taken place in the house, some of which have already been recounted in the novel, others have yet to be. This painting is *about* the painter. A closer look at the list corroborates this, for such an inspection reveals an interesting pattern of letters. I shall transcribe the first four elements of the list to exemplify this pattern:

1. The Coronation at Covadonga of Alkhamah's victor, Don Pelage
2. The Russian singer and Schönberg living in Holland as exiles
3. The deaf cat on the top floor with one blue & one yellow eye
4. Barrels of sand being filled by order of the fumbling cretin. (Perec 1987: 228; my emphases)

The pattern of 'e's moves back a space at a time, until element number 60 which begins with an 'e'. From item 61 to 120, the same pattern is repeated but this time using the letter 'g'. Finally, from 121 to 179 there is a pattern of 'o's, thus spelling 'ego'. (In the French there is the same pattern, although it spells '*âme*' (soul).) All around the artist—his soul or ego—are the events, stories, others of the house. Indeed, I (will) want to argue that the artist can only construct himself within this community of others; Valène's subjectivity is one that is formed from the memories/stories that people (the storeys of) the apartment-block in which he lives.

By way of a conclusion to this section, I would like to return to the stairs—that is, to Valène on the stairs—to chapter seventy-four, 'Lift Machinery, 2'. Like the others with which I've dealt, this chapter does not indicate a character: throughout its course its protagonist is referred to only as 'he'. In fact I have no grounds whatsoever in assuming that it is Valène—but that won't stop me. It begins:

> Sometimes he imagined the building as an iceberg whose visible tip included the main floors and eaves and whose submerged mass began below the first level of cellars. (Perec 1987: 358)

There follows an amazing feat of what Bachelard would call oneirism. 'Valène' dreams extra levels—each one below the first—that are inhabited by a fantastic, Borges-like, world; coupling ordinary, everyday things like bags of fertilizer and busts of Beethoven, with intricate networks of tunnels, canals, railway lines and steaming, clanking, grinding machinery. The lowest level is the most mythic:

> and at the very bottom, a world of caverns whose walls are black with soot, a world of cesspools and sloughs, a world of grubs and beasts, of eyeless beings who drag animal carcasses behind them, of demoniacal monsters with bodies of birds, swine and fish, of dried-out corpses and yellow-skinned skeletons arrayed in attitudes of the living, of forges manned by dazed Cyclopes in black leather aprons, their single eyes shielded by metal-rimmed blue glass, hammering their brazen masses into dazzling shields. (Perec 1987: 361)

As Bachelard writes, to descend into the cellar is to dream. 'Valène' is dreaming his dreams, constructing them from the apartment-block *in which he lives*. With each storey that Valène climbs he either constructs or re-constructs the stories of his memory. In *The Poetics of Space* Bachelard writes (I here transcribe the American translation of the text—it must be remembered that the Americans do not distinguish between 'story' and 'storey'):

> When we recall the old house in all its longitudinal detail, everything that ascends and descends comes to life again dynamically. We can no longer remain, to quote Joë Bousquet, men with one story [*étage*]. 'He was a man with only one story [*étage*]: he had his cellar in his attic'. (Bachelard 1969: 26)

It is Valène's personal space that is described in terms of the life, the stories of the life, of the apartment-block itself. Valène's dreams, his memories and his own stor(e)y are inextricably intertwined: each slides over the other and into the spaces of the house. 'Valène', Perec explains in a conversation with Gabriel Simony, 'is a name I had chosen as the pseudonym of an epoch' (Perec 1989: 18–19); my translation). The name Valène comes to stand for an epoch: Valène the artist, whose stationary picaresque about the stories/storeys of the apartment-block takes no time at all and yet spans hundreds of years, signifies an age. It is the age of the de-centred, fluid, subject. Valène—the name, the character, the subject—names that which is unfixable and nameless, and so comes to name us all.

Perec, then, articulates—particularly in *Life: A User's Manual*—not only the contemporary philosophical notions of subjectivity, but also (and more importantly considering the schema of this paper) the Bachelardian notion of the spatial constructing of the subject. We have witnessed the construction of Valène; we have also seen him called a pseudonym for an epoch. A pseudonym—this is important. This single word encapsulates what it is to be a subject; not only an individual subject, but the subject of a time. The time is a disguise that space takes on in order to be lived in. The subject wears the same clothes, though the colour of these clothes is determined by the space in which they are found. Valène, the name of the subject, is a pseudonym that can only be constructed by looking at the stories/storeys of the house. This subject is one that flows, it is fluid; this subject is spaced-out.

Notes

I would like to thank Dr Leslie Hill for his valuable comments made on an earlier draft of this paper and Debbie Marshall for her editorial help. Mistakes, inaccuracies and general incompetences, however, can be nobody's but mine.

1. Cf. one of Nietzsche's aphorisms in *Beyond Good and Evil*:
   'I have done that' says my memory. 'I cannot have done that' says my pride, and remains inexorable. Eventually—memory yields. (Nietzsche 1966, Section 68: 80)
   It is interesting to note that Freud relates, while discussing resistance, that the Rat Man quotes this passage from *Beyond Good and Evil* to him: (1979) *Case Histories II: 'Rat Man', Schreber, 'Wolf Man', Female Homosexuality*, p. 64.
2. Further references to this text will be to the translation (Bachelard 1969) and will be made in the main text of this paper, following the relevant passage.
3. Further references to this text will be to the translation (Perec 1987) and will be made in the main text of this paper, following the relevant passage.
4. This work was to have been called *Lieux où j'ai dormi*.
5. Further references to this text will be to the translation (Perec 1988) and will be made in the main text of this paper, following the relevant passage.
6. NB '*Hache*' (in English 'H'—'aitch') is also the word for 'axe'.
7. It is interesting to note the etymological link between 'story' and 'storey'. ' Storey', *The Oxford English Dictionary* (1989) tells us, is derived from fourteenth-century Anglo-Latin *historia*, thus having the same derivation as 'story'. Furthermore, '*Historia* as an architectural term, may have originally denoted a tier of painted windows or of sculptures on the front of a building'. In its other sense, and that from which we understand 'story', *historia* means 'a painting or sculpture representing a historical subject. Hence, any work of pictorial or sculptural art containing figures'. So we can picture a storey as a particular floor on which a particular story is told.
   The texts I am working with, however, were written in French; how, then, does the word *étage* relate to this? The *Littré* (1963) gives the following as one of its definitions of *étage*:
   Proprement séjour, station * Terme de droit féodal, lige étage, ou, simplement, étage, obligation des vassaux liges de résider un certain temps chez le seigneur, afin de le défendre.
   As well as signifying a level of a building *étage* denotes the specific relation a servant must have to its master. In occupying a proper station as a vassal, a servant also occupied specific living quarters. These two definitions do not have as little in common as it may at first appear. For if we remember the proper relation that Homer had to his masters, we can see that the telling of a story fulfils such servile obligations. Yet this story of Homer has further important ramifications. The epic story performed the function of genealogical valorization for the noble families of Ancient Greece. The Bayeux Tapestry realizes the same end; though it has more of a relation with 'storey' as it is housed on one floor of a specially constructed building. The epic story, like Hegel's master/slave story, seeks to construct a subject position.
   These points delineate the area upon which this section in particular, and the essay as a whole, is articulated.

Bibliography

Bachelard, G. (1938), *La Psychanalyse du feu*, Paris, Librarie Gallimard.
Bachelard, G. (1958), *La Poétique de l'espace*, Vendôme, P.U.F.
Bachelard, G. (1969), *The Poetics of Space*, (tr. Maria Jolas), Boston, Beacon Press.
Bachelard, G. (1987), *The Psychoanalysis of Fire*, (tr. A.C.M. Ross), London, Quartet Books.
Freud, S. (1976), *The Interpretation of Dreams*, (tr. James Strachey, eds James Strachey & Alan Tyson), Pelican Freud Library 4, (ed. Angela Richards), London, Penguin.
Freud, S. (1979), *Case Histories II: 'Rat Man', Schreber, 'Wolf Man', Female Homosexuality*, (tr. James Strachey), Pelican Freud Library 9, (ed. Angela Richards), London, Penguin.
Greek-English Lexicon (1897), (eds Liddell and Scott), eighth edition, Oxford, Clarendon Press.
Hegel, G.W.F. (1977), *The Phenomenology of Spirit*, (tr. A.V. Miller), Oxford and London, O.U.P.
Homer (1984), *The Iliad*, (tr. Robert Fitzgerald), Oxford, O.U.P.
Josipovici, G. (1985) 'George Perec's Homage to Joyce (and Tradition)', *The Yearbook of English Studies*, (Anglo-French literary relations special number), Vol. 15, 179-200.
Lacan, J. (1979), *The Four Fundamental Concepts of Psychoanalysis*, (ed. Jacques-Alain Miller, tr. Alan Sheridan), Harmondsworth, Penguin.
Littératures (1983), printemps, No. 7 (Special Georges Perec edition).
Littré (1963), tome 3, Paris, Editions Gallimard/Hachette.
Locke, J. (1977), *An Essay Concerning Human Understanding*, Fontana Library, Fount Paperbacks, Glasgow, William Collins & Sons & Co. Ltd.
McAllaster, M. (1984), 'Bachelard twenty years on: an assessment', *Revue de littérature comparée*, avril-juin, No. 2, 165-176.
Motte Jr., W.F. (1984), 'Le Puzzle de/dans *La vie mode d'emploi* de Georges Perec', *Romance Notes*, Spring, Vol. 24, part 3, 207-213.
Nietzsche, F. (1966), *Beyond Good and Evil*, (tr. Walter Kaufmann), Vintage Books, New York, Random House Inc.
The Oxford English Dictionary (1989), second edition, Oxford, Clarendon Press.
The Oxford Latin Dictionary (1982), (ed. P.G.W. Glare), Oxford, Clarendon Press.
Pankow, G. (1972), 'La dynamique de l'espace et le temps vécu', *Critique*, février, Vol. 28, No. 297.
Perec, G. (1970), *La Vie mode d'emploi*, Paris, Hachette.
Perec, G. (1974), *Espèces d'espaces*, Paris, Editions Galilée.
Perec, G. (1975a), *Tentative d'épuisement d'un lieu parisien*, (ed. Christian Bourgois), Paris, Union Générale d'éditions.
Perec, G. (1975b), *W. ou, le souvenir d'enfance*, Paris, Editions Denoël.
Perec, G. (1987), *Life: A User's Manual* (tr. David Bellos), London, Collins Harvill.
Perec, G. (1988), *W, or, The Memory of Childhood* (tr. David Bellos), London, Collins Harvill.
Perec, G. (1989), *Entretien (avec Gabriel Simony)*, Paris, Le Castor Astral.
Rée, J. (1987), *Philosophical Tales*, London, Methuen.
Schwarz, P.J. (1985), 'The Unifying Structures of Georges Perec's Suspended Memoires' *International Fiction Review*, Summer, Vol. 12, part 2, 71-73.
Voloshinov, V.N. (1976), 'Discourse in Life and Discourse in Art (Concerning Sociological Poetics)', in *Freudianism: A Marxist Critique*, New York, Academic Press.
Voloshinov, V.N. (1986), *Marxism and the Philosophy of Language*, (tr. Ladislav Matejka and I.R. Titunik), Cambridge, Massachusetts, Harvard University Press.

14 The Death of Orality and the Rise of the Literate 'Subject'
David Wilson

Papers always seem like a good idea when someone suggests that you write one, but when it comes down to the crunch I always change my mind. Is the topic really appropriate? Is the topic interesting? And, after several nights toil, I usually change my mind and throw it in the bin. Unfortunately, on this occasion, it would appear to be more embarrassing to do so than not to do so, and so you unfortunate souls must suffer the consequences.

There is an extent to which this paper is uninteresting. Little of it is my own work, so I am not sure that it possesses the brazenly original cutting edge that makes a paper interesting; and the arguments, such as they are, possess a dubiousness that would make most academics' hair curl in frustration. Why do I get myself into this position? Sleepless nights of worry, and confidence flowing down the drain with the bubbles of bath salts! There is only one answer: the flagrant presupposition on which this conference is based needs rooting out into the daylight and it is interesting enough and irritating enough for me to be dumb enough to volunteer to attempt to do it.

'The *Coming* of the Subject: *Making* the Self from 1789–1989'. It's a good title isn't it? And most presumptuous. Firstly, the *coming* of the subject suggests that there was a time when there was no subject, sometime just prior to 1789. A time when there was no subject? Were there really no subjects prior to the Enlightenment? It is an odd claim that must hinge on an odd understanding of the word 'subject'. Is it really claiming that there were ten thousand preceding years of people who were not 'subjects', not 'human' in some sense? Secondly, *making* the self, a rather murky little sentence that could suggest that selves are made by others or that selves make themselves. If we run the title completely, *The Coming of the Subject: Making the Self from 1789–1989* then there is a clear hint that the subject and the self are the same thing, that the coming of the subject is a making of self; that prior to this, before 1789, there was no subject-self. It seems then that the title could concede that there were subjects of some form before 1789 but not subject-selves; that after 1789 we have the arrival, the making, of a subject-self. What does such a claim mean? Why in 1789 does this subject-self start to be made? I have said that this paper is on dubious ground. It is on dubious ground because of the very presupposition of this conference, a claim that after 1789 we have a subject-self and prior to this, what? For the moment let us just call it a subject.

It is a brave and foolish philosopher who offers answers; philosophy is the art of asking questions, yet it seems that I have put myself in the position of being brave and foolish even if I am going to offer other people's answers.

What is so crucial about 1789? What is so different about a subject-self? How many thousands of writers, how many academics all put forward the idea that somehow modernity starts in the seventeenth and eighteenth centuries, that somehow we were all different after that in some crucial manner? The Enlightenment, the Reformation, the scientific revolution, the exploration of the globe, the rise of capitalism and consumerism, the Industrial Revolution are all given as causes of modernity, with Descartes and modern philosophy, modern literature, art, academia, political and economic structures and now, apparently, subject-selves as effects, although which is the cause and which the effect of which on what rather depends on who you read. It strikes me, and I hope you, as being rather suspicious. Why are we led to believe that for thousands of years nothing *really* happened; that in the last two hundred years everything of importance occurred; that *this* is the period in which the history of humanity was dramatically altered into modernity? Some writers try to show a continuous chain of historical events leading to a climax, others claim it was a disruptive occurrence, like an unexplained thunderbolt from God. Most limit their explanations to one field, one phenomenon of the period, relevant to their discipline or field. Few dare to give a general account and those that do so are criticized for reducing modernity to a single cause, modernity being complex and we moderns being too complicated for simple explanations. But there *is* an interesting link between all the great changes of the period, and if it is not a single cause *per se*, it does stand as their necessary condition, a condition without which they could not have occurred as they did. This necessary condition is the printing press. Elizabeth Eisenstein (1979) has written a very detailed account of this in her two volumes *The Printing Press as an Agent of Change* and I do not here propose to go into the details of this intricate academic text. I shall, however, briefly indicate how it is a necessary condition for the Enlightenment and for what we call modernity by briefly considering two of the most crucial movements of the period.

Many of you I am sure, are busy sitting and scratching your heads as to the nature of this claim. The alphabetic letterpress was, after all, invented in the fifteenth century and I am suggesting, with Eisenstein, that it may be used to explain seventeenth- and eighteenth-century phenomena. Is there not just a little bit of a temporal gap? If this bothers you I suggest that you read Eisenstein's original text as she does chart its development through this period in some detail. You must realize that in a world of slow communications, new inventions spread slowly and their effects disseminate slowly. The world was not at the time orientated towards texts in a way that it is now and the printing press only slowly developed its own future. But let us consider the two movements that I have promised to you.

Firstly, we have what is known as the Reformation, a movement away from the centralized Catholic Church. We are given many hundreds of reasons for its occurrence and told never to underrate its importance. Central to its thrust was decentralization away from papal and priestly control of Biblical interpretation. More and more churches sprang up offering varying dogmas, and central to most of them was the notion that each *individual* was capable of reading and interpreting the Bible, even if under the watchful eye of a minister or elder; each *individual* was responsible for increasing their own holiness with Bible study, each *individual* was responsible for their own soul. Consider how such a theology is possible without the printing press. Certainly it was to be found in monastic institutions before this, but the monasteries, the Church, controlled the texts and this is precisely the central issue in this conflict. How could the text move into a public arena without popular access to the Biblical text itself? How much sense does it make to encourage individual Bible reading and interpretation with one Bible between so many thousands of people? It clearly makes no sense at all; indeed, it is hard to see how it can even become an issue. The Reformation must have, as its necessary condition, popular access to the Bible and this was not possible without the printing press. It is interesting to note here a reciprocal movement in the Catholic Church at this time, with the monastic institution of confession becoming widespread as a practice for the Church community as a whole. Again this is a movement towards the individual, even if it is a movement to try to control the individual, and appears symptomatic of the period of the Reformation.

Secondly, in this period, we have what is widely known as the scientific revolution. Why? Observation of the natural world had been around for a long time, all peoples have theories of causal explanation that may be called a science of some form? The ancient Greeks even had a form of abstract scientific theory. Why then, do we call this period a scientific revolution? Consider science in the medieval era. Manuscripts take a very long time to copy and copyists very often did not understand what they were copying. Accurate reproduction of charts or complex drawings was almost impossible. Eisenstein asks us to imagine a culture where few people had even seen an accurate picture of anything never mind a book. Hand-done technical drawings tended to deteriorate with copying because the copyist, unless supervised by an expert, often didn't know the subject of the illustration and changed bits to make it seem better. Thus a picture of a camel may eventually end up looking like a horse. The same, of course was true for the text itself. Copyists were notorious for changing the bits that they didn't quite understand, to make more sense. Even, therefore, if you managed to get a copy of a treatise, it was often far from the original text. Exact scientific writing was almost impossible to disseminate. Now consider the effects of the printing press. The mass accurate reproduction of verbal statements, pictures and diagrams now becomes possible. Exact observation can now be verbalized in an exactly repeatable form. Print allows for the widespread distribution of exact scientific observations that may be tested, repeated and criticized elsewhere. It was such a process that allowed Galileo to make his telescope, by reproducing it from a Dutch text and improving upon it. We all know the implications of what followed. Science was now able to leave the realm of a few isolated and brilliant experimenters to build up a body of *texts* which could now widely disseminate in months instead of years and retain their original information. Without this, what we now know as modern science is impossible: the printing press is the necessary condition for the textual foundations of modern science itself.

From these two movements, I believe all the others can be inferred: exploration, the Industrial Revolution etc. I am sure that we are all familiar with the ideas of Weber (1978), and Campbell's *The Romantic Ethic and The Spirit of Modern Consumerism* (1987).

Now, I am not claiming here that print *causes* any of these phenomena. It does not *cause* science, machinery, exploration, Church reform etc. But it permits their explosion in the period that we have subsequently called the

Enlightenment. Print is a necessary condition of this explosion. Well, so what? It's a pretty mundane thesis, let's face it. Eisenstein takes two volumes to put the case, but at the end of the day aren't we merely saying that print is the necessary condition for the mass production of books and that these are the necessary condition for the spread of the Reformation into the Enlightenment and beyond? Isn't this rather an uninteresting and uncontentious point? And surely we haven't even started to find our subject-self. We have been told, however, by the title of this conference that the subject-self develops somewhere in the middle of this explosion that we know as the Enlightenment, so where is it? Since print seems to be a necessary condition for the other developments of the period, shouldn't we perhaps wonder if it isn't a necessary factor for this elusive making of a subject-self? It doesn't help that we haven't yet really decided what we are looking for and yet perhaps we have already had a few hints. The Reformation was a move away from an external, collective and centralized body to an emphasis on the individual—an emphasis permitted by books. Is this perhaps what we are looking for? Let us recall what we have actually said that print does. We have noted that it wasn't a cause but a necessary condition. It allows for the accurate mass reproduction of writing (and drawings) which in turn allows for the Enlightenment revolutions. It allows the process of writing to leave the churches and courts and to slowly permeate the wider community. In the case of the Reformation, it permits the movement of a theology that was *already* found in the Church, an individualistic theology, to the wider community. A movement to individualism permitted by, and apparently going hand in hand with, books, and I don't think we can now limit this to printed books, for this individualism existed in the monasteries prior to print where only hand-written texts were available. Print merely allowed this theology to spread its texts outside of the sacred walls. Since we are searching for the subject-self and this is the only clear movement to individualism that we have found—although we can't yet be sure if it is the same thing—shouldn't we follow it to its root?

But let us now approach this from a different angle and see if we end up with the same picture. Let us approach it from a different writer, namely Michel Foucault. Some of his most renowned philosophical histories trace changes through the Enlightenment and there are some interesting parallels in his conclusions. If we take *Discipline and Punish* (1977) as an example, we find firstly an exploration of changes in the nature of punishment from the eighteenth century onwards. It is a move from a publicly visible system of punishment with *external* concentration upon the body, to a concentration upon correcting the *internal* motives of an individual in private. Secondly, we can trace an exploration away from the *unaccountable* feudal 'subject' to the development of human science; of the definition and objectification of an *individual* to an item of abstract knowledge. Tracing the rise of what he calls 'discipline' in various institutions, Foucault shows how it permits separation, identification, visibility and judgement of individuals which renders them accountable and controllable. What is most interesting is that as one of its necessary conditions, discipline has writing. Disciplinary writing involves compilations of documents, the record, the examination, the register, the timetable etc: individuals become individuated by a network of writing which allows them to be classified by comparison to a 'norm'. What is even more interesting is that this represents a spreading of the use of writing from the courts and monasteries to the population at large. He notes *specifically* that the individuation of discipline does not suddenly arrive, but has long been in existence in the courts and monasteries. Most influential of all was the monastic model which had divided up time, space and individuals with writing for centuries.[1] It was this monastic subject that Foucault was exploring upon his death and in order for us to explore this we will have to draw on various interviews: in *The Foucault Reader* (1984), *Technologies of the Self* (1988) and volume three of *The History of Sexuality: The Care of the Self* (1986). He was by now, he claimed, interested in how subjects acted upon or understood themselves and was investigating this through the concept of *the care of the self*. Originally, in early Greece, this concept, caring for the self, was the care of one's *activity*, an active political and erotic state, the creation of the self as a work of art. It was an *externally* dependent notion, caring for one's role and position in life and developing it to the best of one's ability. Foucault traces the slow change from this idea of the care of the self through its development via the use of notebooks to record daily activities; to the stoic usage of recording what was done against what should have been done; through to the monastic usage of writing for vigilance, the total examination of the soul or the self. By now, care of the self means denying the world and the body and trying to recover an immortality of which one has been deprived. It means concentrating upon one's internal states, examining one's self for hidden thoughts and impurities lest Satan enters your soul. Foucault (1988: 28) says:

> In traditional political life, oral culture was largely dominant and therefore rhetoric was important...by the Hellenistic age, writing prevailed and real dialectic passed to correspondence. Taking care of one's self became linked to constant writing activity. The self is something to write about, a theme or *object* of writing activity...The new concern with self involved a *new experience* of self. The new form of the experience of self is to be seen in the first and second centuries when *introspection* becomes more and more detailed. A relation developed between writing and vigilance...experience of one's self was intensified and widened *by virtue of this act of writing*. A whole field of experience opened which earlier was absent.

A whole experience of the self which earlier was absent is permitted by writing. Doesn't this seem rather an interesting claim?

We now have built the following picture: that print allows for the possibility of the Enlightenment and that part of this movement was a movement to individualism from a previous monastic model, an individualism that seems to have been permitted by writing itself. We are still searching for our subject-self and seem to have come a long way back from the Enlightenment and yet we will still pursue it. If writing permits a certain form of individualism how does it do so? How is this different from an individualism without writing? There is a vast array of literature on this issue, but I propose to use the thesis of Walter Ong's text *Orality and Literacy* (1982) in order to outline the generally expounded differences.

Ong asks us to imagine a culture with no writing at all.[2] It's tough, how tough will soon become apparent. Words can never be seen, only heard. You can 'look up' nothing, record nothing except in oral formulas. Words are totally linked to sounding, and sound only exists as it vanishes, it cannot be frozen and never exactly repeated. This means that words in oral cultures are events, speaking is an action. Words materialize from inside people, reveal and give meaning to the fleeting moment. Oral cultures generally consider words to have great power, power of sound production itself from deep inside the body and power over things. How do you consider the story of Adam's naming of the animals in Genesis? As stupid? An irrelevant tale? And now consider what power, what comprehension you possess without names: oral cultures often have a greater respect for words because of the awareness of this power and as a result they often actually speak less. I was fortunate enough to live with a Sioux medicine man for a while and it was noticeable how little he spoke and how little we in fact need to speak. Words, to the Sioux, not only traditionally held great power, but were given with your life's breath and were therefore not given lightly. We are all aware of what happened to the Indian peoples when they faced white literates who had lost all respect for the very words that they spoke.

When we talk of naming here, it is most important to note that we do not mean the same thing as labelling. Labelling comes with writing and is an abstract written tag attached to an object. Naming is an involved, orally active, immediate relation to a being in a shared world. It is a revelation of a part of that world. I think that this will become clearer as we go on.

The point that is most crucial to Ong's thesis, however, and to Havelock (1963) and others before him is that an oral subject has a different method of thinking and that writing changes this. Clearly, an oral culture can only know what it can recall, there is no other method of preservation. Is this the same as learning a poem or a theorem verbatim and reciting it as we were all taught to do in school? How does it organize its material in order to recall it? If someone comes up with a long analytic proof of a proposition, how is it to be remembered? Come to that, how is a long analytic proof possible in the first place? The only method is to think memorable thoughts. It sounds silly doesn't it? Like a piece of trash advice from a 'B' movie — 'think memorable thoughts my boy' — but how else is it to be done? Oral memory is preserved in mnemonic formulas, is heavily rhythmic, full of balanced patterns, repetitions etc. Every device you can think of to aid recollection is used. Proverbs are a classic example, and we're not talking here about an occasional 'red sky at night shepherds' delight': these mnemonic formulas form the substance of memory itself. For example Indian elders and medicine men when giving judgement or diagnosis will do so on the basis of tradition, just as in literate society, but it will be given on the basis of proverbs or other mnemonic formulas (and is often given *in* proverbs or other mnemonic formulas) in which the knowledge of the tradition is contained. Thought in an extended form is impossible, or at least unrepeatably useless, without them. Thought and speech themselves are framed by the patterns necessary for recollection. This is not to say that it is not sophisticated, it most certainly can be. If you haven't been fortunate enough to travel among oral peoples yourself, then you may at least be familiar with some of the oral characters in the writings of Albert Wendt or Chinua Achebe. What is crucial to realize, however, is that the possibility of what or how a thing is said is different, is shaped by the limits and the potentialities of the discursive practice itself, to use a Foucauldian phrase.

Ong lists several characteristics of oral cultures and formulas which I now propose to give you as I think they will be helpful to our question.

First, they are additive rather than subordinative. Events are given in long accumulative lists rather than tied together in long, flowing more grammatically interesting phrases.

Second, they are aggregative rather than analytic—what we perhaps know better as cliché. An oak will be a mighty oak, a warrior will be a brave warrior etc. The adjectives tend to stick to the word concerned as their formulas help to aid recall. Our remnant of such culture is contained in fairy tales and heroic epics; a hero/ine is far more memorable than Joe Bloggs down the lane and is a necessary element in oral story recall. Today such tales are for children or historians and there has been a mass move in literature away from clichéd stories with heroes; it seems we no longer have any need for them.

Third, it is redundant or copious. Writing is externally continuous: if you lose your place reading, you simply reread it. In an oral situation this isn't possible, the line of thought may be lost; repetition is a necessary element in keeping the speaker and the listener on track.

Fourth, it is largely conservative or traditionalist. Only by repetition, by voicing, is knowledge that has been gained kept existent. Therefore elders, as custodians of the peoples' memory, command great respect.

Fifth, it is agonistically toned. Proverbs and riddles are not used merely to store knowledge but for intellectual debate or combat, countering with a proverb with an opposite point to challenge your opponent's prowess. Reciprocal name calling, jibing and so on, is far more characteristic in oral, than in literate culture. In a lived oral world, where inter-personal relations are necessarily high, this leads to loudly voiced antagonisms as well as attractions. (If we think here of some of our stereo-typical views of other cultures, we tend to think particularly of Spanish, Portugese, Italian or West Indian women as being loud and aggressive. If you realize that until recently many of them were still oral, this might perhaps explain the origins of some of our biases. Closer to home we might think of our attitudes to Scouse or Irish women. I think that this particularly applies to women as they were the last major group to become literate in our society. I can't prove any of this, but it does seem to me to be an interesting line of enquiry for someone to pursue.)

Sixth, it is participatory rather than objectively distanced. Learning needs communal identification with the known, as knowledge is a common, verbal inheritance. This means that the audience will participate in, say, a story telling and the narrator will alter the story slightly to fit the audience, often taking on the character of the hero in the telling of the tale. It is not a distanced telling. Oral societies are therefore by and large, what Ong calls homeostatic; that is they live in the present, the past is altered to suit the needs of the present telling. It is a myth to think that all oral memory is a learned verbatim repetition of a set of lines. An oral poet possesses a story line and a vast store of mnemonic wordings, which are woven together to give the past present relevance; the story changes slightly with every telling. Similarly a genealogy that is no longer required to be recited for political reasons will drop out of existence and those which are rendered are adjusted to flatter the present hearer. Ong cites recent research amongst current Slavic oral bards to illustrate his case (1982: 59). The research has shown that a bard delivers 10–20 ten-syllable lines per minute, but that although the meter is kept regular, a poem is never sung the same way twice. The same formulas and themes often recur but are stitched together in a different manner every time depending on the occasion, mood of the poet and audience reaction. Oral culture, then, is situated in a fundamentally participatory present, it is not static.

This means, finally, that it is close to the 'life-world'. Oral cultures conceptualize and verbalize all their knowledge with close reference to their lived present world. It is not possible or necessary to abstract out of it to any great degree; people and objects are assessed in relation to a total life-world situation. Where is the use, or the point, or indeed the method for complex analytic abstraction?[3] The same applies to the subject. Self analysis requires a partial removal from situational thinking, from the lived world. The individual identifies with, and is identified by, his or her external situation. In Africa I came across similar examples to those which Ong cites from Luria[4] and found them bizarre at the time, but I didn't know what I was in the middle of then: 'How are you today?', 'Oh, the children have eaten today thank you'. Here again we touch on the original understanding of the care of the self which Foucault outlined for us. It is the care of the external states of the self, activities of the present situated life-world. Oral culture does not deal in abstract categorical definitions, complex internal self-analysis etc. It is a fundamentally situated and pragmatic lived world.

Now we have to be careful here and I don't think that many writers in this field are *careful* enough. Oral societies do have concepts of the individual subject but they are not abstracted, which makes it very difficult for Western literates to access them. They are always given in the context of external relations to the world or society. Consider these Twi proverbs:[5]

> The clan is like a cluster of trees,
> When seen from afar, appear huddled together,
> but which would be seen to stand
> individually when closely approached.

> One finger cannot lift up a thing.

> If one man scrapes the bark for medicine, the pieces fall down.

And perhaps most relevant is the image of the Siamese crocodile (I believe it is represented by the image of a bird in European folklore), with two heads representing individual will, and a common body and stomach representing the community. Only by co-operation is the good of all individuals obtained. Individual abstraction from the common good, the given life situation, is self-destructive; the crocodile rips itself apart: 'When a man descends from Heaven, he descends into human society'. All that I am pointing to here is that individualist and communal tension is considered in oral thought. There are oral notions of a subject and it is dangerous to suggest that there are not. For convenience we shall call it the oral subject. Now, Foucault suggested that writing opened up a new experience of the subject and he is far from alone in this. Let us briefly consider how, again through the work of Walter Ong.

First, writing establishes autonomous, context-free discourse. It cannot be contested directly because it is separated from its author. A book is challenged by writing another book, yet even this will never change what is said in the first text for as long as it physically exists. Direct debate is no longer necessary for the preservation or the growth of knowledge. Words are no longer dependant on actual sounding.

Second, therefore, words become objects — things that may be seen. Sound

THE DEATH OF ORALITY AND THE RISE OF THE LITERATE 'SUBJECT'   167

is transposed from the aural field to a visual field; words are transferred to a dead page to be resurrected verbatim at a future date. This would appear to have subtle psychological effects by causing a move from a sound-dominant culture to a sight-dominant culture. Sight isolates, sound incorporates; vision dissects, it is directional; sound is all about you, envelops you in a way that vision does not. You can immerse yourself in sound in a way that you cannot immerse yourself in sight. Ong (1982: 72) interestingly points to Descartes as a sign of this shift, who demands clarity and distinctness, a visual ideal; an auditory ideal is harmony, say perhaps the older ideal of the harmony of the spheres.

Third, and perhaps most fundamentally for our purposes, texts destroy fundamental oral situatedness. They allow for the possibility of abstraction by separating the knower from the known. Ong has taken this from Havelock (1963) and it is worth briefly considering it. Around the fifth century BC many historians agree that something odd took place. There was a noticeable change in Greek grammar and syntax, and in addition the concept of an interior soul arose. By the fourth century BC it was deeply imbedded in Greek self-understanding. This, Havelock claims, represented a clear move away from the traditional oral culture prevalent up until this point. As we have noted, in oral culture the performer and the audience identify themselves with the characters in the story being unfolded before them. Each person has to preserve, by repetition, what is known, but in so doing they are not required to form unique and critical convictions of their own, even if this distancing were possible; merely to retell the story, to give it new life and present relevance and to identify with and imitate its characters. Oral subjects follow remembered precedents. If we take Achilles as an example: he is governed by his acts, his responses are governed by his situation, by remembered precedents, not by interior crises or motives. The knower and the known are in some sense the same, Havelock suggests. Social roles define one's obligations — one's actions are judged by these obligations and previous precedents to form community diagnosis of character. The care of the self, care of one's action. Why does this change? Because of the changing technology of communication, says Havelock. Around this time the Greek alphabet had been perfected and gained increasing usage. The use of writing removes the need for oral mnemonic traditions. Thought/knowledge no longer has to be spoken or recited, no longer has to be remembered and is therefore no longer locked into the mnemonic formulas previously necessary for its self preservation. Precise, long, non-repetitive, non-aggregative, non-redundant verbalization is possible, as it may now be recorded. And the homeostatic nature of thought may change; it is no longer necessary to make the past immediately present in order to preserve the tradition, for it is written down. It no longer needs to be identified with in such a way. The reasons for action slowly move away from tradition and into the self. Writing has separated the knower from the known, they are no longer *so obviously* co-identical. Reading and writing is a private activity, a withdrawal from the world and allows for questioning, categorization, labelling, listing, abstract definitions and other forms of objectification, as the subject may now bracket itself off from the world both to objectify the world and itself. Introspection is a form of objectification, and still lives in a community of sense given by language, only now it is in unspeaking books. Havelock at this point does a fascinating analysis of Plato's removal of poets from the

Republic—ie oral poets, the oral tradition. By book ten, Plato (1982) has sufficiently established the individual psyche to reject the old oral mnemonic tradition on the basis that it 'is making yourself like somebody else'; he denounces it as 'a surrender of one's self, a manipulation' (recollection and example having been the aim of oral education). Plato instead argues for the 'polity in one's self', the necessity of inner self-consistency and control.

I have a suspicion that we have now found our subject-self. The subject that at least believes it possesses and controls itself, may objectify and criticize and correct itself, as opposed to a subject that is externally responsive and models itself on exterior states rather than interior. This subject-self appears to arise with literacy. We are, however, a long way from the Enlightenment. But it must be noted that literacy simply did not arise with a big bang: the process that we have been describing took a very long time. Even after literacy had gained a hold, it was restricted to a select band of people due to the limited numbers of texts. It was mostly restricted, of course, to the Church and courts. Most interestingly there is plenty of evidence to suggest that texts were initially used to supplement rather than replace oral culture—we still talk of auditing (hearing) the accounts. This seems to have been the case in medieval Europe, where, of course, and most interestingly, texts were in a secondary tongue, namely Latin, rather than in the vernacular. To totally undermine oral attitudes, Ong suggests, writing needs to be fully internalized. When a secondary tongue is taught as a literary tongue and the vernacular remains oral, it is clear that strong oral attitudes remain. Examples of this can be found across the board from Africa to North America. There is a tale of a native Indian, an old pupil of my school, who was asked, because of his good education, to go and give a defence of tribal land in an oil pipeline enquiry. His defence was, 'Land? I do not understand what you mean when you talk of buying and selling land. All I hear is the crying of unborn children.' How does this stand up in a White court of law? His oral roots overrode any literate education. I hope you can see from this, that this is not merely a problem of historical interest but of vital significance for understanding many contemporary cultural clashes. Obviously this means that the distinctions which have been drawn between oral and literate subjects are dubious. Perhaps it is a valid distinction between a clear cut primary oral subject, of which there are remarkably few left, and a deeply internalized Western literate subject; but in between there are ten thousand shades of grey. Since literacy is supervenient on the oral, we not only have varying grades of literacy and secondary literate tongues confusing matters, but also the fact that all literate subjects have a degree of orality. In addition, many of the things that literacy supposedly induces are found in traces in oral traditions, so this model is not necessarily as clear cut and valid as it may at first appear. If we also consider the fact that this Ongian thesis is only pertinent to Western literacy and cannot incorporate Chinese, Arabic or any other form of script that does not fully transpose sound onto the page, then we must conclude that this model is not sufficient; that the terms 'oral' or 'literate' do not necessarily mean precisely that. We stand, if anything, in need of a slightly different terminology for it still appears to me that we have clearly distinguished two forms of subject, and that literacy plays a key role in the transition between the two. This obviously needs more thought.

I am not sure that this conclusion should necessarily surprise us, particularly those of you who are familiar with Foucault. There is a very useful framework that may be extrapolated from his texts[6] which perhaps frames this paper and its many connotations, as well as the work of Foucault himself. In the *Archaeology of Knowledge* (1972) we find the idea that discursive practice entails and is entailed by knowledge. His work into discursive practices is known as his Archaeological period, and he later dismissed this work as he moved into what is known as his Genealogical period in which he concentrated on power relations. In *Discipline and Punish* (1977) we find the idea that knowledge entails and is entailed by power. In his final period he again appears to dismiss this earlier work and suggests that he is now interested in the self-interpretation, or hermeneutic of the subject. It seems to me that all of his work falls within the same formula and merely concentrates on different ends of it. If we run it all together, we get Table 1, delineating the periods of Foucault's writings as they seem to me to correspond.

Table 1

Archaeological	Hermeneutic of the subject	Genealogical
Discursive practice $<=>$	Knowledge $<=>$	Power

We should not, therefore, be surprised to find ourselves coming to the conclusion that a change in discursive practice changed the nature of the subject and the existing power relations, which was of course part of what the Enlightenment was all about. Personally I don't see how the elements of this formula can be separated.

So what are philosophers to make of this model of orality and literacy which we have been busy expounding? It is an illuminating model to apply to certain texts. Plato, we have seen, had a negative reaction to the oral tradition whilst Aristotle had a more positive reminiscence. This split taints the whole of the Western philosophical tradition. If we look at another key figure, Hegel (1977), we find that the movement of spirit in his *Phenomenology of Spirit* may be seen as a move from the world of Antigone, which he outlines as oral (they were 'characters' and not 'subjects'), through Roman written law, to the alienated state of the modern, internalized — ie literate — subject. Since Hegel is the origin of most modern, continental alienation theory, it is interesting to speculate if it might not be literacy itself that has allowed for the possibility of the modern 'alienated' subject. May we not conclude from this that literacy may not be such a good thing? The same may be seen in the writing of Hannah Arendt (1958) where the most fundamental human capacity — speech as political action — is primarily oral in character. Arendt's texts are an attempt to reclaim it as modern man has alienated himself from it. All these hints, which could form entire papers in their own right, are merely to point out that apart from the more obvious examples, almost all modern continental philosophy could be interpreted as stemming from the crisis in humanity permitted by literacy, namely the crisis of modernity, of a human being separated off from the world. Is a capacity that separates human beings and communities by thrusting them into internal dependence, or, on the other side, that allows for the objectification and destruction of the world with science and industry, desirable, for all its benefits? The United Nations thinks so: it actively promotes the right of everyone to read and write. Education is constantly thought of in Western literate terms, not in terms of traditional oral education that in many cases might be more appropriate. Now I don't want to get into any judgements here, because writing is necessary to enter the established power relations and how can we deny that chance to anyone? Yet consider the havoc it releases in so many once strong communities, denied access to the privileges of power for race or other reasons, and yet destroyed by being hypocritically given the means to do so. I believe that we arrogantly call it development. Consider also the intellectual imperialism that emanates from our august establishments—for example the separation between sociology and anthropology. In the main, sociology studies Western literate societies, anthropology, oral or 'primitive' societies. I am frankly not convinced that anthropology is much more than the sociology of 'niggers', of so-called primitive minds that we find hard to understand. If you consider this unfair of me, consider that if I go to, say, Ghana, to study traditional African philosophy I am accused of doing anthropology. If a Ghanian comes here to study philosophy, of course, they are doing serious academic study. These problems apply across the board. Oral traditions and knowledge are simply not taken seriously in mainstream academia; they do not fit into literate power relations and self-conceptions, the 'we know better, of course' attitude. Language departments even have a tendency to label oral epics and poetry 'oral literature'—a total nonsense. The power relations of literacy are totally weighted against orality. Simply because African philosophy is not abstract and sanitized it does not mean that there is no reflective experience of the world that we may call philosophy. Here we need a redefinition of philosophy away from its literate Greek roots.

I am not entirely sure where to leave this paper. I have made it very general, I hope general enough for you to follow without being tedious, and by and large I have ignored the philosophical problems that this paper keeps screaming at me, although I have pointed at the directions in which they lie. It is clear that the assumptions of this conference, which we were trying to uncover, do have an arguable, if contentious basis. We have been considering in this volume the rise of the literate subject and it is illuminating how many of the papers concentrated on the use of writing for the development of a self, the self-creation of a subject. Yet I hope that I have also made clear that these distinctions that we have raised, indeed this entire area, needs a lot more work and could have a fundamental effect on many academic sacred cows.[7]

Notes

1. I should make clear that Foucault himself explicitly denies that monasticism was the direct model for discipline, the former he claims was a negative production of the subject and the latter a positive production. (eg *Discipline and Punish* (1977: 137–8). I have argued, however, in an unpublished paper, that Foucault misses the point of monasticism, this being the positive production of a soul for God and that the Panopticon principle of discipline merely replaces God with man.
2. My account, here, of Ong's thesis is paraphrased largely from chapter 3, of Ong (1982).
3. The original delivery of this paper included quotes from Ong (1982: 50–55) which give interesting illustrations of this point.
4. Soviet psychologist and linguist (1902–77). For a selection, see Luria (1978).
5. I have taken these proverbs from chapter 10.2 of Professor Kwame Gyekye (1987).

The translations I take to be his own.
6. I should perhaps make clear that, as far as I am aware, I am the only person to have extrapolated this formula from Foucault.
7. I wish at this point to thank Phil Shaw and Peter Stockwell for organizing such a splendid conference; to thank Reverend Dr. J.M. Wilson and Dr. A.D. Smith for proofreading this script; and, of course, to thank my mother, Mrs. J. Wilson, for typing it!

Bibliography

Arendt, H. (1958), *The Human Condition*, Chicago, University of Chicago Press.
Campbell, C. (1987), *The Romantic Ethic and the Spirit of Modern Consumerism*, Oxford, Basil Blackwell.
Eisenstein, E. (1979), *The Printing Press as an Agent of Change*, two vols, Cambridge, Cambridge University Press.
Foucault, M. (1972), *The Archaeology of Knowledge*, (tr. A.M. Sheridan Smith), London, Tavistock Publications Ltd.
Foucault, M. (1977), *Discipline and Punish: The Birth of the Prison*, (tr. A. Sheridan), Harmondsworth, Penguin.
Foucault, M. (1984), *The Foucault Reader*, (ed. P. Robinow), Harmondsworth, Penguin.
Foucault, M. (1986), *The History of Sexuality: Vol. Three, The Care of the Self*, (tr. R. Hawley), New York, Pantheon Books.
Foucault, M. (1988), *Technologies of the Self: A Seminar with Michel Foucault*, (eds Martin, Gutman and Hulton), London, Tavistock Publications Ltd.
Gyekye, K. (1987), *An Essay on African Philosophical Thought: The Akan Conceptual Scheme*, Cambridge, Cambridge University Press.
Havelock, A.E. (1963), *Preface to Plato*, Oxford, Basil Blackwell.
Hegel, G.W.F. (1977), *Phenomenology of Spirit*, (tr. A.V. Miller), Oxford, O.U.P.
Luria, A.R. (1978), *The Selected Writings of A.R. Luria* (ed. Michael Cole), White Plains, New York, M.E. Sharpe.
Ong, W. (1982), *Orality and Literacy: The Technologising of the Word*, (New Accents, ed. T. Hawkes), London, Methuen and Co. Ltd.
Plato, (1982), *The Collected Dialogues*, (eds Hamilton and Cairns), Bollinger Series LXXI, eleventh edn, Princeton (N.J.), Princeton University Press.
Weber, M. (1978). *Selections*, (ed. Runciman, tr. E. Matthews), Cambridge, Cambridge University Press.

Index

Achebe, Chinua, 164
Aldiss, Brian, 110
Amis, Martin, 138
Di Antonio, R., 127
Arendt, Hannah, 169
Austen, Jane, 108
Arnold, Matthew, 76

Bachelard, Gaston, 7, 146–158
Bal, Mieke, 114–115
Balzac, H., 135–136, 138–139, 144
Barthes, Roland, 86
Bataille, Georges, 4, 6, 9, 13–15, 18–20, 24–26, 30–35
Bateson, F.W., 99
Battaglia, Rosemarie A., 56
Battersby, Christine, 6, 10, 40, 83
Baudelaire, Charles, 71, 83
De Beaugrande, Robert, 103–104
De Beauvoir, Simone, 122, 125, 137
Beethoven, Ludwig Van, 28
Bell, Hesketh, 58
Belsey, Catherine, 42
Bersani, Leo, 41
Blanchot, Maurice, 15, 26
Bloom, Harold, 14, 18, 72, 75–81, 83
Borges, Jorge Luis, 121
Bourdieu, Pierre, 8
Bradbury, Ray, 7, 101–112
Braddon, Mary Elizabeth, 61
Bradley, A.C., 137, 144
Breton, André, 30, 32–33
Le Bris, M., 10
Brontë, Charlotte, 6, 33, 49–57, 138
Brontë, Emily, 6, 28–48
Browning, Elizabeth Barrett, 6
Browning, Robert, 48
Bruns, Gerald L., 72
Buñuel, Louis, 13
Burke, Edmund, 31
Burne-Jones, Philip, 59
Byron, George Gordon, Lord, 6, 28, 31, 41

Callinocos, A., 10
Campbell, C., 161
Chapman, R., 144
Cixous, Hélène, 9, 121, 127, 130–131
Coleridge, Samuel Taylor, 2, 6, 22
Cook, Eleanor, 79
Crane, Walter, 61
Cranston, M., 122–124, 127–128, 133
Crick, Bernard, 85
Cruger, Julie Grinnell, 61
Culler, Jonathan, 80–81, 135–136

Dali, Salvador, 13, 155
Davie, Donald, 96
Davies, S., 42, 48
Deleuze, Gilles, 1–9, 14, 13–14, 17, 25, 146
Derrida, Jacques, 1, 3–4, 6, 8–10, 15, 18–19, 22, 25, 48, 83, 105, 146
Descartes, René, 5, 160, 167
Dick, Philip K., 110
Dickens, Charles, 4
Dolezel, L., 107
Doyle, Arthur Conan, 61

Eagleton, Terry, 102
Eisenstein, Elizabeth, 7, 160, 162
Eliot, T.S., 49, 72, 83
Ellis, Henry Havelock, 60
Ellison, Jane, 144
Emerson, Ralph Waldo, 68

Felman, S., 135–136, 138–139, 142
Ferrero, W., 59
Fielding, Henry, 109
Fitz, E.E., 121–122, 129, 131–133
Fletcher, William, 64
Foucault, Michel, 1, 3–4, 9, 162–4, 166, 168–171
Fowler, Roger, 108–111
Fowles, John, 7, 113–20
Freud, Sigmund, 14–15, 123, 130, 135, 139, 144, 146, 148, 157

Friedman, Milton, 102
Friedrich, Caspar David, 15
Frost, Robert, 97
Fry, Paul, 69, 82

Gasché, R., 10
Gaskell, E., 48
Genette, Gérard, 113–120
Gilbert, S., 39
Gleick, J., 106
Goffman, Erving, 107
Gordon, Julien, 61
Greenaway, Peter, 7, 12–13, 15–16
Grove, Robin, 47
Gueldry, Joseph Ferdinand, 60
Guattari, Felix, 3, 5, 7, 9, 13–14, 25, 146
Gubar, S., 39
Le Guin, Ursula K., 104
Gutman, Huck, 56
Gyekye, Kwame, 170

Hall, Mary Harrington, 103, 106–107, 111
Hamilton, Ian, 96
Hardy, Thomas, 99
Hartmann, Franz, 60
Havelock, A.E., 164, 167
Héger, M., 48
Hegel, G.W.F., 4, 7–8, 13, 16, 18–22, 24, 157, 169
Hemans, Felicia, 6, 29
Hemingway, Ernest, 108
Homans, Margaret, 31, 39
Humphries, M., 144

Jacobus, Mary, 144
James, Henry, 49
Jauss, Hans Robert, 104–105
Jennings, C.E., 60
Jennings, Elizabeth, 39
Johnson, Michael, 105
Jones, Chuck, 103, 106–107
Joyce, James, 49, 76

Kafka, Franz, 109
Kain, R.M., 56
Kant, Immanuel, 1–2, 4–10, 14–15, 23, 25–26, 146
Keats, John 98
Kraft-Ebing, R. Von, 59
Kristeva, Julia, 6, 9, 121, 123–125, 127, 130–131

Lacan, Jacques, 29, 40, 56, 123–124, 136, 144, 146

Lacoue-Labarthe, P., 15
Landon, Leticia, 29
Langbaum, Robert, 49
Lanser, S.S., 115
Larkin, Philip, 5, 93–100
Larkin, P., 26
Lehman, John, 91–92
Lentricchia, Frank, 77–78, 82–83
Lessing, Doris, 105
Levinson, S.C., 103
Lindstrom, Naomi, 123
Lispector, Clarice, 6, 121–134
Locke, John, 149
Lombroso, Caesar, 59
Lowndes, Frederick, 59
Lucas, F., 126
Luria, A.R., 166, 170
Lyotard, Jean-François, 9–10, 14–16, 18, 25–26

McEwan, Ian, 1, 3–4, 137–145
McSweeney, K., 117
Mallarmé, Stéphane, 71–72, 83
De Man, Paul, 18, 24
Marryat, Florence, 61–66
Marryat, Captain Frederick, 61
Marx, Karl, 146
Melville, S., 26
Metcalf, A., 144
Miller, J. Hillis, 28–29, 39
Millgate, Michael, 99
Milton, John, 28
Mitchell, Juliet, 138–139
Moi, T., 121–122, 124, 127–128, 130–131
Montefiore, Jan, 40
Morrison, Blake, 93
Munch, Edvard, 61
Murdoch, J., 66

Nancy, J-L., 15
Newquist, R., 117
Nietzsche, F.W., 4, 6–7, 9, 13–14, 146, 157
Nodelman, Perry, 113
Norris, Christopher, 10
Nunes, B., 133

Ong, W.J., 7, 163–168, 170
Orwell, George, 5, 85–92

Palls, T.L., 133
Peitgen, H-O., 106
Peixoto, Marta, 121, 124–126
Perec, Georges, 7, 146–158

Piranesi, Giovanni Battista, 1, 3, 9
Poe, Edgar Allen, 70-71, 76, 83
Preminger, A., 83
Pritchard, William, 99

Queneau, Raymond, 18, 26

Rilke, Rainer Maria, 19, 23-24, 26
Rimmon-Kenan, Shlomith, 114-115
Ronberg, G., 116
Rops, Felicien, 59
Rose, Mark, 110
Rossetti, Christina, 6, 29, 39-40
Rousseau, Jean-Jacques, 48
Ruskin, John, 7, 19, 22-24
Rutherford, J., 144

De Sá, O., 133
Sanchez-Eppler, Karen, 22
Sartre, Jean-Paul, 123, 125, 128
Saupé, D., 106
Schlegel, Friedrich, 15, 26
Scholes, R., 56
Serres, M., 26
Shakespeare, William, 137, 144
Shelley, P.B., 15, 76-77
Simmons, R.F., 106
Simony, Gabriel, 156
Simpson, P.W., 111
Stapledon, Olaf, 107
Starzyk, Lawrence, 29, 39

Stevens, Wallace, 5, 10, 68-84
Stoker, Bram, 58
Sychrava, J., 10

Tennyson, Alfred, Lord, 12
Thomas, R.S., 96
Tolson, A., 144
Tuke, David H., 60

Uspensky, Boris, 108

Valéry, Paul, 71, 83
De La Vega, Garcilaso, 83
Vermeer, Jan, 13

Walker, David, 73
Wallace, Robert K., 28
Ward, Geoffrey, 25
Watson, S.M., 26
Weber, M., 161
Weedon, C., 124, 133
Wendt, Albert, 164
Whitman, Walt, 76
Willbern, D., 144
Williams, Linda, 36
Williams, William Carlos, 72
Wolfe, Peter, 118
Woolf, Virginia, 49
Wordsworth, William, 6-7, 15-24, 26, 41, 69, 77, 80